"One Man, One Vote" is the slogan that symbolizes one of the great political reforms in American history. In 1962, the Supreme Court ruled, in *Baker* v. *Carr*, that malapportioned voting districts violated the U.S. Constitution. Former Chief Justice Earl Warren later called it "the most vital decision" of his turbulent years on the Court. In the decade that has followed *Baker* v. *Carr*, reapportionment has radically altered the composition of our governing bodies at every level. The hard-won reform is now the law of the land.

By mid-century, Tennessee, like most states, was changing rapidly, its population shifting from the farms to the urban centers. But the state legislature continued to be overwhelmingly rural, and the cities were getting shortchanged. Everyone understood this situation, but to alter it seemed nearly impossible. Happily, the robust world of Tennessee politics spawned a band of young lawyers determined to press the case for reapportionment in the courts, and to succeed. Gene Graham calls them the American Levellers "because their obsession was with the same general principles — equality, suffrage, parliamentary reform — that moved their earlier English counterparts to topple Charles I and then to attack the republican Cromwell for being too much the aristocrat." *One Man, One Vote* chronicles the fascinating interplay between these colorful crusaders and their foes.

No one knows where the slogan One Man, One Vote first came into use, but Japanese students have chanted it as they snake-danced through Tokyo streets. German students, and later French students, echoed those chants as they ripped up cobblestones or bore signs crudely lettered with the phrase. It was the

point by Bernadette
g Catholics in the

an, One Vote stands
t nonviolent reform
that the Establish-
to the orderly ex-
ho protest or attack
rms the hope that a
able civilization to
still move ahead in

ennessee, Gene Gra-
tionment movement
ean, and won a Pul-
fairs reporting. "My
at Harvard in 1962–
seeds of this story
work on how little
how *Baker* came to
nd why."

ONE MAN, ONE VOTE

BAKER v. CARR and the American Levellers

BY GENE GRAHAM

AN ATLANTIC MONTHLY PRESS BOOK
Little, Brown and Company — Boston—Toronto

FIRST EDITION

T 11/72

Quotation from "The Shame of the States" by John F. Kennedy,
© 1958 by The New York Times Company. Reprinted by permission.

Library of Congress Cataloging in Publication Data

Graham, Gene S
    One man, one vote.

    "An Atlantic Monthly Press book."
    1. Apportionment (Election law)--United States.
I. Title.
KF4905.G7   342'.73'07   72-5743
ISBN 0-316-32296-2

ATLANTIC—LITTLE, BROWN BOOKS

ARE PUBLISHED BY

LITTLE, BROWN AND COMPANY

IN ASSOCIATION WITH

THE ATLANTIC MONTHLY PRESS

Published simultaneously in Canada
by Little, Brown & Company (Canada) Limited

PRINTED IN THE UNITED STATES OF AMERICA

For my high school principal,
Carmon McWade Graham,
a teacher of social studies, and his wife,
Opal Swann Graham,
my parents.

Acknowledgments

In the decade since *Baker* v. *Carr* triggered one man, one vote, I have talked to hundreds about it. This includes everyone who occupied a major role in the case and its essential forerunner lawsuits, and with many who came to know its principal characters years later.

I am partial to these men and to their cause; otherwise, I might not have written this book. With most of them I have been acquainted, and with some of them warm friends. Let this work — history, journalism, whatever it is — therefore be judged with the reader's knowledge that I was deeply, personally involved with its subjects. For twelve years, I covered the government beats of Nashville, Tennessee. I reported on the forerunner lawsuit, *Kidd* v. *McCanless,* as it developed, and a few years later I was covering the federal bench of U.S. District Judge William E. Miller, whose court was the home of *Baker* v. *Carr,* when that lawsuit arose. On the editorial page, I supported this reform. In the course of this study, I came to know most of those men with whom I was not already acquainted.

I am deeply grateful for the cooperation of each of the principals who made these contributions to "oral history." Taped interviews were conducted with Mayne Miller and Tommy Osborn, with Charles W. Baker and Joe Carr, with James Cummings and Maclin P. Davis, Jr., with Chancellor Thomas Wardlaw Steele, Daniel Magraw and Frank Farrell, Judge Miller, former Nashville Mayor Ben West, Charles Rhyne, Harris Gilbert and Archibald Cox.

Other such interviews were conducted with Miss Ella Ross; Mrs. Robert Rush Miller, the mother of Haynes and Mayne; Mayne Miller's wife, Mariko; John Seigenthaler, Robert Kennedy's former aide. There were scores of less formal interviews — with George McCanless, Gwendolyn Terasaki and Daniel Harkins; Professor Kenneth Wallace Colegrove; John N. Atkins, Hobart Atkins's brother, and his faithful aide, Miss Mildred McRae; with John Jay Hooker, Jr.; with Tom Osborn's widow, Dottie; and with the friends who supported him, Jack and Iva Lee, and Molly Todd. In Nashville alone, the list of contributors seems endless.

I am particularly grateful to former Chief Justice Earl Warren for his generosity in discussing the effect of *Baker.* I am indebted to the Graduate Research

Board of the University of Illinois for making most of these interviews possible. The board's grant of funds to defray expenses was a contribution without which it is unlikely that this project could have been undertaken.

One learns in such an experience that a book, like a reform movement, is never a one-man affair. Contributions to this one, beyond that of the University, ranged from Wyeth Chandler's courtesy in opening to me the correspondence files of his late father, Walter Chandler, to the criticism and encouragement of Dean Theodore Peterson of the University of Illinois College of Communications, who lent invaluable aid in reading and editing the manuscript. The wealth of taped interviews was transcribed by Miss Diana Crawford and Mrs. Barbara Sutton. While I completed my research in Tennessee, close to the subject, Lieutenant Governor John Wilder and Senate Majority Leader William Peeler were kind enough to put me to work for the Eighty-seventh General Assembly, an experience which enabled me to appraise the changes between that Assembly and the six other legislative sessions with which I had come in contact during a seventeen-year newspaper career with the Nashville *Tennessean*. It was enlightening to watch the Assembly, with its complex of interests, attempt to struggle at once with a self-reapportionment squaring with the 1970 census and a congressional redistricting requiring the elimination of one congressman. One could appreciate more fully why legislatures chose not to wrestle with the subjects, and why court action was an absolute necessity in this particular reform.

My year as a Nieman Fellow at Harvard University in 1962–1963 probably sowed the seeds of this story. It was during a course in constitutional history taught by the late Professor Robert McCloskey that I first became aware of the huge gaps in my own knowledge of American history. Of judicial history, I knew little beyond the landmark events and cases, and less of the background to these: *Marbury* v. *Madison, Chisholm* v. *Georgia, Dred Scott,* the Franklin D. Roosevelt court-packing effort. McCloskey made event and participant come to life in past cases and set my thoughts to work on how little posterity would likely know of how *Baker* came to be, who made it happen and why. I knew quite a bit of the story, of course, having just come from years of following it in Tennessee. But already, at Harvard, graduate assistants were talking to the young of *Baker* v. *Carr,* with great self-assurance, as if "constitutional authorities" and judges with steel-trap legal minds deliberately plotted it all. No motivation beyond the law and no flesh and blood or emotion whatever. No respect for a good slogan, even!

No one knows where that slogan — one man, one vote — came into usage. But then it is doubtful if the first utterance of *"Liberté! Egalité! Fraternité!"* is known either, though those who mounted its rhetoric have their proper place in history. The individuals who spawned the one-man–one-vote movement also deserve such a place. This volume, then, is a pursuit of the movement through those who contributed to it, and an examination of the conditions that compelled them to do so. Germane in such an endeavor is the aphorism of one of the book's figures, James Cummings, the rural power in Tennessee legislative affairs for so many years; "If you want to know, go to the head of the spring." This is what this book tries to do.

Contents

PROLOGUE

One man, one vote.

The phrase rings with justice. It is revolutionary rhetoric. Yet the one-man-one-vote revolution left no blood upon the streets of the nation. No shots were fired on account of it. The phrase grew into the language so imperceptibly that no one seems to know its origin. The reform itself was accepted, despite dire predictions, with scarcely a ripple of protest from the general populace. Though it left some public officials unhappy, they got nowhere with campaigns against it.

The one-man-one-vote movement was perhaps the most important and sophisticated political reform in American history. It was, and is, the American equivalent of England's "rotten boroughs" reform. The case that started it was, as former Chief Justice Earl Warren properly termed it, "the most vital decision" rendered during his tenure on the United States Supreme Court. I would go further and place one man, one vote among the most important developments in the world's history of egalitarian ideas.

Japanese students have chanted one man, one vote as they snake-danced through Tokyo streets. German students, and later French, echoed those chants as they ripped up cobbles or bore signs crudely lettered with the phrase. It was the catchphrase used at one point by Bernadette Devlin and her protesting Catholics in the Ulster uprisings. Yet, during similar tumultuous times in America, one man, one vote stands as a living testimonial that nonviolent reform through law is possible, that the Establishment does indeed bend to the orderly expressed desires of those who protest or attack its shortcomings. One man, one vote, if ever so dimly, holds out hope that a system of law may yet enable civilization to settle its differences and still move ahead in peace.

This is a book about the men and women who began the one-man-one-vote revolution. I call them the *American Levellers* because their obsession was with the same general principles — equality, suffrage, parliamentary reform — that moved their earlier English counterparts to topple Charles I and then to attack the republican Cromwell for being too much the aristocrat. I have traced "that all men are created equal" back far enough beyond Jefferson, Locke and Montesquieu to believe they borrowed this radical notion from the English Levellers, that ultra-republican Puritan sect of seventeenth-century zealots, who got the idea from the Christian fathers.

The methods of these American reformers assuredly were not identical to those of John Lilburne, William Walwyn and Richard Overton, or of Thomas Rainborough and John Wildman. But there are startling parallels in ideals, goals and origins. The original Levellers took root in urban-suburban London in 1645–1646 among supporters of Parliament during the first Civil War and its battles between monarchy and representative government. They argued for a real sovereignty based in the Commons, upon the people, as opposed to kingly and lordly power. They cried out for manhood suffrage and a redistribution of parliamentary seats. This redistribution, they felt, when coupled with annual or biennial sessions, should make the Commons truly representative. They argued for natural rights and complete equality before the law. And when Parliament disappointed them, they turned to the people and tried to capture the army.

There are personal parallels, too. Of all the English Levellers, none was more intense than the agitator Lilburne, of whom the regicide Henry Marten could say, "If the world was emptied of all but John Lilburne, Lilburne would quarrel with John, and John with Lilburne." He had his American counterpart. Young Haynes Miller of East Tennessee was a compulsive crusader, described by his brother as "one of the flower children born out of due season." But Haynes was far too activist to settle for blossoms; Ralph Nader is a

[5]

nearer Puritan model. And, like Lilburne, he cherished debate. "I had hundreds of conversations with him," said his friend and associate Tom Osborn. "He might pick up the phone in Johnson City and call me one morning, then show up at the house that night [some three hundred miles distance] to continue the argument. . . . He would be dissatisfied with the way a telephone conversation came out and he would come down and spend maybe two days to dispute some point." Osborn himself was not without kinship to Lilburne. Both he and Haynes Miller were inclined to the shortcut — direct action or confrontation — in the interest of some cause they thought noble and just.

William Walwyn the theologian-thinker and pamphleteer of Interregnum England, was nearer the mold for American Levellers, though. A member of the upper middle class, as were all the American reformers, Walwyn was successful enough in business to provide quite adequately for a wife and twenty children. But his Christian concept drove him, in *The Power of Love* (generally attributed to him by scholars) to counsel his readers:

Looke about you and you will find in these woefull dayes thousands of miserable, distressed, starved, imprisoned Christians: see how pale and wan they looke: how coldly, raggedly, & unwholsomely they are cloathed; live one weeke with them in their poore houses, lodge as they lodge, eate as they eate, and no oftener, and bee at the same passe to get that wretched food for a sickly wife, and hunger-starved children (if you dare doe this for feare of death or disease); then walke abroad, and observe the generall plenty of all necessaries, observe the gallant bravery of multitudes of men and women abounding in all things that can be imagined: observe likewise the innumerable numbers of these that have more than sufficeth, . . . and the wants and distresses of the poore will testifie that the love of God they have not.

Walwyn, like his contemporary John Milton, was intellectually driven to such a point of concern for people beneath his station by the Biblical teaching that God is no respecter of persons. Just under God, if not beside Him, Walwyn enshrined reason, and this theme runs through his *Compassionate Samaritane*. Having begun with God's position, his mind forced him to a deep belief in equality. This, in turn, logically suggested the illegitimacy of kings and lords and such. *Vox populi, vox dei.* Power, then, must necessarily reside in the Commons, and the volume of no member's voice should exceed that of another. The natural corollary of this reasoning made Walwyn one of the earliest advocates of free press and speech. For it was as obvious to him as to Thomas Jefferson many years later that self-governors cannot govern without information and the widest possible marketplace for ideas. Thus Walwyn pre-wrote the First Amendment concept in *Compassionate Samaritane* by scoring those who aspired

to be masters of the Presse, of which they are lately become by an Ordinance for licensing of Bookes, which being intended by the Parliament for a good & necessary end [namely] the prohibition of all Bookes dangerous or scandalous to the State, is become by meanes of the Li-

[7]

cencers (who are Divines and intend their owne interest) most serviceable to themselves (scandalous bookes being still disperst) in the stopping of honest mens writings, that nothing may come to the Worlds view but what they please, unlesse men wille runne the hazard of imprisonment, (as I now doe) so that in publike they may speake what they will, write what they wil, they may abuse whom they will, and nothing can be said against them.

The parallel between English and American Leveller ends at method, of course, but then the seventeenth-century Englishman could never have dreamed of turning to the courts for an honest resolution of rights. The American Levellers had that option and they pursued it, some of them with all the zeal and intensity of modern Lilburnes, all of them with the reason and logic and "perswasion" that Walwyn worshipped. They changed the course of history.

Book One

THE REFORMERS

1

Why Charles Baker
Sued Joe Carr

Joseph Cordell Carr, the Tennessee secretary of state, was in Memphis on business. He had an hour or so to kill before his meeting of the state Board of Tax Equalization and he decided to use it to introduce himself to the man who sued him six years before and thereby pegged both their names everlastingly into the textbooks of American history.

Unannounced, big Joe Carr stepped into the sixth-floor office of Charles W. Baker, chairman of the Shelby County Quarterly Court.

"I figured it was about time we met since everybody keeps using our names together," he said. It was December 1965, when Joe Carr sat down with Charlie Baker for the first time to confront the irony of their situation. Perhaps the most significant thing these two men had done to earn their places in history was to migrate, like so many millions of their contemporaries, from a rural birthplace to a career in an urban setting. For it was the steady migration to cities during more than half a century, a massive shuffle which created sharp alienation between the American people and their governments, that led to *Charles W. Baker, et al* versus *Joe C. Carr, et al.* These principals, as in many lawsuits, were more symbols of the problem and how it came to be than real antagonists in the battle to solve it.

It would be difficult to overstate the results of the landmark lawsuit *Baker* v. *Carr.* The United States Supreme Court ruled on the case on March 26, 1962. By the end of that decade it had redrawn much of the political map of the nation. By the end of this one, the 1970's, it will have completed the job by applying the 1970 census so that each man's vote must count the same as his neighbor's in every American election from village council and district school board to state legislature and the Congress of the United States. It was a reform so vast as to amount to a revolution.

Baker v. *Carr* alone did not do it all, of course. Other lawsuits followed to define, to implement and refine its finding, to apply it elsewhere within the American system. But *Baker* v. *Carr* opened the floodgate by reversing a Supreme Court decision in an Illinois case which for sixteen years had dammed all efforts to bring about this reform. The historic Illinois case was *Colegrove* v. *Green,* decided in 1946. It produced the "political thicket" doctrine with which Associate Justice Felix Frankfurter for many years entangled all progress in the twin efforts to redistrict the Congress and redistribute legislative seats in state legislatures throughout America.

Illinois, 80.7 per cent urban, renowned for its famous dichotomy between the "Cook County" and "Downstate" crowds, should have been an ideal seedbed for this movement. And indeed, the issue of legislative reapportionment had long been a fiery one in Illinois. For, as C. Herman Pritchett has written:

The Northwest Ordinance of 1787, the Illinois Enabling Act of 1818, the Illinois Constitution of 1848, and the present Constitution of 1870 [a new one was adopted December 15, 1970] all provided for two houses based upon population. From 1818 to 1901 both houses were redistricted fourteen times in conformity with population changes. In 1870 Cook County contained only 14 per cent of the state's population. But by 1900 it had grown to 38 per cent, and 1901 was the last reapportionment that could be put through the legislature because the population growth of Cook County would have had to be recognized.

Accordingly, fights broke out between rural and urban blocs over Chicago's representation in Springfield in the constitutional convention of 1920, again in the legislature five years later. At one point, Chicago threatened to secede from the state unless something was done to give it a better deal. Illinois citizens turned to the courts as early as 1925, again in 1930, in efforts to shake up the balance of power in the Statehouse. These having failed, a group of Chicago and suburban university professors decided on a congressional strategy at the end of World War II with *Colegrove* v. *Green*. When this, too, failed the more malapportioned industrial states gave up for a while.

In Tennessee, though, the shifts in population and hence the growing gaps in equity were slower in coming about. Too, through chance and circumstance of history, the state produced an unusual band of young attorneys and reformers of the Don Quixote stripe, spoiling for battle and fired by idealism. Some arose like the English Levellers out of an urban-suburban setting, others from an Abolitionist region long held down by political injustices left over from the American Civil War.

The case was rooted in the peculiar nature of Tennessee. The oldest cliché about Tennessee is true: it is three states in one. A long, narrow parallelogram, 600 miles corner to corner, averaging only 115 miles across, it cuts east to west across three distinct regions, and the geology of each left its unique mark on the inhabitants who settled there. In the one-man-one-vote movement, this was particularly pertinent with respect to East Tennessee, whose hills and small farms produced no economic need for slaves, and whose inhabitants thereby became rabid Republican Unionists when the Civil War split the state. But East Tennessee's topography and natural resources encouraged early industrialization so its population grew while its share of political power shrank.

Rural politicians from the more agricultural Middle

and West grand divisions, both losing population, were aware as well of another political fact. They saw it coming as early as 1901, the same year Illinois called a halt to legislative redistricting.

From West Tennessee, that rolling-to-flatland third of a state extending from the north-flowing Tennessee River westward to the great Mississippi, the people were moving with the slope of the land toward Memphis. In Midstate, bounded by the Tennessee on the west and the Cumberland range on the east, another third poured off the Highland Rim and down into the basin of Nashville. In East Tennessee, a great valley caught between the Cumberland and Allegheny chains, the same process sent streams of migrants flowing into Knoxville and Chattanooga. Between them, these four metropolitan centers, ranging in size from a quarter to three quarters of a million people, today account for about half of the population of Tennessee. But when the movement toward them began, then swelled to floods at the end of World War II, the political power stayed behind on the cotton flats, the hills and the ridgeland farms.

On the floors of the Tennessee General Assembly, the politicians congregated every two years and sliced up the big tax pie, parceling out to the state's political subdivisions — counties and towns and cities — whatever was left after funding Tennessee's statewide services. But the money did not get divided equally, because there was no equity in representation. According to population, Shelby County (Memphis), for example, was entitled to perhaps as many as twenty representatives, including senators, in the General Assembly. In point of fact, the powers allotted only nine representatives in the Assembly, senators included. For a half a century, starting in 1901, these powers had simply ignored a mandate of the state constitution:

Article II, Section 5. *Apportionment of representatives* — The number of Representatives shall, at the several periods of making the enumeration [every 10 years by requirement of Section 4], be apportioned among the several counties or districts, according to the number of qualified voters in each. . . .

Section 6. *Apportionment of senators* — The number of Senators shall, at the several periods of making the enumeration, be apportioned among the several counties or districts according to the number of qualified voters in each. . . .

Because this same unbalanced legislature set the metes and bounds of congressional districts, a citizen of Shelby County (or of East Tennessee) was shortchanged in the U.S. Congress, too. The Memphian's congressman represented three times the number of persons as did the two West Tennessee rural congressmen in adjoining districts. Shelby County was the home of Charles Baker, and these inequitable conditions were the origin of *Baker* v. *Carr*.

Charles William Baker was born near the hamlet of Drummonds, twenty miles north of Memphis, and grew up in nearby Millington, another small town. The Navy built a huge base there as World War II began, and at its end, booming Millington village and Memphis were growing close to each other. When Baker came out of the Army in 1944, he found Millington almost a suburb of Memphis. He went back to his job at O. C. Branch's store and became the manager, but he had come home with a political yen, like so many other returning vets that year. In 1950, Baker ran for two offices and won both — one the full-time job of mayor of Millington, the other, that of Millington's member of the Shelby County Quarterly Court, a fiscal, legislative body that ran the affairs of a rapidly urbanizing metropolitan area where more than 600,000 people then lived. In September 1954, after four years on the court, Charles Baker was elected its chairman, an influential full-time job with an office and sizable staff in downtown Memphis. He was then forty, a big, black-haired man in hornrims, good-natured and easy-appearing, whose smile was a bit impish and whose speech was the slow flatland drawl indigenous to his stretch along the Big River.

New people, new urban problems pressed down upon Memphis and Charles W. Baker. These new inhabitants arrived in separate black and white streams, each presenting to Baker and his government colleagues enormous problems demanding of money. The Anglo-Saxon sons and daughters of west Tennessee poured into Memphis, to become professionals and merchants and to build or to service the new manufacturing plants springing up and the spreading suburban shopping marts. Up from rural north Mississippi, too, from across the river in east Arkansas, down from the bootheel of southern Missouri others came to blend pastoral and small-town upbringings into the familiar postwar style of suburban living.

West Tennessee has been often and accurately described as a northward projection of Mississippi. As the field-hand jobs petered out in both states, the black descendants of those once enslaved by King Cotton rolled into Memphis, too. Their residences spread in a tight but broadening band around the business heart and some shoved into the suburbs. With every move outward the tension grew, but move they had to, prodded by urban renewal and the building of inter-state highway loops. Many of them cluttered government offices each week on "welfare day" while others landed tough, hard jobs with the governments — garbage collectors, street cleaners, utility jackhammer men. Their 36 per cent presence was felt by City Hall, and by Charles W. Baker.

Yet Baker's congressman spoke with one-third of a proper voice and his state legislation with less than half his legitimate force. This was taking its toll in tax dollars. Of farm subsidies, there were enough from the national capital; of farm tax exemptions, aplenty from the state capital in Nashville. But urban governments went hat in hand; Charles Baker and others decided to sue. "We felt like if the legislature would reapportion itself according to the constitution," he said, "we could get a better break on state revenues coming back to our county."

Charles Baker's name led the lawsuit on the strength of his official position, though Baker well knew what the cause was about. And it was Joe Carr's position as secretary of state that put his name at the top of the defendants' list. Both these men would later feel personally the political effects of the lawsuit that bore their names.

Like Charles Baker, Joe Carr was born in the country and moved with his family into the city. He was ten when his family moved from his birthplace at Cookeville, Tennessee, eighty miles due east of Nashville, to the state capital; his father had been elected to the state legislature. The elder Carr arrived in Nashville for the great Women's Suffrage Session and when the Assembly ended, he stayed to work in the office his son was later to occupy, secretary of state.

Joe Carr cut his teeth on politics. He was fifteen when he took his first state job as a Senate page. He was in the highway department and served as legislative clerk of one sort or another every two years when the General Assembly convened, advancing to chief clerk of the House in 1939. He organized Tennessee's Young Democrats in the 1930's and became national secretary of the organization in 1941. The same year, a joint session of the General Assembly heavily weighted with Democrats elected Joe Carr secretary of state. In the years since, his absences from that office have been rare. During one of them, while Carr did brief World War II service as an MP, his wife kept his office warm.

Following *Baker* v. *Carr,* partisan jobs would not be so safe, however. In 1968, the traditionally Democratic General Assembly was radically changed by *Baker.* Through reapportionment, the Republican party made large gains in East Tennessee and the GOP-leaning suburbs. The once-solid Democrat margin in the Tennessee House melted to a House divided evenly 49–49–1. The lone independent and a defecting Democrat delivered the GOP its first House speaker in half a century. Only the Senate, where the Democrats clung to control, salvaged Joe Carr's job.

The effect Charles Baker felt from his own lawsuit occurred a bit later in his own Shelby County Quarterly Court. In April 1968, the Supreme Court extended to the twenty thousand units of local government across the land the same one-man-one-vote standard that *Baker* v. *Carr* set in motion. Baker's own magisterial district was remapped within the year under federal court order. (He managed to be reelected.)

Such local political shakeups, such changes in the partisan balance of states were commonplace effects of *Baker* v. *Carr.* Republicans gained in some states, notably in the South, Democrats in others. But in almost every state in the Union, the lawsuit shifted legislative power toward the urban centers. For Tennessee was far from alone in this sort of population shift.

The fastest-growing states had the most malapportioned legislatures and Florida's was widely known as the worst of all: at that time a majority of the members of both its houses represented districts which together contained less than 15 per cent of the state's population. The majority bloc, known as the "Pork Chop Gang," consisted chiefly of legislators from the rural counties of north Florida, which once contained the bulk of its population. But almost all of Florida's later growth — a huge 79 per cent between 1950 and 1960 — took place in the southern coastal counties, which were grossly shortchanged. Coastal states bore the brunt of America's internal postwar migrations, as if some giant centrifugal force had spun the populace outward toward its seashores. California was another case in point: In 1962, it was 86.4 per cent urban with a growth factor of 49 per cent for the decade 1950–1960.

These vast internal migrations — the Charles Bakers and Joe Carrs multiplied — not only deposited too many persons on too little land, but tore them away from trusted institutions and left them feeling powerless. By the 1970 census, a full 70 per cent of the nation's people jammed 2 per cent of its land. Only 5 per cent of America's people remained on that 49 per cent of its area still classified "farmland." Where the populace jammed together, it fought all kinds of pollution, personal tensions, often each other. And when it voted, its votes didn't count much.

Such problems tossed up by the great migrations naturally arrived first on the coasts, and Earl Warren's intimate familiarity with them as governor of California contributed to his later evaluation of *Baker* v. *Carr* as the most important decision of his tumultuous tenure on the United States Supreme Court. As governor, he struggled with those problems while "every day California awoke with fifteen hundred new citizens and every Monday morning we had a new city of ten thousand people to serve" with water, schools, sewers, highways, houses, hospitals, parks, etc.

"A great many other problems would have been solved if that rule [one man, one vote] had been in effect earlier," he said. Warren took special note of two major areas — the crisis in American cities and desegregation in the South. Had Negroes in the South been permitted proper representation in government, he suggested, democratic means might well have solved many of the nation's vexing racial problems. He laid particular emphasis, however, on the problems brought about by migration to and growth within American cities.

"Our cities are in crisis," he said, "and are in great danger of disruption to a point that threatens the entire fabric of our society." This might have been averted, he said, if urban problems had received their just consideration in American legislative bodies at the proper time. That proper time, he added, was as the growth took place.

But Warren thought even 1946, when the *Colegrove* case was decided, "very late" to produce a reorientation in national priorities in time to avert the deep convulsions of violence and dissent that were to rock America in the 1960's. As the *Colegrove* case had underscored, Congress as well as the state legislatures

[22]

were overbalanced in favor of farm-bloc politics long after the economy shifted significantly from farm to factory — a shift that laid new emphasis on urban renewal and housing, on clean air and water, street cleaning and building, garbage disposal and core-city tensions.

In general, Congress was far more sensitive to this shift and to its problems than were the legislatures. Nevertheless, the fact that Charles Baker's urban congressman represented three times the number of citizens as did the two rural congressmen in adjoining districts had its effect, particularly when nationally multiplied. Georgia's congressional seats were among the most flagrantly malapportioned. Its largest district had a population of 823,680 while the smallest had a population of 272,154 — a disparity of 551,526. In Texas, the largest and smallest congressional districts had populations of 951,527 and 216,371. And in Illinois, *Colegrove* v. *Green* was provoked by disparities in district populations that ranged from 112,116 to 914,053.

Professor Kenneth Wallace Colegrove, a Northwestern University political scientist, lived in the district with 914,053 and thus was chosen to be lead plaintiff in the lawsuit he and a group of colleagues from the University of Chicago filed. Their suit sought an at-large election of all congressmen, alleging the invalidity of the 1901 districting act. The Green named as defendant was Dwight H. Green, then governor of Illinois. He was spiritually on the plaintiffs' side; that year, Governor Green had appealed to the 1945 legislature to "correct the inequities of our congressional apportionment under which Illinois now has both the largest and smallest congressional districts in the United States, one nine times the size of the other." Marshall Field, the wealthy department store and publishing tycoon of Chicago, underwrote the lawsuit and Urban A. Lavery, a prominent Chicago attorney, agreed to take the case without fee.

The decision dismissing Kenneth Colegrove's lawsuit was announced June 10, 1946, and it was an odd decision, split 3–3–1, delivered in unusual circumstances. One justice, Robert Jackson, was away as prosecutor at the Nuremberg war crimes trials. Chief Justice Harlan Fiske Stone, in the midst of the arguments, suffered a heart attack on the bench. He died April 22.

As it turned out, it was Mr. Justice Frankfurter's opinion that was stamped on *Colegrove* v. *Green,* and some legal scholars still express a sense of awe at how he managed to make his "political thicket" doctrine into nearly a constitutional principle. Professor Robert B. McKay, associate Dean and professor of law at New York University, has written:

The Frankfurter opinion was nothing less than a judicial *coup de grace,* for it managed to reverse, or at least cast doubt on, an established line of (reapportionment) cases, announcing the new rule as a dictum in a minority opinion supported only by an earlier concurring opinion [in the case of *Wood* v. *Broom*] which was itself undocumented. This might be appropriately described as triple bootstrap.

It was in this same opinion, speaking for only three of seven members of a nine-man Court, that Frankfurter delivered his famous lecture:

> To sustain this action would cut very deep into the very being of Congress. . . . Courts ought not to enter this political thicket. The remedy for unfairness in districting is to secure State Legislatures that will apportion properly, or to invoke the ample powers of Congress.

The writer of that passage was not well acquainted with the late Paul Powell, a powerful statehouse politician from rural southern Illinois, or what sort of attitude or action he might have taken to preserve his district. For all his knowledge of legal theory, Mr. Justice Frankfurter could not have known the practical politician State Senator Joe Bailey Cobb of Oklahoma, or the inner workings of north Florida's "Pork Chop Gang." He seems not to have understood why a Georgia congressman whose district lines depend upon his state's General Assembly would be unready to "invoke the ample powers of Congress" to balance a system which, by its very imbalance, kept Eugene Talmadge in power in Atlanta. Or why Everett McKinley Dirksen, from the Downstate district of Illinois, might just have sufficient clout on the national scene to block such possible invocation.

And Justice Frankfurter never knew a certain trio from the ridgeland of Tennessee — Walter M. (Pete)

Haynes of Franklin County; I. D. Beasley of Smith County; and James H. Cummings of Woodbury, Cannon County — three of the finest reasons one could imagine why Charles W. Baker had to sue Joe Carr.

Four years before their landmark lawsuit arose, however, young reformers in Tennessee had laid the groundwork, first with a head-on legislative attack on the rural powers in Nashville and then with a lawsuit of their own. Their failure with both attempts became prerequisites to the later success of the one-man-one-vote movement. The reformers set out separately in two groups, one band arising from the Nashville suburbs, the other from the mountainous Upper East reaches of Tennessee where the state's own history began. But they quickly merged their efforts when they arrived at common targets: One was the *Colegrove* decision and the necessity to overturn it. The other was Cummings, Beasley, Haynes and company, legislative brokers for the rural oligarchy that then ruled Tennessee.

2

James H. Cummings and Maclin P. Davis, Jr.

Jim Cummings, Pete Haynes and I. D. Beasley were country lawyers, all from the midstate Rimland, and they came to be known as the Great Triumvirate on Capitol Hill, or sometimes as Tennessee's Unholy Trinity.

Together, they ran the show on the Hill for twenty or thirty years, off and on, and most of that time was spent in battle with the "city slickers," notable among them the boss of Memphis, E. H. Crump. Old-timers love to tell how Cummings and his two sidekicks consolidated their power in Tennessee.

As the 1935 session was about to begin, Pete Haynes aspired to the job of House speaker and its considerable powers. The trio had already formed an association and were sharing a hotel room for the session. But Boss Ed Crump was tall in the saddle of state politics that year, and he had picked Jim Corn to be his House speaker. So sure was Crump that all was under control that he went away for a health dip at Hot Springs, Arkansas. His legislative *chargé d'affaires*, Frank (Roxy) Rice, was off to the Rose Bowl in Pasadena.

Had he chosen, Beasley could have made it to Hollywood or to Broadway. He was a natural mimic, possessed of the rare talent that could hear a voice, male or female, absorb it, mock it to flawless perfection. While Cummings and Haynes rounded up friendly votes for Pete, then, I. D. placed a series of telephone calls to pro-Crump legislators around the state. Representing himself as Rice, he told them Crump had changed his plans and was supporting Haynes for the House speakership. When the calls were completed, and before the Crump forces could recover, Haynes was the speaker. The legends are legion concerning the stunts this trio pulled in the next few years — Haynes with his skillful gavel, Cummings as floor leader, Beasley with his own special talents — as they flexed their muscles and built their machine. One could choose not to heed the stories, but only at the risk of losing a bill, an appropriation or the job of a friend. Dealing with the legislature meant dealing with the rural bloc, and that meant with Haynes and Cummings and Beasley. They knew where the tax money was, and they decided how to distribute it.

But the times were changing swiftly in 1955. More people than Cummings liked to acknowledge had poured down from the highlands of his Cannon

County, away from Short Mountain into Murfreesboro and on into Nashville. They had slipped away from the dogwood and red-budded hills of Beasley's Smith County like waters down the Caney Fork River, and in Pete Haynes's Franklin County — places like Estill Springs and Farris Chapel, Await and Owl Hollow, Lexie Crossroads and Beans Creek no longer could hold them. The population was shifting, but Cummings and colleagues still held the power for the seats on the Hill hadn't been redistributed for fifty-five years and Jim Cummings had no notions of leaving Woodbury.

"I believe in collecting the taxes where the money is — in the cities — and spending it where it's needed — in the country," he would say, echoing his Populist credo. Deeply ingrained within him, too — though he would never quite say it — was the not uncommon Jeffersonian notion that somehow cities, by nature, are evil and that country people make better citizens and public officials.

For years before the 1955 session, Jim Cummings had been putting his rural background and these rurally rooted philosophies to work on Capitol Hill in a very practical dollar-and-cents manner. It might be generalized that most of urban America before the postwar period shared Cummings's Jeffersonian distrust of cities. They moved there only because they had to and as soon as they arrived they began to think of a way out. A plot of green in the suburbs was the most practical solution, and millions chose it. Only

[29]

when this process began to require that the streets be patched (their building had been amortized in the house mortgages) and new schools constructed did America's new suburbanites begin to come to a fiscal dawning. In Nashville, Tennessee, the awakening began when Jim Cummings took a deep nap.

His widely publicized snooze took place in the House chamber February 24, 1955. The next morning, in three-column format, his slumber was chronicled on the front page of the morning capital-city newspaper, the Nashville *Tennessean*. Years later, in the same good humor with which he accepted it at the time, Cummings explained:

"Well, as a matter of fact, it was not a session of the legislature. It was a meeting of the Education Committee assembled in the House chamber. I remember it very well, and, ah, we had worked long hours the night before formulating the bill and revising various provisions. . . . I said, ah, the next day on the floor I might have been taking a little nap during the hearing that day, but if they looked back to the section that had provisions regarding distribution of funds to my county, they would find my fingerprints on the pages of that draft."

The bill to which Cummings referred was Tennessee's General Education Act and, having thrown his rural bloc behind the administration's sales tax increase to finance the act, Cummings had exacted his price. All night long, or most of it, February 23, he had been seeing that the final draft contained a certain clause:

"Provided that no county . . . shall receive less state school capital outlay funds annually than was distributed to such county for school capital outlay purposes . . . for the fiscal year 1950–51."

In practical terms what this meant was that counties like Cummings's, with diminishing population, and thus fewer schoolchildren, continued to get the same money for building schools. Their per-pupil allotments, then, went up while counties of great growth around the urban centers got proportionately less per pupil each year. As the numbers grew in Davidson County (Nashville), the schools turned to portable rooms and surplus World War II barracks, sawed up and hauled in, to absorb the overflow from the fecund homes of the suburbanites.

Cummings's fingerprints on a bill were known in Tennessee as a "guarantee clause," and his power did not end with school capital outlay funds. He also influenced the distribution of school funds for regular operational expenses. The effect was enough to prompt a study group to declare:

"Conspicuous among these special privileges is the so-called 'guarantee clause.' . . . With Alice in Wonderland logic, this argues that counties which have enjoyed special privileges in the past should be allowed to retain them indefinitely because they are now accustomed to them!" In 1952–1953, Tennessee sent $97.99 a pupil to state school systems outside the four metropolitan counties and cities. In those urban areas, though, the average amount was only $63.67 per child. After the 1955 session, the situation grew worse.

Application of this logic did not end with school funds, either. Cummings and cohorts also finger-printed the formulae distributing two state road funds before 1955, and added a third — the Federal Aid Secondary Fund — that year. They divided these revenues as follows: (a) one half of the fund, share and share alike to each of the ninety-five counties, regardless of need; (b) one fourth on the basis of road mileage; (c) one fourth on the basis of population.

The rural bonanza here, of course, was that first half, and Cummings himself was later to say: "We were honest about that. I am sure my fingerprints got on that, too, because the, ah, we were launching on a program of state highway construction — the primary system as well as the secondary farm-to-market and mail road programs. And that fund was supplied from state gasoline tax collected throughout the state. And we provided for a certain percentage of it by counties across the state. . . . We got what might be called a fair, er, share — some might say a lion's share — of that fund."

It was that sort of attitude of state legislatures and their Jim Cummingses throughout America that played a huge role in the urban crisis and the fund starvation that helped to bring it about. The effect was every-where; the Pork Chop Gang distributed to each of Florida's sixty-seven counties, for example, an equal portion of the state's race-track revenue. This meant a return of about twenty cents a person for Dade County (Miami), but sixty-one dollars a person for rural Liberty County. The rich cities, creatures of the legislatures, could do as they pleased — as long as they went by the capitol hills to do it. There they received scant home rule. For every legislator knew that city halls were not to be trusted. It was part of every rural representative's deep belief that the cities had plenty of money, a secret horde hidden away somewhere out of which anything could be done, with some still left to grease the palms of mayors and aldermen, ward heelers and syndicate gangsters. In 1955, in Tennessee, this myth came under attack.

The young lawyer who took on Cummings and his system in the Tennessee legislature that year was, on the surface, an unlikely crusader. Maclin P. Davis, Jr., had not heard much about the need to redistrict the General Assembly, in fact, and he thought so little about it that his eight-point platform for the Democratic primary had made no mention of it. He was for better and consolidated public schools, though himself a private school product. He favored a domestic relations court to handle the Chancery and growing circuit court logjams of divorce and custody cases produced by a rapidly expanding metropolis. And he was of course committed to "good and efficient government."

Davis and Cummings were a study in contrasting styles and backgrounds, both prototypes of the men elected to state legislatures by rural and urban constituencies in the 1940's and 1950's. The older man was a fourth-generation politician from his county, which his great-grandfather settled in 1812 and then represented as constitutional convention delegate when the postwar Tennessee charter was drafted in 1870. Cummings started running for public office as soon as he became eligible to vote and by the time the 1955 legislature convened his seat in one house or the other was considered virtually a proprietary item. He was elected invariably with token or no opposition; a Cannon Countian would have considered it presumptuous if not brash to run against Jim Cummings.

Maclin Paschall Davis, Jr., was also of pioneer stock; an ancestor had begun the family fortune with a successful Tennessee distillery (Cascade, George Dickel) and his grandfather made millions in Cuban banking and sugar before retiring at forty to become an intimate adviser to Democratic Presidents. But a well-known name, while an asset in Davidson County, was hardly enough to assure a twenty-eight-year-old youngster not long out of Vanderbilt law school a seat in the General Assembly. Mac Davis had to run very hard and have some luck to win one of the six House seats then apportioned to an underrepresented metropolitan county. In fact, Davis went to bed election night thinking he'd lost, and this circumstance had much to do with his decision to take on Cummings.

Davis had spent the election-night watch hours at the suburban home of neighbors and supporters.

[34]

Among those present were the Lees — Jack and Iva — and the Osborns — Dorothy and Tom. Tommy Osborn, fresh out of the Nashville city attorney's office, was a member of the same law firm as Davis. He had advised the younger lawyer and worked in his campaign. Osborn had often discussed how the rurally based state legislature was shortchanging city taxpayers. As the returns came in that night, Davis's neighbors discussed the injustice of Nashville's allocation of only a half-dozen House seats and two in the state Senate.

Davidson County's delegation to the General Assembly was then elected "at large." That meant the top six vote-getters from a field of forty-six candidates who ran that year would be the winners. But Davis, in the wee hours, was running seventh and he appeared to be out of it. Weary, he went off to bed.

"I went to bed thinking, a little bit bitterly I guess, that if our community had the number of seats it should have had, ol' Mac Davis would have been elected," Davis said. He awoke to discover he had won the sixth seat by a scant three hundred votes.

Young Mac Davis did not forget. In the four months between the primary and the legislature's opening day in 1955, he probed the constitution, studied census figures, doodled lines on blank maps of Tennessee. And on the day he was to take his oath, he walked up the Hill like countless young legislators before him, and since — with stars in his eyes and one bill in his briefcase that would save the Republic. His bill would reapportion the state legislature.

Beyond his personal experience, another force was driving Mac Davis, Jr. Less than five years out of law school, he considered himself (and still does) a political conservative and a strict constructionist in matters of constitutional law. Today, beyond the *Baker* v. *Carr* decision, there is not much about the Warren Court record with which he agrees. By personality, he is persistent (friends say to a fault) and he is a stickler for the tiniest detail. He can be annoying in a lawsuit because "he just won't give up, even on a minor point." In 1955, it is safe to say, the legislature found him so, too. For he managed repeatedly to remind its members not only what the constitution of Tennessee provided, but that each of them had solemnly sworn with him "that I will faithfully support the Constitution of this State."

"For me," Davis still insisted, years later, "there was no choice. We had to do what the constitution said or we were violating our oaths. If the constitution is violated, our system of law collapses and we become a government of men, not law." This view — and Mac's personal traits — cast against the intransigence of the Assembly, were the ingredients that managed to so dramatize the situation in Tennessee as to arouse urban leadership. Even in 1955, it was aroused more to words than to action; urban interests in the legislature, and those outside in the lobbies, were unwilling to risk the swift retribution they feared if they crossed the rural powers on the Hill.

Davis was different in that he had nothing to lose.

He was no official in any local government, as were many of the Assembly members. He had no list of powerful clients who might feel the wrath of the statehouse crowd if he got too far out of line. He had brought to the Assembly credentials of heritage to match those of Jim Cummings. His ancestors were as deeply rooted, fully as early, in Volunteer soil. But young Davis was no match for Cummings in the skills of parliamentary infighting or cloakroom intrigues. Before Davis could get his reapportionment bill into the hopper, the rural bloc had wind of it and sponsored one of its own, ostensibly written by Representative Ray Dillon, a gangling young lawyer from Crossville, high on the Cumberland Plateau. Dillon's bill was a ploy and he himself voted for its rejection, a motion that carried 62 to 33. The Tennessee constitution, having just been skirted, was then invoked to bury the subject. Under terms of Tennessee's charter, once a bill is rejected, no other bill bearing on the same subject can be considered in the same session of the Assembly. One must wait two years to bring up the issue again.

Davis, however, would not accept Jim Cummings's way. Dillon's bill was rejected January 13 and two weeks later young Davis was still insisting on consideration of his bill. Taking it over to the state attorney general's office, he demanded a ruling on its legality and got instead a departmental letter declaring it was the legal department's opinion that it should not try to determine if Davis's bill was constitutional but should await "a judicial determination."

Waving this letter, Davis went to the floor, sparking a two-hour parliamentary wrangle. Cummings took the floor for a long, rambling and hilarious speech that endured for one hour and twenty-two minutes. Davis's efforts to fight back were throttled. At the conclusion of Cummings's rich recital, salted with rural aphorisms, Davis sought the floor on a point of personal privilege. Representative Dale Glover, of Obion County in rural Weststate, objected that Davis was arguing the question. He was gaveled down by House Speaker James Bomar, from rural Bedford County. Davis's bill was then rejected 60 to 34.

Years later, Davis could recall Cummings's speech with a chuckle: "I remember quite well that he conceded I came from good and honorable Coffee County ancestors, but that if my bill passed, my ancestors would lose representation." The freshman had violated the rule not to be heard and the word circulating at the session's end was that the rural bloc was not going to allow any bills through the House bearing the Davis name. In the closing hours, when the Assembly traditionally engages in a few foolish hijinks to celebrate adjournment, Mac Davis, Jr., was presented the body's huge crying towel.

One of the Davis casualties that year was a bill regulating small loan operators, a measure known as the "Loan Shark Bill." Tommy Osborn, who had helped Davis with his reapportionment efforts, worked the

Assembly corridors for this bill, too. Coming over to Nashville to lobby for it was a young East Tennessee attorney. Mayne Miller had met Tom Osborn and the two were casual friends. Miller and his brother, Haynes, had also been probing the reapportionment issue, a matter of high interest in malapportioned East Tennessee. Mayne Miller was around for nearly two months of the session. When his wife came to Nashville to visit, the Millers, the Osborns, the Davises and the Lees spent several evenings together. They talked at some length of what they had seen and experienced. They saw little hope of convincing the legislature to take an action which would mean, for some, the end of their public service. It was, they concluded, too much to ask of men like James H. Cummings, whose world revolved around Nashville.

The legislature would never, never redistrict itself. At their social gatherings, the young attorneys determined to merge their interests and apply their profession. They were convinced that the only hope was to turn to the courts. Before the 1955 session was out, this band of lawyers and their reformist supporters would draw up and file an important — even imperative — forerunner lawsuit to *Baker* v. *Carr*.

3

The Miller Brothers
and Tommy Osborn

The lawsuit worked up by the young attorneys during
the 1955 session of the Tennessee General Assembly
became known as *Kidd* v. *McCanless*. It was significant in the one-man-one-vote movement because it
served to exhaust the state judicial remedies of those
complaining of debased ballots in Tennessee, and
gave them ample justification to seek relief later in the
federal courts.

Although Tom Osborn and Mac Davis joined in the
lawsuit before it was filed and Osborn helped draw the
final pleadings, the Miller brothers were the prime
movers. While Mayne Miller was lobbying in Nashville, indeed, his brother and law partner, Haynes, had
been drumming up prospective plaintiffs back home
in Johnson City.

It was appropriate that *Kidd* v. *McCanless* had its

origins in Upper East Tennessee, geologically and historically the state's oldest section. In this ancient corner governments were born and out of it the earliest inhabitants flowed down the Great Valley with the Clinch, Holston and French Broad tributaries toward Knoxville and Chattanooga. Others who had helped establish there the Watauga government, Tennessee's first capital and the "lost State of Franklin" bored up through the high notch of Cumberland Gap and down the Cumberland Valley as it snakes out of Kentucky through the midstate knobs to settle Nashville.

No other section of Tennessee was worse abused by the legislative inequities of the 1950's. For no other section had been so staunchly Unionist during the Civil War, and no other section remained more solidly Republican thereafter. The inhabitants who stubbornly clung to the freeborn ideology of this mountainous, picturesque notch were aptly characterized by V. O. Key as "political eunuchs."

That being so, it may seem strange that the Miller brothers were Democrats. They were, in fact, descended from a distinguished and rather aristocratic Confederate line — grandnephews of two of Tennessee's best-known governors, the brothers Robert and Alfred Taylor, and maternal grandsons of a Democratic state supreme court justice and historian, Samuel Cole Williams. Grandfather Williams, the codifier of Tennessee law, dean of Emory University's law school at one time, was a great influence on both the boys after their father was killed in an automobile accident when Mayne Miller was ten, Haynes only seven.

But the Miller brothers had reasons of their own to seek legislative equity for their native region, some related to partisan politics and some beyond. Directly related was the cynical arrangement that had long prevailed between the Democratic Crump machine of Memphis and the established political leaders of East Tennessee, Republican and Democratic alike. Though Crump was now out of power, his successors continued this informal and indeed somewhat covert arrangement whereby Democratic candidates for statewide office were supported in Republican East Tennessee in exchange for federal and state patronage. Any Eaststate Democrat aspiring to local office or a federal post such as, say, congressman, was tossed to the dogs by his own party leaders, as a part of the deal, to keep the Republicans happy; it was next to impossible for an East Tennessee Democrat dwelling among the "eunuchs" to win, anyway.

Mayne Miller had returned to Johnson City, though, for the very purpose of establishing himself as a Democratic candidate for Congress; he wanted no part of a trade with his own party's brokers engaged in the business of keeping Republicans in office in East Tennessee. A more pristine motive, perhaps, belonged to Haynes. He was an extremely intense young man, his Southern town's civil-rights crusader, a soul dedicated to libertarian causes. Both brothers were steeped in their grandfather's writings and both undoubtedly had read from his *History of the Lost State of Franklin* the purpose behind that noble but ill-starred experiment of 1785: "The people of the western counties [of North Carolina] found themselves grievously taxed without enjoying the blessings of it."

Haynes Miller was the sort who would insist upon rectifying such wrong when it cropped up in new format a hundred and seventy years later, just as his ancestors had. In fact, his persistence in righting all sorts of wrongs in late 1954 and early 1955 was the main force prompting his brother Mayne to suggest to him that he look into the inequities of legislative malapportionment.

Haynes Miller, in the fall of 1954, had been scurrying around Johnson City in pursuit of another "project." Only recently returned from France, where he had studied international law at the Sorbonne, Haynes was already locally famous for his "projects." And already his interest in them was causing trouble for the new law firm he had formed with his brother. For one thing, Haynes had sued the railroad, in the interest of safety, to force it to pull up its trackage that ran through the streets of Johnson City. But worse, his campaign for equitable tax assessments in the community had focused unfavorable public attention on the Miller brothers' principal clients, a pair of uncles who owned one of the largest hardwood flooring manufacturing mills in the country.

This was beginning to worry the senior partner in Miller & Miller, Attorneys-at-Law. It was well enough for Haynes, still a happy-go-lucky bachelor, to be spending his time crusading for great causes. But Mayne was a married man trying to earn a living and rally future political support. Late in 1954, therefore, Mayne mentioned to his brother that he should devote some time to legislative reapportionment, a subject Mayne used to discuss over beer with Vanderbilt law school cronies. Haynes Miller was off and running. A few days after this, his mind already at work on the best way to attack this newest injustice, Haynes encountered a friend who had known the Miller boys since childhood, Miss Ella V. Ross, dean of women at the local East Tennessee State College.

"What sort of project are you working on this time?" she asked.

"Legislative reapportionment," he replied, grinning.

"Hey, that's *my* interest," she said. "Let's have a Coke and talk about it." The two stepped into a drugstore. They slid up to the soda fountain and there, in an unlikely American institution, the first plots were laid for a movement that would alter every political institution in their nation.

The cause Mayne Miller handed his brother was neither unknown nor unpopular in East Tennessee. For while the death of the plantation system depopulated rural Middle and West Tennessee, industry had discovered quite early the waterpower and raw stuffs of East Tennessee. Its population accordingly grew by leaps and bounds, filling the valleys and lakeside towns with workers in textiles, in foundries like that owned by Ella Ross's family, in lumber mills like that of the Miller brothers' uncles, in zinc mines, in paper and mercantile trade.

Even before the Tennessee Valley Authority arrived in the Depression Thirties, East Tennessee was changing to an industrial region and the first pressures toward reapportionment were being felt. By the time 1955 arrived, Eastman Kodak was long established in Kingsport, the Atomic Energy Commission boomed in Oak Ridge, the Aluminum Corporation of America had its own Alcoa, Tennessee, south of Knoxville, and Bowaters Newsprint was moving in on the pine-pulp country around Calhoun. Chattanooga was long since known as an "industrial city"; ever more people were flooding in to build up the tourist trade in the Great Smokies around Gatlinburg; coal came up from Scott and Campbell counties, from the deep narrow trough of Sequatchie Valley.

Eaststate people, growing in numbers, facing new problems, were beginning to become restless in their role as "political eunuchs." Some of the more erudite were talking of reapportionment, but others were at the point of open revolt. Returning veterans of World War II — Eaststate counterparts of Charles W. Baker — seized political power in McMinn County by literally driving the Crump-allied oligarchy of Paul Cantrell out of office at the point of souvenir guns. This famous "battle of bullets and ballots" was almost repeated in rebellious Polk County, where a similar uprising dismantled the machine of Sheriff Birch Biggs, one of Crump's most dependable allies in the state's copper-rich but desolate, eroded southeast corner. And that was the political climate in 1948 when Mayne Miller, twenty-five, fresh out of Vanderbilt law school, joined the United States Senate campaign of Estes Kefauver, an underdog East Tennessee Democrat from Madisonville. Miller was one of hundreds of Tennesseans of his age caught up in the 1948 postwar purging of old-line politics. The central target was Crump and the trades he made with brokers of both parties in East Tennessee.

It was during that heated, historic political campaign of 1948 that Mayne Miller came to know Tommy Osborn well. The two had first met the previous summer at the University of Illinois, where Mayne was attending a summer law term and Osborn was visiting his wife's relatives.

Z. T. Osborn, Jr., and Mayne Miller liked each other at once. Osborn, four years older, was already practicing law in Nashville. He was associated with a law firm that had long been close to United States Senator K. D. McKellar, and their friendship shortly had to weather that circumstance. For McKellar was the number one ally of Boss Ed Crump in Tennessee politics and Osborn worked the following summer to defeat the bid of Kefauver to upend the Crump machine while Mayne Miller was helping Kefauver (it was the campaign of the famous coonskin cap). When Kefauver won and rewarded young Miller with a spot in his Chattanooga law firm, Tom Osborn was quick with his congratulations, however. He hadn't been too anxious about the election outcome, anyway. McKellar and Crump, even, had divided over which of two candidates to support against Kefauver, and Osborn had simply owed a debt and had paid it; the McKellar people gave him a real start in Nashville legal circles and — as a poor boy without family connections in a city known as a "son-in-law town" — he had appreciated it.

Osborn and Mayne Miller were attracted to each other more by their common love of politics and propensity for underdog causes than by similar backgrounds. Osborn was the eldest of five children of a circuiting Presbyterian minister — a missionary type, repeatedly assigned by his presbytery to start new churches in Kentucky, Tennessee and Arkansas. Home for the Osborn children was a variety of manses furnished by the struggling small-town and rural congregations their father served. After a couple of years at Centre College in Kentucky, Osborn dropped out to go to work in Nashville, where his family had finally settled. At night he attended law classes at the YMCA there, and passed the bar at twenty-one. It was considered the poor boy's law school.

The considerable talents and the personality of Tommy Osborn did not go unrecognized in Nashville, however, once he got inside a courtroom. His gangling gait and boyish grin were assets that won for him a spreading circle of courthouse friends. There were beginning to be more and more migrants like Osborn and some of these men were reaching the rungs of power in Nashville. He was considered an extremely bright and promising young attorney.

After two years as an assistant U.S. district attorney (where he incurred the political debt to McKellar), Osborn agreed to join the firm of Armistead, Waller, Davis and Lansden. The "Davis" was H. Paschall Davis, an uncle of Maclin Paschall Davis, Jr. Young Mac joined the firm, too, in early 1950.

Osborn was next offered a $9,000-a-year job as city attorney. He took it and the experience was to prompt his entry into the reapportionment tussle. Ben West, the new mayor of Nashville, knew something of the problems he would encounter at City Hall, but the experience was an eye-opening education for Tommy Osborn. For the first time, watching how Jim Cummings and his Statehouse confederates divided the tax money, seeing how desperately Nashville needed funds for its streets, sewers, traffic signals, traffic police salaries and schools, he came to understand the practical implications of the word "reapportionment."

"Now, I knew of the existence of the problem prior to that," Osborn said, years later, "but I did not personally have any genuine interest until I had been exposed firsthand to the way in which the legislature divided the tax money. I realized there was inequitable apportionment but it meant nothing. As a matter of fact, prior to going to City Hall, if anything I approved it. I was more or less for the *status quo*. And it was not until I went over to City Hall and actually saw the abuse to which city dwellers were being subjected, moneywise, that I changed my feelings about it."

Even when he left City Hall following a political disagreement with Mayor West, Osborn did not change his feelings. He now understood that his city and its spreading suburbs, built on a limestone dome, swam in sewage effluent that boiled up through soil that would not absorb it, yet the local governments lacked the resources to do much about this menace. Whether the city engaged in building streets, utility lines or sewers, that underlying rock was a revenue-eater, and the state would not contribute its fair share. When Davis went to the Assembly with his reapportionment plan, then, Tommy Osborn cheered, even coached his younger law associate and neighbor. And when Mayne Miller came over to Nashville, renewed their acquaintance and told of his Eaststate plans, Osborn and Davis were prepared to join the Miller brothers in legal battle. No one promised them a fee; they were doing it all, presumably, on behalf of the people of metropolitan Nashville, who were hardly demanding their services.

It was quite by coincidence that on the same day the rural bloc in Nashville attempted to lay Davis's reapportionment bill to rest, things were set in motion in Johnson City for *Kidd* v. *McCanless*. On the thirteenth day of January, a Thursday evening, thirteen persons showed up for the organizational meeting set up by Ella V. Ross and the Miller brothers. Besides these,

Miss Ross's sister, Mrs. May Ross McDowell, was among those present. So was Grandfather Williams's widow, Isabel Williams, a stern ex-schoolmarm whose concern for politics and matters of state sprang from a time spent in Nashville with the state Department of Education.

During the several weeks since Haynes and Ella Ross had sipped Coke and plotted, both had been busy with the matter off and on. Haynes drove out to the college at the edge of town and with the help of political science professors drew up some maps of Tennessee showing how out of balance the legislature had become and specifically how shorted in representation was the East Grand Division. Ella Ross had drawn her sister in. May Ross McDowell was an attorney; she and her husband also ran the Ross family business, Johnson City Foundry and Machine Works, Inc. They were dedicated Republicans, as was another organizer, Gates Kidd, the local Ford dealer. But they elected a Democrat, attorney Frank Bryant, to head the infant organization — the Tennessee Committe for Constitutional Reapportionment — and they adopted the twelve-point plan of procedure sketched out by Haynes and Ella Ross.

Point Five of the plan was vital: finding individuals or groups in other counties to join in the action; and Memphis, Nashville and Knoxville were specifically mentioned along with Sullivan and Anderson counties. Miss Ross, a tallish woman with graying hair swept back and pinned from a middle part, was a natural for this role. Two years earlier, she had taken leave of her college dean's duties to serve as one of Washington County's delegates to the limited constitutional convention. Tennessee went into that convention of 1953 with the oldest unamended constitution in the world. The state's voters surprised some observers, however, by ratifying in November the amendments adopted by the convention, and Miss Ross got a taste of reform success. During the convention she also broadened her contacts across the state and now she set out to call upon them for help. Her responses were disappointingly negative. No one in neighboring Sullivan County was interested. In Anderson, home of the Oak Ridge nuclear facility, the League of Women Voters invited Miss Ross down to speak, but they couldn't and didn't join the lawsuit, not having gone through the LWV's required procedures. In Knoxville, she was promised, and received, some newspaper publicity. Her overtures to the prestigious constitutional convention delegate from Memphis, Walter Chandler, a former mayor and congressman from the largest city in the state, were politely declined.

The East Tennessee group tried hard for Chandler. In mid-January Miss Ross had a chance meeting with him in the lobby of the Hermitage Hotel in Nashville. They chatted about the formation of the Johnson City group, a few days before, and he sounded extremely interested. Upon returning home, she suggested to Haynes Miller that he write Chandler, and she did so herself. Miller moved quickly at Miss Ross's suggestion. On January 22, he sent Chandler an outline of reapportionment actions dealt with in other states, a brief review of some of Tennessee's pertinent cases and six maps he had made up with his East Tennessee State College friends which he proposed "be given to the newspapers one at a time for six days" to provoke publicity and "clarify the present situation for the Judges." Miller also wrote:

I am sure that you understand that we do not plan to attack the Legislature directly, but ask for a judgment declaratory of the unconstitutionality of the present scheme of apportionment together with such relief as "may be meet and proper."

We think that the Court could order an apportionment itself on the theory that the Constitution is self-executing, since there is one distribution most obedient to the Constitution and mathematically superior to all others; or, the Court could order a state-wide election at large; and finally there is the possibility that at least Shelby, of all the underrepresented counties, could show that it is entitled to representatives now elected by certain other counties in West Tennessee.

But the hope Miller expressed that Chandler and big Shelby County might join in the action was no more than that. On January 31, Chandler acknowledged receipt of the material, which he "read with keen interest, but have not had an opportunity to give thorough consideration to the matter."

The persistent Miller did not give up. On February 19, he wrote Chandler again, reminding him that "we in East Tennessee are just about ready to file an action for the reapportionment of the State in the Chancery Court of Davidson County" and expressing again the "hope that Shelby County will join by intervention or bring a separate proceeding, and we should be particularly reassured if you could personally take part and bolster our forces." He enclosed a new map.

Memphis and Shelby County were playing coy, however, and Chandler did not reply to this letter until June 21, long after the suit was filed. His letter noted why, in effect: the legislature had still been in session. And when Mayne Miller's lobbying visit enrolled Tom Osborn and his friends, Osborn's try for Memphis also fell short. His contact with Shelby County was through Jesse Vineyard, a red-haired assistant city attorney for Memphis whom Osborn had known during his own stint as a city attorney. Vineyard was assigned to the Shelby County legislative delegation as the group's legal adviser during the 1955 session and he stayed in Nashville throughout it. He was interested. A series of letters and other communications flowed back and forth between Osborn and Vineyard during the time the papers were being drawn and prepared for filing and invariably Vineyard sounded encouraging about Memphis's interest. But he was checking regularly with Walter Chandler.

Time was drawing short on the session now, however, and the young attorneys decided they had to move. The name of Gates Kidd, an automobile agency owner who had been elected Finance Chairman of the citizens' committee, led the list of plaintiffs from

Washington County and thereby Kidd stepped into the pages of legal history. Kidd had been made Finance Chairman because he pledged the largest amount toward the lawsuit; he had received a recent personal injury judgment and used the money in this cause. Grandfather's widow, Isabel, was listed among them, simply as Mrs. S. C. Williams. Altogether, there were five from Washington County. Having failed of support in Sullivan and Anderson counties, both of which had strong Democratic contingents, Haynes Miller went over into Republican Carter County, just east of Washington, and there recruited six persons as plaintiffs. And Tom Osborn, in Davidson, added the names of his friends — neighbor Jack Lee and Mrs. James M. (Molly) Todd, who had also served with Ella Ross in the recent constitutional convention. On March 8, 1955, ten days before the General Assembly adjourned *sine die,* Haynes Miller and Osborn tossed *Kidd* v. *McCanless* into the legal mill. The first concrete step toward America's rotten-boroughs reform thus had been taken.

Upon filing the suit, Osborn and Haynes outlined their intent to the press. Osborn called it "the first step in what may be a years long effort to bring equal rights in state government to all the people of Tennessee."

"If we should win in the state courts," Haynes Miller added, "it is practically certain that our opponents seeking to protect a stacked deck in state government will take the issue on up through the federal courts. If we should lose, we certainly do not intend to stop short of the highest court in the land."

The Millers and Osborn did not enter the arena blind. They were thoroughly familiar with *Colegrove* v. *Green;* knew of its "political thicket" pronouncement; were aware that it had been decreed the law of the land by a 3–3–1 split of the United States Supreme Court. They knew that other states, on the basis of that split decision, repeatedly had been turned down. The first paragraph of their original bill made it abundantly clear that they were also well aware of the presence of a federal issue:

"COMPLAINANTS RESPECTFULLY SHOW TO THE COURT . . . That they are now denied the right to equal suffrage in free and equal elections, which right is granted them by the Constitution of the State of Tennessee, and the equal protection of the laws, as guaranteed by both the Constitution of the State of Tennessee and by the Fourteenth Amendment to the Constitution of the United States."

Their complaint attacked the constitutionality of Chapter 122 of Tennessee's Public Acts, the last reapportionment law enacted by the General Assembly — in 1901, despite the every-decade mandate of the state constitution. Even when it was drawn, they argued, the 1901 act was invalid because "no census of qualified voters upon which a proper apportionment could be based was actually made in spite of explicit requirements" in the constitution. The 1901 apportionment, even then, was "unfairly and unequally made," the bill claimed. But in any event, "the Act of 1901 ran its course and became unconstitutional in 1911," when the next reapportionment was due.

They also argued the act was unconstitutional because it denied their clients the number of representatives to which they were entitled, "thereby reducing and debasing [their] right to equal franchise." Moreover, "these complainants are further denied the equal protection of the laws accorded them by the Fourteenth Amendment to the Constitution of the United States by virtue of the debasement of their votes." Haynes Miller's numerous maps made up the exhibits. These purported to demonstrate that "a minority of approximately 37 per cent of the voting population of the State now controls twenty of the thirty-three members of the Senate," and that "a minority of 40 per cent of the voting population of the State now controls sixty-three of the ninety-nine members of the House of Representatives." These were the precise figures cited in *Baker* v. *Carr,* years later, before the United States Supreme Court.

"Thus a minority now rules in Tennessee by virtue of its control of both Houses of the General Assembly contrary to the basic principle of representative government . . . and contrary to the philosophy of government in the United States and all Anglo-Saxon jurisprudence in which the legislature has the power to make law only because it represents the people."

The reformers asked the court, after finding the act unconstitutional, to enjoin the defendant-officials from holding another election under the act. Instead, they asked the court either to require by mandamus an at-large election over the state as a whole, or that the judge himself redistrict the state by mathematically applying the 1950 census "unless and until the General Assembly . . . reapportions."

Besides Attorney General George F. McCanless, the plaintiffs sued the three members of the state Board of Elections — Dr. Sam Coward of Overton County, James Alexander of Carroll County and Hubert Brooks of Washington County. They sued the thirty-seven members of the Republican state Primary Election Commission. They sued the thirty-six members of the Democratic state Primary Election Commission. They sued the three members of each of the county election commissions in the counties from which the plaintiffs were drawn — Washington, Carter, Davidson.

Wanting to make no mistakes, the young attorneys sued any group they felt might have any responsibility. In the first draft of their brief, put together January 10, 1955, by Haynes and Mayne Miller, they had designated the secretary of state the lead defendant, but they later switched to McCanless, whose first name they did not know at the time of the initial drafting. (This was left blank and the attorney general's name was misspelled "McCanliss.")

Listed as sixth defendant among the Republican primary group was Hobart Atkins. The Knox Countian, also an attorney, promptly persuaded his party, which had much to gain, to join the crusade and make

reapportionment its official stand. Such a decision certainly implied an end to the era of historic political
tradeouts by East Tennessee political leaders. Guy
Smith, the Republican chairman and publisher of the
Knoxville *Journal*, agreed with Atkins. So Atkins, the
defendant, switched sides. In Tom Osborn's summary: "We sued Hobart Atkins as one of these [elec-
tion] officials, and Hobart turned around and sued
everybody in the legislature." This cross-action,
through which Governor Frank G. Clement was also
sued, made Atkins both defendant and plaintiff. But
he had joined the Millers and Osborn, convinced they
were right, and this was to be a stance he would never
abandon.

Among those sued by Atkins, of course, were James
H. Cummings and I. D. Beasley. Pete Haynes was not
in the General Assembly that year. But shortly Cummings and Beasley saw that the third corner of the
Great Triangle got into the dispute. They retained his
legal services to represent them. Most of the rest of the
legislature simply designated McCanless and his staff
to defend their interests.

Even so, it was going to be crowded in Chancery
Court.

4

Thomas Wardlaw Steele: West Grand Division

The young attorneys, having gotten their cause to court, soon had to view with mixed emotions an unexpected development: a switch in judges.

They had filed their lawsuit in March 1955, in the Davidson County Chancery Court of veteran Chancellor Thomas A. Shriver, Sr. In April, before the case could be set for hearing, Shriver was elevated to the Tennessee Court of Appeals. Appointed in May to replace him was Thomas Wardlaw Steele, who had never spent a day on the bench.

Chancery courts, which derive from our English legal heritage, try cases in equity, involving principles of law. Sometimes referred to as the "courts of conscience," they are the tribunals in Tennessee where constitutional matters are decided. Their judges are titled "Chancellor," and Steele, barely thirty-three at the time, was the youngest man ever to hold that office in the state.

Though Chancellor Steele's youth made him a member of the generation bringing the reapportionment action, there were nonetheless reasons for concern about his becoming the sole judge of *Kidd* v. *McCanless*. To begin with, the young jurist had deep roots in rural West Tennessee, which had much to lose in any redistricting. Moreover, he had been a member of the Tennessee General Assembly a few years before, in 1949, representing one of the more agricultural districts — Tipton and Lauderdale counties, both of which were shrinking in population the year he was elected (and have continued to wither). Having represented such a rural region, Chancellor Steele, it was feared, might well rule with sympathy for the legislative bloc headed by Jim Cummings. In fact, the rumor was out that he would. Tom Steele himself "learned from friends some years later that shortly after I assumed the bench it had been said Governor Clement appointed one of his friends to the bench to be sure that this case never got anywhere. This amused me at the time, and of course it was certainly the fiction of somebody's imagination and one of those types of courthouse rumors that go around." It was a rumor not hard to believe, however, if one was unacquainted with Thomas Wardlaw Steele, and few associated with the lawsuit at that time could claim they knew him well; he had been living in Nashville less than four years.

The rumors about Tom Steele's appointment were plausible because there was reason to suspect that Governor Frank Clement had little sympathy for the lawsuit. True, he had given some lip service to the principle of equitable representation, but the Governor still had to deal with a rural legislature for some years to come. His relationship with the Assembly in 1955 had been most cordial. With Cummings in his crew, the Governor saw reasonably smooth sailing ahead for the rest of his tenure. He was not anxious to disturb the waters. It was with considerable trepidation, therefore, that Tennessee's young reformers congregated outside the fourth-floor dark mahogany courtroom in the Davidson County Courthouse that humid day, July 6, 1955, for the first argument of their cherished lawsuit before a raw, relatively unknown lawyer and inexperienced judge indigenous to the one section of the state where, try as they might, they had been unsuccessful in mustering support — the West Grand Division.

Had they been better acquainted with Steele's background, the Miller brothers at least might have felt somewhat more assured. Tom Steele's upbringing was not unlike their own. Steele, too, was a member of an aristocratic Democratic family, and was the son of a politically minded attorney. (Wardlaw Steele, Tom's father, by strange coincidence had also died in an automobile mishap, in 1941 while returning to his home on the day he had picked up in Nashville his commission as a member of the Tennessee Supreme Court —

the same bench on which the Millers' grandfather, Samuel Cole Williams, had once sat.)

The son would have been unlikely to betray his father's ideals. There had been a special relationship between Tom Steele and his father. Wardlaw Steele had been a powerful man in West Tennessee. He was a prosperous businessman and a third-generation partner in the state's oldest law firm, Steele & Steele, founded in 1868. He dealt closely with U.S. Senator K. D. McKellar and, through him, with Boss Crump. But he was no Crump puppet; the "Boss" had once opposed his appointment to the federal bench. Steele was a delegate to the Democratic National Convention and he took his young son along. He was chairman of the state Democratic Executive Committee and Tom drove him to its meetings throughout the state. They traveled quite a lot together — down to Memphis on business, to Nashville for political or bar association meetings, to East Tennessee to try some lawsuit. Wardlaw Steele deliberately exposed his son to his business, legal and political activities. It became accepted that Thomas Wardlaw Steele, the angular, bony kid growing up in Ripley, would follow his father into law and politics.

When Tom Steele got his law degree from the University of Virginia in February 1948, he promptly returned to his hometown with the same thought in mind that Mayne Miller had when he returned to Johnson City a couple of years later; he intended to run for Congress. In pursuit of this goal, he declared that summer for the state legislature and he was elected handily. Everyone in Lauderdale and Tipton counties knew Wardlaw Steele's surviving son. But legislative service was soon over and it became apparent to Steele that the congressman from his district, Jere Cooper, had no thoughts of vacating the seat once held by Davy Crockett. Cooper had been a close political ally of his father's and Steele did not wish to run against him. Unattracted to practice in a rural setting, Steele closed the state's oldest law office in September 1951 and, like so many others of his generation, moved his young family off to help swell the population of a growing metropolis.

When Thomas Wardlaw Steele mounted the bench to participate in the initial legal step in Tennessee's landmark reapportionment revolution, it was thus largely by chance that he did so. He was also, when appointed, only "vaguely aware that the lawsuit had been filed." He "knew nothing whatsoever that was involved in it" and had taken no earlier interest in the subject. As a freshman legislator, he had had only the fuzziest awareness of the malapportionment of seats in the body in which he sat. "I must confess," he said, "that as a member of the legislature I was not conscious enough of this to feel any compulsion to do anything about it."

For Steele, *Kidd* v. *McCanless* "came on rather routinely. By that I mean I didn't give any priority to it insofar as the hearing of it was concerned. It got set in the normal course of events and I was under the impression, as I suppose judges often are, that this case really was not considered by any of the lawyers involved or any of the politicians who were following it to be a case of any exceptional interest. It was not, I presume, thought that the case had much chance of success. I had no preconceived attitude about the ultimate results that ought to be achieved in it."

But shortly after he assumed the bench, Steele acknowledged, he decided he had better acquaint himself with the reapportionment situation "and of its potential importance in the political structure of the state. I commenced to try to find out something that was involved in it, and I did."

Steele disclaimed any feeling of trauma or sense of divided loyalties about having to rule on a matter in which his native West Tennessee had so large a political stake, and particularly those rural regions of his boyhood. "I had, I like to think, an ability on the bench to let outside influences not interfere with what I decided to be just in a particular case. I was extremely conscious of this, in one way; but, frankly, during the time that I was considering this case, it did really never occur to me that I might be doing something to my old home district down in Ripley, Tennessee. This thought just never entered my mind."

Tom Steele, the judge, was correct in that position, of course. For it was not Tom Steele, the man, who was "doing something" to West Tennessee. Time and circumstance were responsible for the enormous change taking place in that tobacco and cottonland third of the state lying west of the Tennessee River.

Thomas Wardlaw Steele could not have known where it all was headed the day he mounted his bench to hear the first arguments in *Kidd* v. *McCanless* from an array of legal talent and assorted interests.

James Cummings and Pete Haynes were there insisting that "the legislature shall be the sole judge of its members," that the judicial and legislative branches have lines they *must not* cross.

Mac Davis, Jr., was there with his brief, prepared to show that the law itself could collapse if the constitution's interpretation fell short of its strictest and most conservative construction. It said: You *shall* redistrict.

The Miller brothers were there from the East Grand Division, Democrats arguing a Republican cause, crying for justice, pure and simple.

Tom Osborn was there taking the economic tack, talking in terms of dollars and cents, thinking in terms of sewers and schools.

Hobart Atkins was there, on hand in a partisan cause, hoping the interests of his Grand Old Party could be so strengthened that Tennessee, in time, might even become a two-party state and the Solid South more fluid.

And the defendant, George McCanless, was there, attorney general of Tennessee, ready to remind the young chancellor reared in West Tennessee what the Supreme Court itself had said: This is a political thicket. Do not enter.

Perhaps no young jurist ever faced a more formidable task in his first week on the bench than the one thrust upon Steele. The lawsuit before him, besides being intensely political, involving the very basics of the American structure of government, was also indescribably complex.

The young attorneys for the plaintiffs had sued eighty-seven defendants, in the first place. One of the defendants, Hobart Atkins, in filing his answer and cross-bill, had added to the list the governor, thirty-three senators and ninety-nine members of the Tennessee House of Representatives. Altogether, this brought to two hundred and twenty the number listed as defendants, and some besides Hobart Atkins were on both sides. Representative Maclin P. Davis, Jr., for example, was listed as counsel of record for the plaintiffs; through Atkins's action he was now also a defendant, entitled to file an answer. This he did shortly, on his own behalf and that of his five House colleagues in the Davidson County delegation. But Davidson's two senators chose other means of answering the suit. One, Henry Gupton, joined eighty-two other legislators designating the lawsuit's chief defendant, Attorney General George McCanless, his counsel. For this group and himself, McCanless and his staff of three lawyers filed a demurrer, the legal pleading which in effect says to the plaintiffs, "All that you say may be true, but there is no legal remedy for it." The other Davidson senator, Clifford Allen, was a lawyer, and he chose to write his own answer. All legislatures are full of attorneys like Allen, ready and anxious at any time to enter, with both feet, an exciting legal fray political in nature. Some did. The Shelby County delegation, now drawn into the lawsuit ready or not, answered in a bloc in a friendly response filed on their behalf by Jesse Vineyard.

And Cummings, Beasley and Pete Haynes's stand-in for the 1955 session — Representative H. Frank Smith of Haynes's Franklin County — filed a separate demurrer. Since they had named Haynes their lawyer, the State was obliged to accept the appointment. So the "Unholy Trinity" was reunited again (although briefly, for Beasley died that fall). Governor Clement, having likewise been sued by Atkins's cross-bill, filed a separate demurrer in the court of his recent appointee.

Atop these answers, cross-bills, demurrers, came memorandum briefs (Hobart Atkins's alone ran to forty-three legal-sized pages), preliminary memoranda on legal authorities cited (the Miller brothers and Osborn gave seventy-six cases), cross-defendants' memorandum briefs in opposition to demurrers (Mac Davis filed two, of eleven and five pages, respectively), and so forth. At least one hundred cases were cited, half of them more than once, many of them claiming to be precedents on opposite sides of the issue. Prominent among these cases, of course, was the polestar, *Colegrove* v. *Green*. It was the main thrust of the State's move for dismissal.

This maze was enough to try the scholarship and the patience of a seasoned judge. Steele, it appeared, approached the task with gusto, and shortly it was time for oral arguments. In his small courtroom, five lawyers lined up on either side to take part in what, for attorneys, is a joyous day — arguments. For the plaintiffs: Haynes and Mayne Miller, Tom Osborn, Mac Davis and Hobart Atkins. For the defendants: McCanless, his three assistants, Knox Bigham, Jack Wilson and James Glasgow, and finally Pete Haynes.

"It was," said Mayne Miller, fifteen years later, "the high point of my legal career. I recall that day quite well because Steele was good enough to give us the whole day — told us it was the most important case he'd ever hear; and just have at it and talk in turn as long as you wanted to and have as many turns as you wished. This was fine because when we got up we were relaxed and went to it and I think I changed my argument halfway through and made an entirely different argument from what I intended." Attorney General McCanless had argued that the separation of powers should not be breached, and it occurred to Mayne Miller as he got up to answer "that the purpose of the separation of powers was to prevent the concentration of power in the hands of a few. In the smallest county in Tennessee [Moore], votes counted seventeen to one more than in the largest county. So in my argument I described an Election Day when one man came in and got seventeen ballots, another man got one ballot. He who got only one ballot protested and was told the Supreme Court had decided in favor of the man with seventeen votes. Asking why, he was told, 'Well, the Court

figured that it was because of the separation of powers.' I discussed the basis of the separation of powers
in the theories of Locke and Montesquieu: that it was
intended to prevent the concentration of power. . . .
Strange justification for the seventeen-to-one vote!"

Tom Osborn argued that the 1901 act, under which
legislators were then elected, had been unconstitutional even before it had expired, because there was no
enumeration of voters preceding it as required by the
state constitution. It had been enacted to "perpetuate
the gang enjoying minority rule in the legislature" and
"our lawsuit tests whether or not a government of law
as opposed to a government of men can succeed in the
preservation of human rights. Courts of chancery have
stood for freedom of the people," he told the new
Chancellor. "Now history sits again at a chancery door
to see what chancery will do."

Hobart Atkins raised the argument that went back
to the American Revolution. The fiscal inequities
perpetuated by this system, he argued, amounted for
East Tennesseans to "taxation without representation.
If we can't go to chancery court, where will we go?"
Mac Davis, arguing briefly, stuck to his favorite theme
of strict construction. The whole issue, he declared,
was whether the legislature or the constitution was supreme.

The arguments went on for five hours. Once Mc-
Canless had laid out the broad outlines of what the defense would be, he left to his assistants more technical
attacks upon the form of the lawsuit and alleged faults

in its drafting or its choice of defendants that might, by technicalities, get it thrown out of court. Knox Bigham, for example, pointed out that the original suit was brought against election commissioners in only three counties and that even if the Chancellor held the plaintiffs' views to be correct, then any decree would affect those counties alone. He argued that "these cases usually are politically inspired and not addressed to the populace as a whole." Any decision by Steele, then, might be subject to opposite decisions by chancellors over the state and "you can see the utter futility and chaotic effect of such a scheme."

But the defense base was almost solely built on Justice Frankfurter's *Colegrove* assertions regarding the separation of powers and why, therefore, courts ought not to enter the "political thicket." McCanless had struck that theme. Bigham now returned to it: "They want you, the Chancellor, to pass a reapportionment act but I don't think that any court would take unto itself such arrogant power to destroy another branch of government." And Pete Haynes, on behalf of Jim Cummings, I. D. Beasley, and without question himself, landed on it hard: "There is nothing plainer in Tennessee law than the constitutional language on separation of power between the judiciary, legislative and executive branches of government. For the courts to write a reapportionment bill would be to destroy that power delegated to the legislature." If anyone present felt that Steele was that presumptuous, they underestimated him. He had no such notions in mind.

It had been two months between the appointment of Chancellor Steele and the day of arguments for *Kidd* v. *McCanless* and the young judge had spent some of his time during those months studying the background of reapportionment. He was not too pleased with the briefs or the arguments, high-principled and stirring though they were. He was looking for help. "I must confess to you," he said, "that in the very beginning, the presentation of the case, both by argument and briefs, was not really too helpful to me because the attorneys had not gone into the case as deeply as I thought it deserved."

"After I started studying the case," Steele said, years later, "I became convinced it would ultimately end up in the Supreme Court of the United States, regardless of what the decision I made was, or what the other courts did after I decided. I studied the case rather consistently and rather deeply for approximately four months. During that period of time I was hearing other litigation and deciding other litigation, but this was almost a continuous process of trying to read everything I could find on the case, both that which had been cited to me, and that which had not been cited to me.

"And then purely sitting around thinking and thinking and thinking what ought to be done about this thing. I suppose if there was one determining factor that governed the decision I ultimately reached, it was that this was the situation similar to other situations which come along infrequently in our political history where something had to be done. I made up my mind that the people will tolerate a situation only so long, particularly where it involves a clear violation of their basic constitution, and I couldn't believe that the courts, by virtue of judicially declared doctrines of nonintervention, were helpless and powerless to give relief where other political branches of the state government had refused relief, and blatantly so.

"Philosophically, I suppose this was the most dominant thing in my thinking. I finally got to the point where I knew I had to decide the case after four months was up and I started writing the decision." Almost the entire decision, which finally ran to fifty-three typewritten legal-size pages, was written on a weekend at the Steeles' home. Steele dictated with lawbooks and briefs spread all around him; his wife Frances wrote his words down longhand.

"I felt that I had both reached the conclusion and expressed it in a manner that I was completely satisfied with. When I did that, I released the opinion totally unaware of the apparent impact it was going to make on the politics of the state." The date was November 21, 1955.

There are, in the legal trade, lawyers known as "arguing" lawyers and others known as "briefing" lawyers. Tom Osborn, the Millers, Pete Haynes, they were "arguing" types, skilled in oratory and repartee, fast on their feet. Tom Wardlaw Steele was a bit of both, but his strength lay in the brief. He was scholarly, gifted with the power of clear, straight logic, capable of articulating his reason in precise terms. The opinion he handed down was considered masterful.

In orderly fashion, he had consolidated all the complex issues to three: "(1) The Court's jurisdiction of the subject matter of the suit is attacked and assailed on the grounds that the bill presents a political or legislative question, which cannot and will not be determined by the Judiciary; (2) The jurisdiction and power of the Court to grant any of the relief sought by the bill is challenged on many grounds; and (3) The constitutionality of the Act assailed is asserted, thus making an issue upon that question."

Tom Steele did not believe then (and does not believe now) that the courts had any business reapportioning legislatures. Steele stood firmly for separation of powers and quickly disposed of the Governor's part in the lawsuit by sustaining his position that the court had no authority over him. With the same logic, he sustained all the demurrers filed by all members of the legislature. Some legislators had filed no replies at all; they were dismissed as defendants on the judge's own motion.

He further reduced the defendant list by ruling that neither of the party primary boards, having no power, were proper parties to the lawsuit. The case was reduced to a contest between the original plaintiffs on the one hand, then, and McCanless and election officials on the other.

Having cut the lawsuit down to size, Steele could approach the major question: Did his court have jurisdiction? It was the question of the *Colegrove* decision, which Steele cited: "An examination of the decision in *Colegrove* v. *Green, supra* . . . discloses that a majority of the Court did not approve and sanction the above-quoted doctrine [the political thicket]," Steele wrote. He pointed out that Justices Frankfurter, Reed and Burton concurred in the *Colegrove* opinion, expressing the judgment of the Court. "Mr. Justice Rutledge concurred in the result reached, but did not concur in the opinion that the Court had no jurisdiction of the subject matter. His conclusion was that while the Court had jurisdiction of the subject matter it should decline to exercise its power to afford relief in a case of that type. Justices Black, Douglas and Murphy dissented from the conclusion reached therein, and it was their opinion that the Court not only had jurisdiction of the subject matter, but should exercise its power in the premises. It will, therefore, be seen that four of the Justices in that [*Colegrove*] case were of the opinion that the Court had jurisdiction of the subject matter of that suit, and only three Justices were of the opinion that it did not." To cap this, Steele cited eighteen cases to support his position that his court was cloaked with jurisdiction. But he felt he had jurisdiction in any event "on the general principles of reason and the fact that justice must be done."

Having taken jurisdiction, Steele declared the 1901 Tennessee apportionment act no longer valid because it "has expired by its own provisions and according to the intent of the Legislature which adopted it." Any future election held under its malapportioned terms, he declared, "will be held without any legal authority whatever."

He stopped short of injunctive relief — calling that prospect "premature" — or of ordering an at-large election. Rather, he turned to the other branches of government, whose territory he would not invade, to put the house in order. He "presumed" Governor Clement would "exercise his constitutional power and duty to call the Legislature into special session" to enumerate and reapportion as required by the constitution. He further presumed the legislature would do its duty: "That such result will not occur is inconceivable to this court."

Would the existing legislature be a legal one, since the 1901 act was out? He said, "That the present General Assembly may thus act as a *de facto* body, the court entertains not the slightest doubt." It was, indeed, a judicial coup, turning the onus upon the Governor, the legislature itself, or, as we shall see, upon Tennessee's supreme court. Frank Clement did not like it one bit. "He can't do that! He just can't *do* that!" he told his press secretary, Howard Anderson. But his appointee had done it.

5

"Fiat Justitia Ruat Caelum"

Steele's ruling in *Kidd* v. *McCanless* produced a wave of euphoria among its supporters and unexpected praise for the young jurist. He was not alone, of course, in receiving the plaudits. Walter Chandler, then serving an interim term as mayor of Memphis, wrote to congratulate Haynes Miller, who had tried so hard earlier to get him to participate in the lawsuit: "If the Supreme Court of Tennessee has real courage the vexing question of reapportionment will be decided correctly." He urged Miller and his associates to call on Memphis for future help and so did Jesse Vineyard, his assistant city attorney, in a similar letter December 9 to his friend Tom Osborn.

Steele, who "had some apprehension from the very beginning as to how this would be treated by the appellate courts" was now encouraged to feel "that maybe the Tennessee Supreme Court might go along with the decision." His ruling had been, after all, no more than "a mere warning to the Governor and the legislature that they had to do something about this or ultimately the courts would."

The opposition of the Governor and legislature had been underestimated, however, and all the favorable metropolitan press reaction overestimated. Political power suddenly began to flex its muscle. Governor Clement, despite his announced devotion to the high principles involved, made it quite plain that his administration would support the appeal that everyone had expected all along. And some felt they read in the vigor of the Attorney General's pursuit of this appeal a hint of the Supreme Court's own leaning.

One has to know something of the unusual judicial system in Tennessee to understand such an interpretation. The attorney general is appointed by the five judges of the Tennessee Supreme Court, who are elected by the public. (In practice, though, most of the justices first mount the bench in much the manner that Tom Steele was named to chancery — by gubernatorial appointment when a vacancy occurs.) By custom, the attorney general has been a native of the section of the state that does not already have two justices on the supreme court; thus, each of the three grand divisions is accorded, ostensibly at least, equity in the justice apparatus.

As this system operates in Tennessee, the judiciary is more often sensitive to legislative than to executive pressure, once the justices get on the court. For once appointed, they have to be periodically reelected, and the state legislators are capable of both discouraging opposition and of supporting them at the grass-roots level should opposition develop.

The effect the nuances of such a system have on a court and its officers might well be pondered. At all events, in Tennessee it was considered that a challenge of the state legislature was a considerable burden for young reformers to bear to the steps of the state supreme court. The reception the reformers got, they felt, was somewhat less than hospitable and left upon them bitter marks that endured.

On the court representing Middle Tennessee at the time were Chief Justice A. B. Neil of Nashville and Justice Pride Tomlinson of Columbia. West Tennessee had Justice John E. Swepston of Memphis and Justice Alan M. Prewitt of Bolivar. East Tennessee had only Justice Hamilton S. Burnett of Knoxville, and it was for this reason that an East Tennessean, McCanless, held the post of attorney general and reporter. All were, of course, Democrats. Before them to argue that blustery March 5, 1956, were the Miller brothers, Tom Osborn and Hobart Atkins, the counsel for the Republican party.

Even today, Mayne Miller seethes when he recalls that scene before the Supreme Court of Tennessee. His brother, Haynes, took a considerable risk with his health to appear. The day before the arguments took place he left his hospital bed, against the better judgment of his doctor, to be present in Nashville; the week before he had undergone surgery for a slipped disc, a back problem that had given him trouble for some years. When Haynes Miller walked to the podium to present his argument, then, he faltered and almost fell. The Nashville *Tennessean* reported, "Miller's face was pale as he clutched the edge of the table with one hand after he made his way slowly to a point before the judges. . . . His hand resting on the table trembled. Twice he asked the Supreme Court whether any Justices had any questions. Twice silence greeted him." But Miller got his argument out anyway and his voice gained strength as he swung into it: "If democracy means that the people have a right to rule, we have no democracy in Tennessee. It is not possible for a majority of citizens to control the state." The younger brother's argument was much the same one he had presented earlier, but greatly abbreviated. Chief Justice Neil had seriously limited the time for the entire case, upsetting the Millers.

"The Chief Justice wouldn't let us have any additional time," Mayne Miller recalled. "There was a great contrast between him and the attitude of Tom Steele, the chancellor who heard the case. That morning [in the supreme court] there were several cases that had been passed in on briefs and this meant that other arguments that the court had allowed time for weren't going to take place. So the court had time to hear us; the court simply was unwilling to hear us.

"We had to rush our arguments and I remember in

the middle of mine I made one of those stupid mistakes where you put in a negative, you know, when you didn't mean to, and you've said the reverse of what you meant to say. And I started to unwind it and straighten it out and I suddenly realized that not one of them had caught it. They weren't listening!"

Mayne Miller acknowledged that he became angry when, in the midst of his argument, Chief Justice Neil left the bench and walked out of the room. In something close to rage, then Mayne called attention to the court's motto: *Fiat Justitia Ruat Caelum,* "Though the skies may fall, let justice be done." "I drew their attention to this in what I regarded as an appropriate way," Miller commented, years later. George McCanless remembered that the elder of the Miller brothers "made quite a lot of the motto."

As Tom Osborn recalled, "Our argument didn't really go well before the Tennessee Supreme Court. I think we had an hour to argue; Haynes really could hardly get into the subject in less than *two*. Mayne wanted to argue. And of course I wanted to argue. And we had to save a place for the people who had joined us as complainants; the Republicans wanted to argue. As a result, the argument went poorly. It did not go well at all." Osborn was not terribly disappointed with his own short talk, but then he was "better equipped to make a brief argument than either Hobart Atkins or Haynes." If things went better for Osborn in the arguments, however, he was soon to be in serious trouble with the justices.

Tom Osborn had already nettled some of the justices, apparently, with a portion of his appeal brief which he had labeled PURE ARGUMENT. Osborn used the same "fable" he had used before Chancellor Steele. It went as follows:

"It is the first Monday in January in the year 2000. The state legislature is convening in Nashville, Tennessee. One of the defendants to the cross-bill, perhaps Mr. I. D. Beasley, takes his seat in the House of Representatives. Another of the defendants, perhaps Mr. James Cummings, is taking his seat in the Senate. The federal census, about to be released, reflects that they are the only inhabitants of Cannon County. . . .

"Three blocks away and on the fourth floor of the Davidson County Court House, citizens from Carter, Washington and Davidson County are in chancery pointing out that in the forty-five years passing since 1955, their votes have become further debased to where the vote of Mr. Cummings and Mr. Beasley outweighs the value of their vote 200,000 times.

"The Attorney General argues that these citizens have no right to appear in court, that the hurt they complain of is the hurt of all the people of Tennessee and that since their hurt is not special within his interpretation of the word hurt, they have no right to complain. The Attorney General is arguing that the question is political and that in apportioning legislative seats the men in the legislature and not the words of the constitution are the supreme law of Tennessee. He argues that chaos would result if the citizens of Tennessee were allowed free and equal suffrage as guaranteed by the constitution.

"Will he cite *Gates Kidd, et al.* v. *George F. McCanless, et al.,* decided in Chancery at Nashville in 1955 as authority for his argument?"

On April 6, 1956, a month and a day after the arguments, the court reversed Chancellor Steele's opinion and it did so on grounds that infuriated the intense young men who had poured so much of their time, and by now a considerable amount of their money, into the fight. Osborn's reaction, in turn, infuriated the court.

The court's unanimous reversal of Tom Steele was a relatively short verdict, written by Mr. Justice Swepston. After the usual review of the case pleadings, the supreme court agreed with all Steele's findings with respect to dismissing defendants, refusing to reapportion the legislature, withholding the suggested remedies of injunctive relief or at-large elections, etc. The key questions of whether the court had jurisdiction or whether the 1901 act was unconstitutional it skirted altogether (or pretermitted, to use the legal term). It made no determinations concerning the basic justice of the existing system.

"We think the Chancellor was in error in applying the *de facto* doctrine," the opinion read. The court went on to say, "It seems obvious . . . that if the Act of 1901 is to be declared unconstitutional, then the *de facto* doctrine cannot be applied to maintain the present members of the General Assembly in office. . . .

"The ultimate result of holding this Act unconstitutional . . . would be to deprive us of the present Legislature and the means of electing a new one and ultimately bring about the destruction of the State itself." The next morning's newspaper ironically commented under the editorial heading of *Fiat Justitia Ruat Caelum*: "In other words, the skies might fall if justice were done."

Tom Osborn's bitterness also spilled over into the press that day. Contacted for comment immediately after the court's opinion was released, he called it "absurd" and added: "Instead of deciding our case, the justices set themselves up a case and decided it. They overlooked the nature of the complaint made and the relief requested. They tried a little different lawsuit from the one we brought." He went on to explain that the legislature was created by the constitution, not by any apportionment act, and that invalidation of an apportionment act would not destroy the legislature. "Our lawsuit was that the reapportionment act was not a valid act. We did not challenge the right of any individual to be seated in the legislature."

Meeting in private the next day, the court voted to disbar Tom Osborn. Before this became publicly known, however, the clerk of the court, David Lansden, a brother of Osborn's former law partner, intervened in Osborn's behalf with the justices and they agreed to relent — on the condition that he would publicly apologize for his impertinence, which he did. Thirteen years later Osborn could recall the incident with less bitterness but with no less conviction that

remedy for unfairness in districting is to secure State legislatures that will apportion properly." It is remarkable how the myth persisted that this might happen. The Tennessee Supreme Court's decision was hardly delivered, for example, before two of its justices, including the one who had written the opinion, relied again upon this notion to rationalize a decision that both knew and confessed did not contain equity. Justice Swepston, who was from underrepresented Memphis, suggested in an interview with the Memphis *Commercial Appeal* the day following the opinion that urban areas in Tennessee could obtain fair representation if urban candidates would make reapportionment the main issue of their campaigns. Mathematically, it could never have happened; a glance at Haynes Miller's maps would have shown that the pledge of every urban legislator to devote his full energies to the subject would not, at roll-call time, have much changed the vote.

A month beyond the decision, another of the justices created something of a sensation by publicly admitting that the law on which the court had been asked to rule "unquestionably is unconstitutional." Justice Hamilton S. Burnett, who later became chief justice, offered as remedies, however, only the *Colegrove* nostrums and defended the court's reversal of Chancellor Steele.

"The solution of the reapportionment problem lies in the people themselves," he said. "I hope that reapportionment will be made the paramount issue in every legislative race this year. Every candidate of the House and Senate should be pressured into coming clean whether he is for or against reapportionment. Then the people can choose those who pledge themselves to comply with the plain provisions of the Constitution that there shall be a reapportionment every ten years on the basis of the decennial U.S. Census. [In fact, the constitution provided for apportionment on the basis of enumerated voters.] In that way we can get a legislature that will enact a fair and just reapportionment law."

A terse statement written again by Justice Swepston refused Tom Osborn's petition to rehear the *Kidd* case on June 8, 1956, a necessary preliminary to an appeal to the United States Supreme Court. On July 17, Osborn appeared in the office of the Supreme Court Clerk with a page-and-a-half document giving notice of appeal. He invoked the Fourteenth Amendment. But Osborn learned that his good friend Mayne Miller had had enough when he sent him copies of this appeal notice. Mayne wrote back from Johnson City:

I certainly hope you have the money to go on up with it. From time to time I have seen something in the paper on finances and it has not looked promising. I plan to write off the amount I put into this lawsuit, that is the unreimbursed amount, several hundred dollars, but I am not in position to incur any further loss.

Shortly after the adverse decision by Judge Swepston, I told Haynes that I was withdrawing; that I thought it useless to file a petition to rehear and that I opposed an appeal to the federal court. I realize he must not have so informed you so I wanted to tell you now. It is perfectly all right that my name be used if you feel it is desirable but I have never favored going to Washington on the matter even if relief would be forthcoming, anyhow. I was rather of the opinion that Haynes had decided to drop it, but I guess when some expense money came in he changed his mind. I would, however, appreciate being kept informed of the case so that I could discuss its status with the Washington Countians who originally brought it should they ask me about it.

The rather "states-rights" position Mayne Miller took in this instance was one he was to change before long. "I read the testimony of the mayor of Nashville, Ben West, before an intergovernmental committee," Mayne explained later. "He was begging the group not to recommend the return of federal revenue to the states on any sort of revenue-sharing basis. He told how some of the tax money already being returned to the states was being distributed by the rural legislatures. It convinced me, finally. And I changed my position."

Mayne Miller's unawareness of the depth of this problem at the time of appeal is symptomatic of the perspective with which he and his brother approached the issue from the outset. It was one based primarily on principles of equity, rooted in their philosophical concepts of democracy and its ideals. The more pragmatic Osborn, though concerned with such matters, had come into the lawsuit for the very reasons West cited: practical inequity, unfair division of money, economics. He, too, however, was attracted to a states-rights stance, and he was far more conservative politically than either of the Millers, inevitably supporting candidates on the right of center. With sympathy, then, Tom Osborn replied to Mayne Miller's withdrawal: "I will not place your name on the material filed in *Kidd* v. *McCanless* henceforth. I think your judgment is pretty good about the matter; I hate to be critical of the [United States] Supreme Court for its continuing interference in state affairs and then in the next breath ask them to meddle further."

Haynes Miller, too, for entirely different reasons, was about to move out of the lawsuit; when the matter finally reached the decision processes in the highest court in the land, only Osborn and Hobart Atkins would remain with it. The restless Haynes Miller helped prepare the appeal papers, but even before the case reached the Tennessee Supreme Court, he was mapping plans for an overseas assignment. With Tom Osborn's assistance, he landed a post with the United States government. His assignment would give him a chance to use his French — in the exciting Asian peninsula once known as French Indochina. It would give him a chance to give scope to his basic humanitarian instincts, helping a poor and underdeveloped nation — Laos — and its people in their struggle for better conditions. It would fit beautifully into his liberal concepts of building a better world. Foreign aid dealings.

Haynes left the country at about the time Tom Osborn and Hobart Atkins were filing the required jurisdictional statement with the United States Supreme Court. (Such a statement, citing precedents, attempts to convince the high court that it has jurisdiction in a particular case.) Osborn and Atkins were still short of the amount of money they felt it would take, but they were also confident that sufficient funds to cover expenses would flow in quickly in the event the Supreme Court accepted jurisdiction. Since June they had been trying to raise the money and now, in September, the deadline for filing was on them and the gamble had to be taken.

The matter of money was something of a wry joke among the losers by now. Osborn recalled later: "Mayne and Haynes and I . . . all of us lost money. I think the last bill on it was eleven or twelve hundred dollars, which Ward Hudgins and John Barksdale [his law partners] and I paid. Hobart Atkins had undertaken to raise us some money, and Hobart sent me a check for two dollars. That was all he could raise. I still have the check. I told Haynes and Mayne that I better just keep it. Think it would be a better souvenir than to have the two dollars."

Osborn and Atkins had not quite three months to wait for the Supreme Court's answer. On December 3, 1956, giving no reason, it declined to review *Kidd* v. *McCanless*. From its very beginnings, the State's only substantive plea against the lawsuit had been the rule of *Colegrove*, Justice Frankfurter's rhetorical "political thicket." And at least for now, the thicket was not to be entered. Hobart Atkins said he could not think of any further action to be taken: "We had hopes the Court would consider the suit, but now it looks like it's final. It is a big disappointment to me."

Tom Osborn contained his temper this time, resigned to the decision. "I suppose that's the end of our fight," he said. "We had a sound proposition, I thought, but since the United States Supreme Court won't handle it, that puts an end to it."

For now it was over. *Fiat Justitia Ruat Caelum:* The sky had fallen in on the young American Levellers' drive for justice.

Interlude

A BRIDGE AT ST. PAUL
Frank Farrell and Dan Magraw

One thousand twisting miles of the Mississippi River separate Memphis, Tennessee, and St. Paul, Minnesota, but the two river-bluff cities have much in common beyond the historic stream they share.

The West Grand Division of Tennessee surrounding Memphis was next to the last region along the Mississippi cleared of Indian title; the territory around St. Paul–Minneapolis was the last. Andrew Jackson, in 1818, bought out the claims of the Chickasaw in Tennessee and helped lay out Memphis on property in which he and his law partner, Judge John Overton, had personally invested. The following year, halfway between Minneapolis and St. Paul, the United States government built Fort Snelling on a small tract of land at the junction of the Minnesota and Mississippi, acquired from another Indian nation by Zebulon Pike.

As Memphis grew and prospered from Jackson's purchase, so St. Paul rose from the land cession transaction of 1837 when the government bought from the Sioux, or Dakotas, a triangle between the Mississippi and St. Croix rivers. Near this triangle's lower tip, St. Paul was founded a few years later. Both cities grew quickly and were still growing in the mid-1950's, when both played important roles in the one-man-one-vote reform. The Industrial Revolution, which had meant cotton gins for Memphis, was grain-harvesting and ore-mining machines for Minneapolis–St. Paul. The effect was the same on both; machines displaced men on the land while building jobs for them in cities. Minnesota's Twin Cities accordingly filled with the sons and daughters of grain farmers from the southwestern and western plains, the offspring of iron-ore miners from the far northern ranges, just as Memphis had swelled with the black and white migrants described earlier.

The rural legislators of Minnesota were a decade later than Tennessee's in reacting to all this growth. But in 1913, the miners and farmers saw what was happening and called a halt to the required redistricting of the Minnesota Legislature. It had stopped in the Volunteer State in 1901. In both instances, the legislators were violating similar terms of their respective constitutions, for in the matter of reapportionment requirements, Minnesota's constitution had been modeled on Tennessee's.

By the time of the 1970 census, Minneapolis–St.

Paul was America's most dramatic example of suburban growth, just as Memphis had jumped from far down the list to seventeenth place among the nation's metropolitan centers. In 1960, the central Twin Cities had a combined 796,000 people, compared with 686,000 in their surrounding suburbs. By 1970, the situation was reversed; the cities held 741,000, their suburbs 1.1 million. The pattern was everywhere in America — Denver, Omaha, Birmingham, Milwaukee. But long before 1970, young reformers like those in Tennessee set out to make Minnesota recognize this growth and its legislature live up to its oath. Inside the Minnesota Legislature, no one did more to bring to public attention the apportionment inequity than state Representative (later Senator) Alf Bergerud, a lawyer and president of a grocery chain. Bergerud represented the most heavily populated House district in Minnesota. Session after session, near the Legislature's opening, he put into the hopper what came to be known as the "Bergerud Bill." His bill appeared with such regularity it became something of a joke among the legislators. It was not funny to Bergerud. He spoke for 107,256 persons in the 36th South House district of the county named for the first white man to visit St. Paul, Father Hennepin. His district was 471.1 per cent larger than the "ideal" district, which would have had a population of 22,767 had the House districts been perfectly divided. With the same certainty that the Bergerud Bill arose, it was buried by rural legislators.

Witnessing the ritual with growing disgust, then with fury, was a young state employee, Dan Magraw.

Magraw was first exposed to the legislative situation in his native state in 1950, as part of his job with a New York consulting firm of certified public accountants. When his assignment was completed, he decided to stay on in the employ of Minnesota, a decision that gave him a ringside view of the perennial reapportionment efforts of Bergerud in 1951, 1953 and 1955.

"There are a lot of things, I suppose, that triggered my interest," Magraw explained, "but one that I remember most vividly was the unbelievability of legislators, individually and collectively, simply refusing to act as required by the constitution." One personality in particular impressed Magraw. "Carl Iverson, a member of the Minnesota House for many years, and quite an orator, a tall man with a big shock of white hair and a strong Swedish accent, would always rise to his feet during these periodic debates on the floor of the House and declare that so long as he served in the Minnesota Legislature there would never be redistricting." Magraw had encountered the Jim Cummings of Minnesota.

It was difficult for Dan Magraw, untrained in the law, to understand why there appeared to be no remedy for a situation so obviously at odds with the American ideal of equality and in open violation of the Minnesota constitution. After four years with the state, he resigned in late 1954 to accept an administrative position with Investors Diversified Services of Minneapolis. At about this time Magraw moved his family into a new house in St. Paul, only a few blocks from the Mississippi River bluffs he had explored as a boy. Living across the street was the family of Frank Farrell, an attorney for the Northern Pacific Railroad. The Magraws and the Farrells were the same age; they soon found they had many things in common from child-rearing problems to politics.

"We became fairly friendly and talked about many things and one of them was this redistricting," Dan Magraw has recalled. "Frank initially took the view — I guess the view that most of us had taken before — that you couldn't do much about this from a legal standpoint because it had been tried and failed in the state supreme courts and the federal Supreme Court over the years."

This issue had indeed been tried unsuccessfully in Minnesota, where it remained in the same situation as in Tennessee after the failure with *Kidd* v. *McCanless*. In Minnesota, the case had been *Smith* v. *Holm*. It had arisen in 1945 when Jay W. Smith, a candidate for the Legislature, challenged the constitutionality of the 1913 reapportionment act. Smith argued that his Minneapolis district was equal in population to fifteen other counties which had more than five times as many representatives in the Legislature. He won in the Ramsey County district court, but the Minnesota Supreme Court reversed the decision:

"The responsibility to heed the constitutional mandate to redistrict is laid upon the Legislature, and it is,

[99]

at most, only when as of the time of enactment there appears a clear and palpable violation of the fundamental law that the courts could have the power to upset the law." The court held that it did not have that power and therefore the Legislature's "judgment and discretion are its own to exercise or not, as its conscience permits."

To Farrell, the lawyer, such definitive language and United States Supreme Court upholdings of similar notions seemed to settle matters. His discussions with Magraw were mere intellectual exercises, therefore, until the summer of 1956. Farrell then decided to run for the Legislature. Magraw enlisted in his campaign. While preparing for Farrell's campaign that fall, Magraw ran across a federal district court decision from Hawaii that caused Farrell to think about the issue from a new perspective.

The case, *Dyer* v. *Kazuhisa Abe*, had been decided in February of that year. Since Hawaii was then still a territory, it did not offer a strong precedent. But, as Farrell noted later, he thought it did hold out some promise. At least the court had held "that the failure of the territorial legislature to reapportion denied the citizens of Hawaii the equal protection of the law." Like Mac Davis, Jr., and his young lawyer friends running for the legislature in Nashville, Frank Farrell felt that redistricting might be an attractive campaign issue. The district from which he sought election was, after all, one of the most malapportioned in Minnesota. With 62,569 residents, the third most populous in the state, it was 274.8 per cent larger than the "ideal" district. It was peopled by a sophisticated and well-informed citizenry. It lay in the western part of St. Paul, embraced in a hook of the Mississippi river where the stream swings south and back northward again. Within its boundaries are Macalester College, Concordia College, the College of St. Catherine, St. Paul Academy, St. Paul Seminary and the College of St. Thomas. The Ford Motor Company has a large riverside plant in the lower end.

The 42nd South is a huge district and Frank Farrell worked it hard. Having studied the Hawaiian case carefully, Farrell during the course of his campaign "made a statement to the effect that I thought judicial relief was possible but I did not want to involve litigation in the campaign." The statement won him headlines, but not the election. Farrell was first in a field of fourteen during the primary; in the general election he lost to the incumbent by about two hundred votes.

When the campaign was over, Farrell and Magraw decided to bring suit in federal court challenging the legislative districts. Once more they would try through the judiciary to do with the legislative what the young Tennessee reformers had just failed to do. The United States Supreme Court turned back *Kidd* v. *McCanless* on December 3, 1956; at the very moment, Magraw and Farrell were already preparing to give it a go again.

Frank Farrell and Dan Magraw were thirty-six and thirty-five, respectively, when they set out in St. Paul to prepare their lawsuit, *Magraw* v. *Donovan,* and make of it a navigational guide that would do justice to Minnesota's reputation as the North Star State. Daniel Barstow Magraw was the third of four talented sons of a professional bond broker and an extremely civic-minded mother. Two of the sons turned to medicine, two to public service careers. The eldest voluntarily surrendered his career during World War II, however, choosing prison to military service when his concientious objection to war was officially disallowed. The youngest served as a Quaker doctor in China for five years; the brother immediately senior to Dan in the line, Richard, a psychiatrist-surgeon, served for a time in the Johnson and Nixon administrations as a Deputy Assistant Secretary of Health, Education, and Welfare. Richard suspected Dan's interest in reapportionment stemmed from his rearing "in a family of four boys where, for good reason, extreme emphasis was put on fairness."

Frank Samuel Farrell was reared in Duluth in a family filled on both sides with independent businessmen. He turned to law at the University of Minnesota after a brief fling as a salesman and a somewhat longer term as one of those Army pilots of World War II later called back for Korea.

The wide variance between these two men's backgrounds and those of similarly motivated Tennessee men of the same generation testify movingly to the diversity of the nation's bloodstream. But the identical, even singular target of the two groups shouts its evidence of the common ideal that makes us a nation. Yet there was more than ideal. There was a practical side. Urban life in one place was becoming similar to urban life everywhere else in America by the late 1950's, presenting common hardships to Nashville and Memphis, St. Paul and Minneapolis. Rural problems looked much the same in Minnesota or in the Southern hills around Corinth, where young Minnesotans once fell before Tennessee muskets.

In Tennessee, as we have seen, the Miller brothers (and especially Haynes) were the liberal idealists behind *Kidd-McCanless*, Tom Osborn the more pragmatic force, Mac Davis a combination of conservative principle and personal pride. In Minnesota, Dan Magraw was the egalitarian spirit, Farrell the legal and strategic brain. A man of great pride and powerful drives, Farrell had been stung by his narrow defeat in the 1956 election, a near parallel to Mac Davis's experience in Tennessee. It did not help much that he could see the relative ease with which one might claim a legislative seat were he fortunate enough to run from the "rottenest borough" in all Minnesota, right next door to his own district. (The smallest legislative district in the state, the 49th District of Ramsey County embracing the central loop of St. Paul, contained only 7,290 persons. It had no more than 32 per cent of the population living in the "ideal" district.)

Frank Farrell was also a practical man. His first stratagem was accordingly more political than legal, but it was only partially successful. He set out to recruit representatives of the major law firms in the Twin Cities metropolitan area to participate in the lawsuit. Farrell wanted every one of them. He was successful in getting most at the outset by working through junior partners of his acquaintance.

"We thought this was essential to demonstrate to the court that a large number of thoughtful citizens and lawyers had done considerable research on this case. We found out as the litigation wore on that some of the attorneys we had associated with us, because of quiet pressures, had to leave us," he said, "but we were still able to claim representation from a number of prominent firms in the state."

Joining Farrell as attorney for the plaintiffs was a classmate, William C. Meier, Jr. Six attorneys were listed "of counsel" or as being associated with the action: Reginald Ames; William A. Bierman, son of Bernie Bierman, the University of Minnesota football coach; O. H. Godfrey, Jr.; William B. Randall; Joseph A. Rheinberger; and John C. Robertson.

Robertson, another classmate, turned in a valuable contribution — his brother-in-law. The relative, John Avery Bond, had just completed his Ph.D. thesis at Minnesota on the state's malapportioned legislature. Bond's detailed statistical studies of every House and Senate district, its number of representatives, population, and percentage of disproportion would become the appendix of the complaint to be filed shortly, and he would be a key witness when the case came to trial months later.

Farrell also turned to friends for the next task of recruiting plaintiffs. He wanted some of the most malapportioned districts represented, but he also wanted plaintiffs from outside the Twin Cities area. Besides Magraw, then, he called upon John O. Erickson, who practiced law in Minneapolis but lived in the far western section of Hennepin County, where both Senate and House districts were the worst examples of underrepresentation in the state. The 153,455 persons who shared a senator with Erickson lived in a district that was 344.7 per cent above the ideal and a House district 471.1 per cent larger than it should have been. Ruth H. O'Dell, the third plaintiff, was a housewife from Duluth and an active member of the League of Women Voters there. Her district was twice the size it should have been. The final plaintiff — Arthur R. Swan — was another law school classmate of Farrell's, then in private practice at Rochester, a growing community south of the Twin Cities. With such a representative group, Farrell was laying the groundwork for a "class action on behalf of all registered voters — really all citizens of the state."

Selection of defendants in such a lawsuit was important, too, indeed perhaps in some ways even more crucial. Unlike the Miller brothers and Tom Osborn, who had named a long list of statewide primary officials, or Hobart Atkins, who extended it to the entire Tennessee legislature and the governor, Farrell limited his defendants to officials directly concerned with supervising elections in the counties from which his plaintiffs came. (This tactic would later influence the plans of lawyers in *Baker* v. *Carr*.) Some earlier reapportionment actions, Farrell felt, had been lost by directly attacking the Legislature, thus putting two of the coordinate branches in direct conflict.

Farrell's first defendant, then, was the man directly concerned with certifying all election returns in the state, Secretary of State Joseph L. Donovan. Named codefendants with him were officials charged with election duties — the auditors — in each of the four counties: Walter H. Borgen, Robert F. Fitzsimmons, Eugene A. Monick, and Frances L. Underleak.

Farrell was now ready to lay his complaint.

The ten-page formal complaint, with Bond's statistics attached as exhibit, initiated *Magraw* v. *Donovan* when the papers were filed in Minnesota Division, United States District Court on February 19, 1957. The United States Supreme Court's refusal to hear *Kidd* v. *McCanless* was then less than three months old. Frank Farrell had read that case. He knew of the high court's refusal. He may even have known that in the *Kidd* jurisdictional statement, Tom Osborn had cited the same Hawaiian decision from which Farrell's hope first sprang.

It did not matter. The water was pressing upon the dam of American legislative apportionment in the middle 1950's, and other young lawyers like Frank Farrell were already probing lawbooks for a weak point in the dam — in Florida, Michigan, Iowa, Kansas, New York, Vermont, Indiana, Illinois, Oklahoma,

California, Alabama, Georgia. It wouldn't have mattered, for the reason the Tennessee elder statesman Walter Chandler would deliver in his shrill staccato, two years later: "Your Honors! No case is ever decided finally until it is decided *right!*" Besides, Frank Farrell already thought he had a clue where the leak might be found, or opened. He accordingly laid the first ground of his complaint on the language of the Civil Rights Act of 1871:

Section 1983. Civil action for deprivation of rights. Every person who, under color of any statute, ordinance, regulation, custom, or usage, of any State or Territory, subjects, or causes to be subjected, any citizen of the United States or person within the jurisdiction thereof to the deprivation of any rights, privileges, or immunities secured by the Constitution and laws, shall be liable to the party injured in an action at law, suit in equity or other proper proceeding for redress.

His other basic ground had been tried already: the Fourteenth Amendment, dating from 1868. But he shared with many other lawyers a suspicion that the Supreme Court, constantly broadening its doctrines under the two great clauses of the Fourteenth — "due process of law" and "equal protection of the laws" — would sooner or later bring the ballot fully beneath that equal protection umbrella.

When Frank Farrell filed *Magraw* v. *Donovan,* the 1957 session of the Minnesota Legislature in which he had hoped to sit was in session. He "had hoped the suit might stimulate them to action," too, but the body's first reaction was much like its usual acceptance of the Bergerud bill — general levity or an attitude of "What the hell, there's nothing to this."

"We decided not to push it lest they dig in their heels," Farrell said. In due time, the State filed for the defendants its expected motion to dismiss, but the lawsuit was not taken seriously until Farrell and his associates filed their brief. That was enough to alert the defendants that someone had researched deeply and intended to fight; the brief contained fifty-two pages, cited seventy-three cases, ten textbook and digest references, and a score or more constitutional and statutory authorities. The brief's seven arguments began where the American republic had: "Our Government, from its very inception, was founded upon the concept of equality. The Declaration of Independence adopted by the Second Continental Congress on July 4, 1776, asserts as its third grievance as follows: 'He [the King of Great Britain] has refused to pass other laws for the accommodation of large districts of people unless those people would relinquish the right of Representation in the Legislature, a right inestimable to them and formidable to tyrants only.' "

Thus alerted, the auditors of three rural counties intervened in *Magraw* v. *Donovan* in October 1957, on the side of the defendants. At about the same time, Minnesota's League of Women Voters intervened as a "friend of the court," *amicus curiae*, in support of the plaintiffs. The three counties intervening were Grant, Houston and Otter Tail. Farrell was not at all displeased with this development, particularly with respect to Otter Tail County — a hundred and forty miles west of the Twin Cities, it was the most over-represented county in the state and thus helped him underscore a point.

Dan Magraw, meanwhile, had recruited the participation of his former political science professor at the University of Minnesota, the respected Dr. William Anderson, then retired. Anderson's seventeen-page treatise on the effect of reapportionment failure on the American political system was filed as an appendix to the plaintiffs' supplemental brief; it became an important document in developing proof both for the Minnesota case and later in *Baker* v. *Carr*. Anderson had been a member of the Commission on Intergovernmental Relations created by Congress in 1953 and his treatise echoed their warning about the drift of power from the states to the federal government. He placed a large share of the blame for this condition on reapportionment failures.

Some of his words of 1958 today seem prophetic:

The effects upon the minds of young persons resulting from unethical and unconstitutional practices in high places are also worthy of mention. Anyone who has believed in and tried to convey and explain to young people the principles of popular government and constitutionalism, as I have tried to do for many years, knows what can happen in young minds when practice departs so far from principles and pretensions. Here we come to what may be the most crucial issue of all, that of constitutional morality. . . .

This issue of . . . constitutional morality, of abiding by the constitution, cannot be brushed aside as mere idealism. It lies close to the base of all systems of popular government. These systems rest upon such basic ideas as those of mutual respect and confidence among men, and upon keeping faith with all men in all things. When this basis is seriously undermined, and no way can be found for a peaceful and lawful correction of wrongs and the restoration of mutual confidence, the resort to force and violence is not unthinkable.

Anderson also came very close to articulating the one-man-one-vote doctrine in just those words at another point. Tracing the history of representative government, he pointed out that very early "the rule for apportioning representation in the legislature was . . . based squarely and solely upon population. It was people, and only the people, who were to count and be counted in deciding the affairs of state. The principle underlying these arrangements was that of equality: Every man one vote, and every vote to be equal to every other vote."

Anderson felt the equal protection clause of the Fourteenth Amendment was the "most pertinent and most important" approach in *Magraw* v. *Donovan* and he reminded that "those who drafted the Fourteenth Amendment did not limit it to the protection of rights of Negroes." Attacking the "political question" doctrine that had barred Court entry into this field to that time, Anderson argued, "Since the equal protection clause is so worded as to protect any and every person within a state's jurisdiction, and . . . extends by implication to all matters in which equality is important, I believe that it covers important political rights as well as others, including equal representation in the state's legislature." The Supreme Court, he added, had already extended this equal protection to the political field, and specifically to voter rights, in the "white primary" cases, through which Southern states were forbidden from blocking Negro participation in party primary elections.

Anderson clearly felt that a threat to the American system itself was at hand:

"Let minority rules in state legislatures, racial and religious discrimination, and other tendencies of recent years develop much further than they have, and the pretensions of this nation to democratic leadership in the world will be seriously compromised, if they have not been so compromised already," and "if no way can be found to make the equal protection clause truly effective in a case such as this one, I truly believe that government of the people, by the people, and for the people, is already in a state of serious decline."

Magraw v. *Donovan*'s first day in court came on March 21, 1958, more than a year after Frank Farrell had filed suit, and it took that initial hurdle when U.S. District Judge Edward J. Devitt turned down the defendant's motion to dismiss. Accordingly, a three-judge panel, required in such constitutional cases, was set up on March 25. It consisted of Devitt, U.S. District Judge Robert C. Bell, and Judge John Sandborn, a member of the Eighth Circuit Court of Appeals sitting in St. Louis. Farrell considered the last appointment a real break; Judge Sandborn had been a member of the last Minnesota Legislature to obey its constitutional mandate and reapportion the body, back in 1913. He was thoroughly familiar with the issues involved.

A trial on the merits, set for May 2, 1958, consumed one long day in the courtroom of the Old Federal Courts Building in St. Paul. Frank Farrell and his two associates in the trial developed their proof with only four witnesses: Alf Bergerud and Alfred Otto, the legislators from the largest and smallest districts nearby; Professor Anderson and Professor Bond — the retired political scientist and the young one (then at North Dakota State Agricultural College) who had done the graduate study with all the statistical data. Bergerud testified to the difficulty of representing so large a district as he was assigned in the western Minneapolis suburbs. Otto, by contrast, quite willingly testified that from his Inner Loop district of St. Paul, with its small population, he seldom received constituent pressures or even requests for legislation.

John Avery Bond told of the vast population discriminations in the various House and Senate districts, ranging from 16,878 to 153,455 in the Senate with House districts showing even greater inequalities. Professor Anderson added the historical facts and effects. They must have impressed the court, for it ruled, on July 10, 1958: "This court has jurisdiction of this action because of the federal constitutional issue asserted."

That simple sentence alone was a victory. In the face of the defendant's invocation again of *Colegrove* v. *Green* and Justice Frankfurter's "political thicket," a federal court had chosen, a dozen years later, to enter.

It was not ready, however, to draw district lines. "Early in January 1959 the 61st session of the Minnesota Legislature will convene," said the court, "all of the members of which will be newly elected on November 4 of this year. The facts which have been presented to us will be available to them. It is not to be presumed that the legislature will refuse to take such action as is necessary to comply with its duty under the state constitution." (For both sound and effect, it might have come from the Tennessee pen of Chancellor Thomas Wardlaw Steele.)

"We defer decision on all the issues presented (including that of the power of this court to grant relief), in order to afford the legislature full opportunity to 'heed the constitutional mandate to redistrict,'" the court added. "It seems to us that if there is to be a judicial disruption of the present legislative apportionment or of the method or machinery for electing members of the state legislature, it should not take place unless and until it can be shown that the legislature meeting in January 1959 has advisedly and deliberately failed and refused to perform its constitutional duty to redistrict the state."

The clincher, though, was no less than an ultimatum:

"The court retains jurisdiction of this case. Following adjournment of the 61st session of the Minnesota legislature, the parties may, within 60 days thereafter, petition the court for such action as they or any of them, may deem appropriate." For the members of the Minnesota assembly it was a do-or-we-will decree.

"It is a real milestone, a new approach to solution of a problem which has defied solution for a century," commented Robert C. McClure, a professor of law at the University of Minnesota who had been retained as a consultant to the plaintiffs along the way. Dan Magraw, Frank Farrell and the Minnesota men and women they had gathered around their cause had constructed a bridge at St. Paul over which millions of American citizens with debased franchises would pass in the generations ahead, a sturdy and necessary span to *Baker* v. *Carr*.

Book Two

THE
ESTABLISHMENT

1

Congressman-Mayor
Walter Chandler

Had it not been for the success of Dan Magraw and
Frank Farrell in Minnesota, the history-making lawsuit *Baker* v. *Carr* might never have been filed. Certainly it was *Magraw* v. *Donovan* that prompted officials of Memphis and Shelby County to reopen the reapportionment court battle in Tennessee.

The idea for the revival came from David Newby
Harsh, chairman of the Shelby County Commission
during late 1958 when the *Magraw* case first drew national attention. Years later, he recalled that he and
his public official colleagues in Memphis were also
encouraged by a whole new body of law rapidly rising
from the school desegregation case, *Brown* v. *Board of
Education*.

The United States Supreme Court, through repeated
use of the Fourteenth Amendment, was broadening

federal jurisdiction in areas that once had been the exclusive bailiwick of the states. The doctrines thus emerging case by case in the name of civil rights and racial nondiscrimination were beginning to swing into logical parallel with the arguments for reapportionment. If a man could not be denied equal treatment because of his race, how could he be denied the same because of his residence? If one was a federally protected right, why not the other?

In Minnesota, that kind of argument had clearly appealed to a three-judge court, and Harsh thought it might appeal just as strongly down the Mississippi, where another consideration was that Shelby County needed the money which Harsh and his colleagues felt would come if the case was successful. In Memphis, the money shortage was closely identified with a historic circumstance, the effect of which had not been fully felt when the reform movement began — the death, in October 1954, of Edward Hull Crump. The "Red Snapper" boss of Memphis, like so many political strong men before him, left no heir apparent when he died two weeks beyond his eightieth birthday. The power base from which he once ruled Tennessee had disintegrated — eroded away during the half-dozen years since that 1948 defeat by Estes Kefauver and Gordon Browning. Crump, ill and mellowing, had no will to rebuild after this loss. Perhaps the old master recognized that the ingredients for reconstruction were gone.

In any event, it was reluctant and rather belated

recognition by Crump's successors that Memphis could no longer have its fiscal way in Nashville that resurrected America's rotten-boroughs reform. Chief among these successors was Walter Chandler, by far the most respected of the so-called "Crump men" in Memphis. The resurrection took place when Chandler, having been retained by Harsh, filed *Baker* v. *Carr* on behalf of the three governmental entities of the West-state metropolis. Other plaintiffs were recruited by Chandler, but Memphis was behind it. With that filing, May 18, 1959, what might be termed the urban establishment of Tennessee took over, with economic intent, the egalitarian crusade characterized until then by the idealism of the youthful crew that began it.

In the heyday of Boss Crump, no one in Shelby County — least of all Walter Chandler — would have dreamed of the need to bring suit to return a rightful split of state revenue to Memphis. Big Shelby always got its share in Nashville — and some to spare. In many ways Crump, like Richard Daley later in Chicago, was a pragmatic urban reply to a rurally controlled Assembly. But the convenient and sometimes shifting alliances with which Boss Crump controlled the executive branch as a counterweight to the slanted Assembly worked well only for Memphis. The other Tennessee urban centers — Nashville in Middle, Knoxville and Chattanooga in East, and the industry-swollen Tri-Cities of Upper East Tennessee — often suffered. Crump seldom made common cause with them. He was basically a localist, a booster with parochial views. He spent a career building a bigger, cleaner Memphis; he seldom thought beyond that city's welfare. Memphis had no urban allies to shield it, then, when Crump's power crumbled with his statewide defeat in 1948 and ended altogether with his death in 1954. Almost immediately, and in the critical midst of the postwar boom, Memphis began to feel the fiscal pinch.

Walter Chandler was a shrewd and high-minded man. He was scholarly and sensitive, an individual of far greater breadth than Ed Crump, his political sponsor. It is unlikely that he missed the significance to the Memphis treasury of Jim Cummings's support of Governor Frank Clement during the 1955 legislature. At the outset of his gubernatorial tenure (which he had won, with Crump support, two years before), Clement had driven through the Assembly a bill to return to Tennessee cities a one-cent share of the state-imposed gasoline tax. But by 1955 he had become what his background suggested — a bright young lawyer-orator with a small-town boyhood. His personal ambitions and the interests of towns the size of his hometown got far more attention than metropolitan needs. His political judgment here was not wrong; suburban people in Tennessee were, after all, still voting as if they were born in log cabins within farm-wagon distance of a general merchandise store. Frank Clement sensed that his identification with Crump's enemy Cummings was not an unpopular one.

Aware of all this, Walter Chandler still held back. As we have seen, he declined the invitation of Ella Ross and Haynes Miller in 1954–1955 to join in the *Kidd-McCanless* cause. Heavily courted later, he politely turned down all pleas for his support in the appeals. And no Memphis funds were forthcoming when money ran short for Tom Osborn and Hobart Atkins. Chandler's interest was great. He was encouraging, even laudatory — but noncommittal. His reasons seem to have been several.

The most obvious, in retrospect, was that "the organization" simply ceased to exist when E. H. Crump died. Although some sought for a time to preserve the myth of a powerful structure, it was not there. The political cement which for years had given central purpose to Memphis actions was no more. The era of spotless streets and sweet tyranny was ended. No one and everyone suddenly spoke for Memphis and Shelby County. Someone had to put something together again, but the job would take time. And Crump had been dead but a month when young Haynes Miller got the reapportionment gleam in his eye.

Walter Chandler was the ablest among the Crump survivors, but he was approaching seventy. Moreover, eight years before the Boss died, Chandler had walked away from "the organization" and from political life. He did not break off with Crump amidst curses, not even with the color-strewn vituperation for which the Red Snapper was famous; that was not the gentle Chandler's style. He simply resigned as mayor of

Memphis in August 1946, a year before his term was up — disappointed, some said, because Crump had thwarted his U.S. senatorial ambitions; hurt, others said, because the Boss had unburdened himself of some unsympathetic remarks about Chandler's proposals for "pay-as-you-go" city financing. Whatever the motives for his retirement, Chandler was in private law practice when all the appeals for his help came. After a long and honored public career, he held no public office and aspired to none. He was really in no position to respond on behalf of anyone beside himself. Although at about this time he agreed to serve for a few months as interim mayor when Frank Tobey died, Chandler was through with politics. But he was wise enough in its brutal ways to know and fear what the rural Assembly would do to an exposed and Crumpless Memphis if one of his own prestige and background participated in a crusade against that body's composition.

A careful reading of the voluminous Chandler correspondence file also suggests philosophical reasons for his hesitancy in joining the reapportionment battle. Having served in both the legislative and executive branches of government for years, Chandler was somewhat bothered by the separation-of-powers argument. Many of his oldest and dearest friends did not believe the judiciary had any business in this arena, and some of them told him so in blunt letters when he committed himself later. He is bound to have known and understood their feelings beforehand, for he had pondered and discussed the matter much in the period between *Kidd* v. *McCanless* and *Baker* v. *Carr*. Compounding this ambivalence was the states-rights argument, of course. Although a progressive New Deal reformer throughout his congressional career, Chandler was nonetheless a Southern Democrat who, in old age, was not growing more liberal. Repeatedly in his correspondence Chandler went out of his way to rationalize — even for those who had not challenged him — his reapportionment role as that of an advocate of individual rights. He tried hard not to see this dispute as a federal-state conflict but as a contest of the individual versus the state. In April 1962, after *Baker* v. *Carr* had been decided in his favor, for example, Chandler wrote Frank Farrell to acknowledge the young Minnesotan's crucial contribution to the victory, and added:

"Of course, we were met by the cry of 'States Rights' all the way, and the demagogues are still crying the same wail and quoting Frankfurter's cliché about the Federal Courts not getting into 'this political thicket,' but no one seems to appreciate that we have been fighting the rights of the people of the states, and they make up the states, as well as the Federal Government, as you well know."

Chandler also wrote Farrell, "When I read the case of *Magraw* v. *Donovan*, I decided that the time had come for Tennessee to take action, and the inspiration of that decision has carried us along throughout the contest." That sentence alone probably carried the largest clue to Chandler's earlier failure to join the issue in the courts: He did not think the time had come.

Events behind the rejection of *Kidd* v. *McCanless* by the U.S. Supreme Court, however, were enough to convince anyone that Tennessee's legislature was never going to move on this matter until the courts shoved its members, and the *Kidd* case had made it plain enough that the Tennessee courts were not going to provide the shove. That left only the federal arena, but Walter Chandler still lacked the enthusiasm to enter it for a remedy.

He knew, however, there was no alternative. When the *Kidd* case came to a close, the 1957 session of the General Assembly was about to begin. The case had received wide publicity, and the issues were therefore well known to every member of that Assembly. For two years, reapportionment had been a subject of much debate throughout the state, and if the membership had consciences about it, this was a time to make those feelings known. It was a time, too, for testing the practical validity of Mr. Justice Frankfurter's notion that the people could remedy this situation, and the paralleling theories of Justice Burnett and Justice Swepston of the Tennessee Supreme Court, whose interviews after their rejection of the *Kidd* case had suggested the solution lay in electing a legislature pledged to right what both had admitted was a wrong.

Most urban candidates for the legislature that year had made such a pledge, in fact, but of course there were not enough urban votes in either house. The practical result of *Kidd*, then, had been to harden the line of rural legislators and to make correction less likely. With the authority of the United States Supreme Court on their side, most of them apparently felt they had license to perpetuate the inequity. Some even used the high court's decision to legitimatize their own arguments for inaction. The 1957 Assembly accordingly buried every reapportionment proposal that came before it. It even refused to authorize Governor Clement's promised Legislative Council study of the issue. If Chandler had any doubts remaining about what had to be done or its timing, then, they were now resolved. He was ready to put a brilliant legal mind, years of experience and extraordinary organizational and leadership skills to work in what was to be his last, and certainly his most important, reform.

Walter Clift Chandler was seventy-one years of age when he agreed to take up what had been a young man's crusade. He had spent most of those years in cities, and he was convinced that the future of the country, much less that of his community and his state, was at stake.

"People wonder why Tennessee does not grow in population and per capita wealth," he wrote Thomas Wardlaw Steele, who by this time — April 1969 — had left the bench. "One of the principal reasons is the composition of the Legislature. The State will never grow with control of the Legislature in the hands of rural people without vision. This is not a criticism, because every member of the Legislature strives to represent his constituents, but the great progress of the State lies in advancement of the cities, and that can come about only through an understanding of the problems of the cities and a willingness to help them in the efforts which will redound to the benefit of the entire State."

A background such as Walter Chandler's probably could have produced no other conclusion. He was born October 5, 1887, in a growing city of Tennessee's medium range — Jackson — one of nine children of a railway mail clerk. When he was in his mid-teens, in 1902, his family moved to Memphis. He considered that city his home for the rest of his life.

Rearing so large a family in the city on a modest income can hardly have been easy, and young Walter was expected to do his part. He came to understand the city style of living and to recognize an urban problem at the householder's level. The three central streams of his life were the law, politics and the military. He was still a boy when he joined Tennessee's Forrest Rifles, a militia infantry unit, and he later enlisted in the Chickasaw Guard of Memphis. He entered politics in 1916 and was serving in the Tennessee House of Representatives in 1917 when the United States entered World War I. He went on active duty as soon as the General Assembly adjourned. He was an infantry captain in France and for the rest of his life he would write and speak in combat metaphors and plot strategy in military terms. His political association with Crump, thirteen years older, began when he returned a hero, and it took him to City Hall, to Congress and back again.

Even at sixty-five, Chandler was a driving force in Tennessee's constitutional convention of 1953, where, as Shelby delegate and chairman pro tem, he gave heavy support to the convention's important Home Rule Committee. One of the leading lights on that committee, which drafted an amendment that broke the absolute rule of the state over its cities and towns, was a much younger lawyer from East Tennessee, William E. Miller of Johnson City. Bill Miller was a distant cousin of the Miller brothers, Haynes and Mayne. He, too, would shortly play an imperative role in the nation's reapportionment battle.

It was organization, experience, stature, that Walter Chandler brought to that battle in early 1959, reopening it at a crucial time. "He was a fine lawyer, but more especially," Tom Osborn later explained, "he had a presence and a prestige that we younger lawyers did not have." In the corridors of the state capitol that early spring, he stood near the concession stand, a knot of admirers around him, buttonholing old friends, a wizened little man now, his once plump body shrunk from bouts with disease and surgery. His sense of fairness told him to be there, to warn members of the Assembly in which he had twice served that if they did not give relief to underrepresented regions, a new lawsuit would be forthcoming.

A sense of fairness—and strategy. For he was already building his case, his letters make clear, when he came over to Nashville that day. On January 5, immediately after his first conversation with Commissioner Dave Harsh, Chandler had written Jesse Vineyard, who was back in Nashville representing Memphis and Shelby County with the Shelby legislative delegation: "Commissioner Harsh has asked me to look into the advisability of proceeding with the matter of reapportionment of the Tennessee Legislature." And after asking Vineyard to round up his file on *Kidd* v. *McCanless* and to advise him who among those associated with the earlier case "seemed to have the best grasp of the situation," he added: "In the meantime, I am sure you know that it is highly advisable to watch Jim Cummings and see that he does not introduce a phony bill for reapportionment and then move for its rejection."

A few weeks later, Chandler himself talked to Cummings. Cummings recalled it: "He came to Nashville and took counsel with a number of us and expressed the view the court would take jurisdiction of the case and warned us of the consequences and that we had need to take it up and do something about it in the legislature. We all agreed with him," Cummings added. "The question was how. You know, in order to get a bill passed down there [in Nashville] you have to get fifty votes in the House and seventeen in the Senate, and we were never able to get those votes."

In his lifetime, Walter Chandler had been known by the title "Congressman" or "Mayor" and, as he grew older, by a very respectful "Mister." Occasionally, an old-timer would address him as "Senator," and one knew that this went back to the Twenties and his days on Capitol Hill in Nashville. But the one title that stayed with him came from those few dreadful months when the forests of Argonne tested the mettle of so many men. Most of his closest acquaintances called him "Captain." In the early days of 1959, he began to behave like one again. He had been commissioned to win relief in the legislature if he could, but to sue in the courts if he could not. To see the struggle through, he could count on financial support from David Harsh, the Shelby County Commission chairman; Edmund Orgill, the new mayor of Memphis; and Charles W. Baker, the chairman of the Shelby County Quarterly Court. Cap Chandler began to marshal his troops and lay his battle plan.

Chandler did not believe in wasting time. On the very day that Jesse Vineyard's reply to his letter of January 5 arrived, he fired off a memo to George Harsh, a brother and law partner of Commissioner David Harsh, enclosing a complete file of *Kidd* v. *McCanless* supplied him by Vineyard. The memo suggested three things: obtaining a copy of the pleadings in the Minnesota case "in order to follow them as closely as our facts will permit"; a search of the 1955 and 1957 Tennessee acts for any apportionment actions; and the enlistment of attorneys associated with *Kidd* v. *McCanless*. That same day Hall Crawford, an associate of the Harsh brothers, telephoned William C.

Meier, senior partner in the St. Paul law firm of Meier, Kennedy & Quinn, to ask for a copy of the *Magraw* v. *Donovan* complaint. Meier sent it the next day.

At the same time, Chandler set about recruiting his lieutenants. Vineyard had named Mayne Miller, Hobart Atkins and Tom Osborn as "the main people that I would recommend." David Harsh promptly telephoned Guy Smith, the Republican chairman and Knoxville *Journal* publisher, concerning his continued interest and that of the party's counsel, Atkins. Smith assured him the GOP would join the action and that Atkins would participate. The Memphis group knew of Mayne Miller's interest for a few days earlier he had written Mayor Orgill concerning the *Magraw* v. *Donovan* case, and Magraw for copies of the court papers. The case in Minnesota, he wrote, "is on all fours with the Tennessee situation; in fact the Supreme Court of Minnesota had, only a few years ago, refused to grant relief just as our State Supreme Court did."

But Mayne Miller was not available, and Chandler learned of it a few days after an official meeting of the Memphis-Shelby governments was held, January 21, to announce Chandler's formal appointment. Miller was in the throes of a traumatic break with his native state. It was typical of Chandler that he offered Miller, despite his impending departure, "the privilege of signing the complaint if you desire to do so, particularly in view of your great service in the *Kidd* case." From his new home in Casper, Wyoming, Mayne Miller wrote back, a bit sadly, "I regret that I will not have an opportunity to join with you, tilting at the reapportionment windmill once again. You have my fondest hopes for success, admiration for your effort, and, should you succeed, my sincerest astonishment."

Unlike Mayne Miller, Tom Osborn was quick to sign on with Chandler's gathering command staff. In his letter to Osborn, Chandler had diplomatically remembered "that Jesse Vineyard requested me to try to get some money from the Shelby County organization to help defray costs which accumulated on your doorstep. I am wondering if you would still be interested in going into the matter again if a satisfactory arrangement can be made."

Osborn replied that he would be delighted to take part, since he had largely recovered from the monetary injury of *Kidd* v. *McCanless*. Osborn, the single young reformer who had followed the *Kidd* action from first filing to final appeal, also had some suggestions to make this time around. He thought "a good deal of the money lost on the lawsuit was wasted" because they sued too many people and spent substantial sums on statistical material never actually used. He also felt a basic error was made in the presentation of the federal question involved in the *Kidd* case. "When it came time to prepare a jurisdictional statement for the United States Supreme Court I found that we had not pleaded 'a purposeful and systematic plan to discriminate against a geographic class of persons' necessary where equal protection is denied by inaction as distinguished from legislative action."

Finally, Tom Osborn went back to the theme that aroused his interest in the subject in the first place: "Another weakness in our bill was our failure to show the practical result had from unequal apportionment of the legislature. This may not be necessary in strict theory but I now think that it would have been a persuasive matter to have demonstrated the financial interest had by the legislature in the preservation of the status quo — this disproportionate distribution of legislative representation." Walter Chandler penciled a check mark beside that suggestion; it was, of course, the matter that got him interested, too, and that prompted those public officials paying his fee. He soon sent Osborn a portion of it.

The legal team was made now: Chandler, George Harsh, Osborn, Atkins. But Harsh shortly withdrew; he believed his participation might be considered inappropriate since his brother was commissioner. For almost a full year, the team would consist of Chandler, Osborn and Atkins. With Chandler, the subject quickly became obsessive. He gave increasing portions of his time to the effort, for he realized he was in a time bind. The legislature was already in session when the decision was made, and legislative actions would be required to help build his case before the Assembly adjourned *sine die* within its prescribed seventy-five legislative days.

Chandler's first thought had been to force the Tennessee legislature to move by holding over its head, in the Minnesota pattern, a court order which said in effect, "You do it or we will." After he had considered the matter more thoroughly, and after he had obtained copies of the Minnesota suit papers, Chandler abandoned this idea. Time was too short; a court could not really be expected to enter an order against the 1959 Assembly before its adjournment on March 20. And both Osborn and Mayne Miller were advising against a lawsuit that would draw in too many defendants, thus vastly increasing the costs and complicating the pleadings. After studying Frank Farrell's Minnesota approach, Chandler was convinced there was no need to enjoin the entire legislature. He redirected his efforts toward putting before the legislature a constitutional reapportionment bill, warning them publicly of impending legal action if they failed to pass it, and gathering everything he could about the Minnesota case. In drafting his own complaint, he would follow Farrell almost to the jot and tittle.

Chandler went to Nashville to serve his informal warning and to confer with Cummings and other leaders on Tuesday, February 10, 1959. They presented him to the Senate, overlooking that as a former member of the body, thirty-eight years before, he was entitled to its floor privileges. Chandler also saw Guy Smith during his Nashville visit, and Smith reaffirmed the GOP's willingness to sponsor Atkins's participation. Hobart Atkins had been a member himself of the 1957 state Senate, and he had been one of those who attempted in vain in that first Assembly after *Kidd-McCanless* to get the legislature to put its own house in order. Chandler likewise encountered Molly Todd in the legislative wings during his visit, and she informed him of Maclin Davis's efforts with the 1955 Assembly.

Promptly upon his return to Memphis, Chandler wrote both Atkins and Davis for copies of their defeated bills, and he confided to Atkins: "I would like to have a bill pending in the present Tennessee Legislature in order to allege the existence of the bill and the failure or refusal of the Tennessee Legislature to act. In addition, I would like to have the complaint filed in the Federal Court in Nashville during the pendency of the present legislative session in order that the legislature may be apprised of the fact that we expect to use its failure to act as the basis for asking the Federal Court to act."

As it turned out, time was too short for such action, and Chandler and Atkins decided instead to give each member of the Assembly a formal notice of what was about to happen. But before they did, Chandler wanted to have before the body a constitutional bill on the subject. He was also anxious that the issue not be cluttered by too many such bills; in Nashville he had met Senator Robert L. Peters of Kingsport, in East Tennessee, who was planning reapportionment legislation. He wrote Peters, diplomatically asking to see a copy of the legislation before it was introduced. Peters sent it, and Davis and Atkins furnished him copies of their 1955 and 1957 defeats. Using them and Tom Osborn's exhibits from the *Kidd-McCanless* case, Chandler drafted a new bill. He sent it to Jesse Vineyard for the Shelby delegation's sponsorship with the warning that Vineyard should "discuss this matter with our delegation in order to determine when our local bills are beyond the danger point" before dropping it in the legislative hopper. Clearly, Chandler expected instant retribution from the rural members of the Assembly.

On March 2, eighteen days before adjournment, Chandler felt the danger point was sufficiently past to send out his warning letters, personally addressed to each senator and representative. They read:

A number of citizens of Tennessee, especially interested in the proper apportionment of the Tennessee Legislature in accordance with the provisions of the State Constitution, have engaged attorneys at law to institute legal proceedings in the Federal Court if the present Tennessee Legislature does not enact legislation in conformity with the constitutional formula for reapportionment, and the undersigned are among the attorneys engaged for this purpose.

We feel that it is proper to notify you, as a member of the 1959 General Assembly, of the contemplated institution of this suit for reapportionment, which will be based, in material part, on the failure of the present legislature to carry out the mandate of our Constitution. We wish to assure you that there is nothing personal in our approach, as counsel, to the proper solution of this long-standing problem, but we feel that you should have knowledge beforehand of the plan referred to in order to take appropriate action before the adjournment of the present legislature.

With every good wish,

It was signed by Chandler and Atkins. On the same day Chandler had the Shelby delegation release the reapportionment bill, almost a carbon of the one Atkins had sponsored two years before. He also informed Dave Harsh and Mayor Orgill that the formal complaint to be filed in federal court was drafted.

When Chandler's reapportionment bill was introduced, Senator Peters was upset. He had filed his own measure, which contained a slightly different formula; he feared that the difference might create difficulties. Chandler, taking no chances, simply wrote Peters a letter of half-apology. He wanted the legislature to turn down what he knew in his own mind was a reapportionment bill that fit the terms of the Tennessee constitution and he wasn't sure about the Peters bill. Anyway, he strongly suspected both bills would be butchered, and they were at once. The Senate turned down one 14 to 18, the other 13 to 20. The lower house did not even bother with them.

One thing could have foiled Walter Chandler's well-laid plan in the final days of the 1959 General Assembly. Representative James Quillen of Kingsport, who later became the Republican congressman from Upper East Tennessee, introduced in the House a joint resolution authorizing another study of reapportionment by the Legislative Council. The study was useless, the proposal no more than a popular political ploy, but had the resolution been adopted, the pending study might well have offered the federal court an adequate reason for not entering this sensitive area of federal-state relations. But the House cut down the proposal 37 to 45, and Chandler wrote Atkins, chortling a bit:

"Jim Cummings undoubtedly thought he was 'putting a nail in our coffin' when he defeated Representative Quillen's resolution . . . but I think that he did us a great favor, because, if the Legislature had adopted the resolution and kept the matter within its jurisdiction, the three-judge Court might have postponed action until after 1961."

Walter Chandler was in high good spirits when the legislature adjourned. His strategy up to now was working well, and he could turn his attention to gathering plaintiffs. On March 22 he reported to his clients, Commissioner Harsh and Mayor Orgill: "It was necessary to wait until the adjournment of the Legislature before bringing the suit which is based, in part, on the failure to reapportion, and we are now in a position to go forward with this litigation." The same day he asked Atkins and Osborn to round up interested parties in Nashville and Knoxville. His letter to Osborn was accompanied by a five-hundred-dollar check, the first payment Osborn had received since his agreement to help.

Chandler had hoped for broader participation than he got from East Tennessee Republicans. Too many Shelby Countians wanted in in the lawsuit, but elsewhere interest was less than enthusiastic. Atkins responded with only Guy Smith's name, though he promised to survey his other Republican contacts in East Tennessee for co-plaintiffs. But Atkins rejected

Chandler's suggested addition of Senator Peters of Kingsport to the list on the grounds that it would be unwise to include too many politicians. The reapportionment activity of both Peters and Quillen in the 1959 legislature had been part of their rivalry for the mantle of Congressman B. Carroll Reece. After Reece died in 1961, Quillen defeated Peters for the seat. The Republicans had other political problems, too; when the list was complete, therefore, Smith's was the only East Tennessee name included aside from that of Chattanooga's John R. McGauley, who volunteered directly to Chandler. McGauley was president of the Citizens Taxpayers Association in Chattanooga. Although he had his name added as a private citizen, he knew he had the support of his organization's directors.

Another welcome volunteer was W. D. (Pete) Hudson, judge of the Montgomery County Quarterly Court and criminal court jurist. Hudson, rather belatedly, had heard of the Minnesota case through a friend in St. Petersburg, Florida, who sent him a newspaper clipping. (Florida also was by then in the throes of a reapportionment action paralleling the Minnesota and Tennessee situations.) Hudson, too, could be considered "urban establishment," for the same motivations prompted his entry into the lawsuit that triggered its beginning. Clarksville, the exploding seat of Montgomery County, was one of the fastest-growing cities in the state, its populace swollen by nearby Fort Campbell, Kentucky, and by the natural growth phenomenon around any American university, in Clarksville's case Austin Peay State University. Montgomery grew from 44,186 in 1950 to 55,645 in 1960 and the population increase did not slow then. By 1970, its census stood at 62,721. As chief fiscal officer of this rapidly urbanizing county on the Kentucky border northwest of Nashville, Hudson was feeling the pinch, and he knew how the state dollars were being divided.

"Montgomery County is one of the 12 counties that paid 65 per cent of all of Tennessee's taxes and these 12 counties only have 37 per cent of the representation in the Legislature," Hudson complained in his letter to Chandler. "Last year the state took from us and distributed among the smaller counties $850,000 of sales taxes paid from this county. In other words, we paid in $850,000 more than we got back."

Hudson was obviously still seething over the failure of the legislature, recently adjourned, to take any action in the matter. "Unless this State is re-districted and the majority of the people get their just and equitable share of representation in the Legislature, our children will be deprived of their constitutional rights in getting a fair and reasonable part of the taxes paid by the citizens in the larger counties for the education of their children." He concluded: "I am not in favor of accepting promises or any other dilatory tactics to prolong this matter. . . . I will be glad to offer myself as a guinea pig taxpayer as the petitioner if you want me to." Chandler did. Hudson's name, bearing considerable prestige among public officials from the medium-range cities and counties in Tennessee, was pegged to the plaintiff list. On that list, too — through the efforts of Tommy Osborn — went the names of his Nashville neighbor, Jack W. Lee, and Molly Todd, the local League of Women Voters lady who had also joined in *Kidd.*

Shelby Countians rounded out the list of plaintiffs in this original filing, though the petition would be amended to add more before the case was appealed to the Supreme Court. Herbert S. Esch, a friend of Dave Harsh, joined the plaintiffs, along with Roy Dixon, a banker from the northern Memphis suburb of Raleigh. The remaining three were the public officials, Harsh, Orgill and Baker. Baker was listed first, perhaps because his name was first alphabetically, perhaps because, as chairman of the fiscal body he would have influence in obtaining funds from the Quarterly Court. In Shelby County, the Commission headed by Harsh could be roughly compared with the executive branch, the Quarterly Court to the legislative, which set the tax levy rate and appropriated all monies to operate the Commission.

So it was *Baker* v. *Carr.* And Carr was, of course, the Secretary of State for Tennessee. Named codefendants with him were George McCanless, the attorney general of *Kidd* v. *McCanless,* Jerry M. McDonald, coordinator of the state Board of Election Commissioners, and the three members of the state Election Board,

Sam Coward, James Alexander and Hubert Brooks. Brooks, a Republican, later disappointed Chandler by failing to oppose the other defendants' motion to dismiss.

A last-minute prospective plaintiff was Lone L. Sisk, Jr., an insurance underwriter from Oak Ridge who had been selected by his city's Junior Chamber of Commerce to join the suit in their behalf. But his letter to Chandler came during that period in the dying days of April and the first few of May when the lawsuit papers were being bumped around to the various plaintiffs for signing. Efforts to obtain the official participation of the other large metropolitan governments of Tennessee — of Nashville–Davidson County, Knoxville–Knox County, Chattanooga–Hamilton County — had gone awry for one reason or another. But each of these metropolitan centers was now represented at least by a citizen group. The three Grand Divisions at last were united in the reform movement. The papers, finally signed by all plaintiffs, were sent to Tom Osborn for filing in the United States Court, Middle District of Tennessee, Nashville Division.

The site had long since been decided; long ago Walter Chandler had abandoned his first thoughts of bringing the suit in Memphis. On the bench in Nashville, a Republican appointee in 1955 of President Eisenhower, was that former Johnson City attorney who had worked with Chandler on the home rule reform during the Tennessee constitutional convention.

On May 18, 1959, a few days delayed because Osborn had been out of the city, the lawsuit papers were dropped off in the office of U.S. District Judge William E. Miller's clerk. *Baker* v. *Carr* was officially on its way to becoming the law of the land.

2

U.S. District Judge William E. Miller

A lawyer of Walter Chandler's professional stature and personal ethic would never suggest that a jurist of William E. Miller's reputation might judge a case on anything but its merits. But a man of Walter Chandler's keen insight would hardly ignore the obvious facts that judges are human beings who read newspapers and, like other human beings, they are the products of their experiences, breeding and backgrounds.

Judges — the best of them — bring to their benches certain attitudes that make governors and Presidents ponder their appointments to supreme courts and cause senators sometimes to balk at their confirmations. Often these attitudes are formed and frozen in early manhood or even childhood. The great Justice Holmes, it is said, developed his rhetorical skill as a result of his father's custom of rewarding young Oliver

Wendell with an extra dab of marmalade for every clever saying his son dropped at the breakfast table. His phrases, when uttered years later from the nation's highest bench, were elevated to the status of constitutional law. Accordingly, lawyers sometimes refer to Holmes's succinct sayings as "Justice Holmes's marmalade."

The scholarly Justice Frankfurter, a member of a minority group himself, never got over his youthful assignment to investigate the Tom Mooney case and his professional outrage at the treatment of Nicola Sacco and Bartolomeo Vanzetti, the Boston Italian immigrants put to death in 1927 following a trial he considered a travesty. For the remainder of his life, Frankfurter was a jealous guardian of the rights of accused persons and a consistent warrior against press coverage of criminal matters. He had become convinced that the highly competitive Boston newspapers shared in the Sacco-Vanzetti miscarriage by sensationalizing the case, and he laid out that view in a famous *Atlantic Monthly* article and later a book about it. Frankfurter's celebrated insistence on "judicial restraint," moreover, should be measured against the time and circumstance of his appointment by President Franklin D. Roosevelt. FDR was confronted with a conservative Supreme Court obsessed with economic matters at the time; that Court was exercising little restraint in cutting down the liberal, pro-labor economic policies and legislation favored by the President and, incidentally, by his brain-truster appointee, Mr. Justice Frankfurter.

By the time *Colegrove* v. *Green,* the "political thicket" case, arrived before Frankfurter's bench, however, the "judicial restraint" notions he had developed in New Deal days were a dozen years mellower. It is an irony that he should then use these notions to argue — this time from a conservative posture — against the Supreme Court's entry into the field of congressional malapportionment. Nevertheless, the political thicket doctrine had to be overturned if Walter Chandler was to win his lawsuit in 1959, still another dozen years later. If it could be reversed in Tennessee, Chandler felt, United States District Judge William E. Miller was the jurist most likely to do it. There were other reasons of convenience for filing *Baker* v. *Carr* in Nashville, but William E. Miller, the judge sitting there, was the number one reason.

Chandler knew that Bill Miller, at the time a youthful-appearing fifty-one, was an East Tennessee Republican, a native of that section of the state which had been for years the victim of deep voter discrimination. Miller, he knew from firsthand experience, was both a constitutional authority and a constitution-maker, a lawyer whose eyeteeth were cut on Blackstone, a judge who had already demonstrated by liberal implementation of school desegregation in Nashville that he was not bound by the hidebound. He was well aware, too, that Miller was a practical man who knew and had participated in politics. With some measure of confidence, therefore, Chandler could write his colleagues a week after the State of Tennessee on June 8 filed its expected motion to dismiss *Baker:* "It is difficult for me to believe that Judge Miller would grant the motion of the defendants when he is bound to know how grossly unjust is the present apportionment of the legislature. Of course, I expect him to decide the case on its merits," he added, "but I certainly think that we are entitled to a trial on the merits, rather than a summary judgment against us."

Despite that expression of optimism, Chandler was worried. That very day he had read in his morning Memphis *Commercial Appeal* unexpected word from St. Paul which he did not know how to interpret: A special session of the Minnesota Legislature, under the mandate of the three-judge court there, had enacted a reapportionment bill. Was this good or bad? Three days before, Chandler had felt "that the three-judge court in Minnesota would decide the pending case there shortly after the adjournment of the special session of the Minnesota Legislature, and that we might get the benefit of that decision." He did not dream that the Minnesota legislators would actually pass a bill. Now that they had, would the three-judge panel render a decision? Or would Dan Magraw, his codefendants and their lawyer, Frank Farrell, decide they had won their point? Or had the Minnesota Legislature done too little to satisfy the complaints? Chandler wrote Magraw at once, inquiring precisely what had happened in St. Paul and what might now happen.

Whatever the answer, though, he knew his arguments would have to be modified in some manner. And time was short. That same day's mail brought word from Judge Miller that *Baker* v. *Carr* had been set for call the following Monday, June 22.

Considerable confusion surrounded that date. Judge Miller, it seems, had expected the parties to argue the motion to dismiss that day. Chandler misunderstood. And Hobart Atkins had felt, apparently, that the impaneling of a three-judge court was to be an automatic matter. Osborn, appearing for the plaintiffs that Monday, requested and obtained a date for the arguments. Judge Miller named July 6, 1959. He alone would hear the contestants on that day to determine whether *Baker* would be dismissed summarily or a three-judge panel assembled to rule on the State's motion. In cases involving a federal question on a constitutional matter, three-judge panels are mandatory. The July 6 hearing, therefore, would be to determine if a federal question existed. That was indeed a question in view of the Supreme Court's refusal to review the *Kidd* v. *McCanless* case, containing substantially the same issues, involving precisely the same state legislature, less than three years before. That a three-judge panel in Minnesota had seemed to assume jurisdiction in a reapportionment case was no guarantee of the same decision in Tennessee. *Baker* v. *Carr* had arrived at a pivotal point, its life not necessarily at stake, but its future chances for a clean appeal very much in the hands of William Ernest Miller.

The hands and the mind were well equipped for the task. Bill Miller was the son of a judge with twenty years' tenure on the Chancery bench and he had on occasion filled in for his father, once for an extended period when the elder Miller suffered a heart attack. He got his law degree at Yale, capping an interest that began with the precocious reading of Gibson, Carruthers and all four volumes of Blackstone before he completed high school. Miller had never aspired to be anything but a federal judge or a congressman, and when the latter ambition fell 1,473 votes short (of 60,000 cast) in 1948, there was speculation that this up-and-coming young lawyer would someday try again. But shortly after his distinguished 1953 service in the constitutional convention ended, a special bill went through Congress creating a second district judgeship for Middle Tennessee. It would have been customary for a Middle Tennessean to fill such a post, but President Eisenhower went three hundred miles eastward to Congressman B. Carroll Reece's district to tap his man. On March 16, 1955, the appointment of William E. Miller fulfilled Miller's boyhood ambition — and, some cynics said, removed a future threat to Reece.

When the landmark case in the one-man-one-vote revolution began in his United States District Court, Judge Miller had spent four years and two months presiding over some of the most difficult cases in Tennessee legal history. For the rest of his career as a district

[148]

judge, too (Miller was later elevated to the Sixth Circuit Court of Appeals), his court was a lightning rod for a difficult, even bizarre, streak of cases involving a wide range of society's most sophisticated problems. Some of them, as we shall see, were oddly interlocking and drew into them some of the biggest names in America.

William Miller had scarcely arrived in Nashville before they began. *Brown* v. *Board of Education,* the school desegregation case, had been handed down by the United States Supreme Court the year before. Miller donned his robes just in time to catch the lawsuit filed against the Nashville school system to implement that decision. The case would have been a tough one to handle anywhere at the upper edge of Dixie; it was perhaps even tougher in Nashville, for a paradoxical reason. Nashville was an early target of civil rights proponents, not because it was a particularly hard nut to crack but because it was not. A liberal base for progress existed around the city's numerous colleges and universities. The city also contained an enlightened, cultured Negro community, centered at black institutions such as Fisk University, Meharry Medical College, Tennessee State University. The blacks had an abundance of legal talent, including Z. Alexander Looby, a Nashville city councilman, and his young law partner, Avon Williams. The NAACP was a pillar in Nashville. Black men served on the city's housing authority, its school board, and in its fire and police departments. Looby and Williams brought the suit. Out of it, with Miller's guidance, was forged what came to be known as the "Nashville Plan," a grade-at-a-time desegregation of the public schools beginning at the first grade, where, it was believed, less prejudice might exist. Miller's decree suggested that should matters go smoothly, the stair-step plan might move faster than one grade at a time. Neither side was satisfied, but the plan stood; it was widely copied throughout the South.

Miller's flexible, innovative liberality in implementing so ambivalent a term as "all deliberate speed" soon led him to clear entirely new legal ground: In 1957, he established a pattern for determining union responsibility for strike violence by awarding a judgment against the United Mine Workers of America. In that case, the Meadow Creek Coal Company had sued the union for damages, claiming its striking members had destroyed mine property. The union said it was not legally responsible for the actions of its members and cited federal law and precedent to prove it. Judge Miller declared that it was responsible to the extent of $400,-000, however, and when the union appealed his non-jury finding, the United States Supreme Court upheld him.

But Bill Miller had toed the line of precedent, too, when other unique opportunities presented themselves. One, a forerunner of later similar challenges of the Vietnam War, was brought in his court that year by Fyke Farmer, a brilliant if eccentric attorney who was deeply committed to World Federation and peace movements, and who later managed to stay for a short

[150]

while the executions of Ethel and Julius Rosenberg, the couple accused of handing over atomic secrets to the Soviet Union. Farmer attempted to subpoena former President Harry S. Truman into Miller's court to account for what he considered America's unlawful entry into the undeclared Korean War. Farmer had withheld the portion of his federal income tax that he calculated was used to prosecute this "illegal" war. Korea, he argued, was a complete violation of international law, as declared at the Nuremberg War Crimes Tribunal. In dismissing Farmer's challenge, Miller held that courts "have no right or authority to resolve political or governmental questions, or to review issues of governmental policy entrusted to the executive and legislative departments. . . . The foreign policy of the United States is the exclusive province of the executive and the legislative branches of government. . . . It is imperative that courts strictly observe the limitations upon their power."

William E. Miller had both made precedent and observed it, then — and on "political questions," too — when he took control of *Baker* v. *Carr*. What this might bode for reapportionment was not altogether clear; his decision in the Farmer case suggested an unwillingness to cross traditional lines of power separation, but his other rulings gave clues that he was not totally bound by the past.

As coincidence had it, still another case pending in Judge Miller's court when *Baker* v. *Carr* arrived contributed an unusual, and certainly a most influential, factor to the ultimate success of the one-man-one-vote movement. For it was a "Teamster case" and it brought to Tennessee a young attorney for the highly publicized McClellan Subcommittee who would later become Attorney General of the United States — Robert F. Kennedy.

The jury trial of Glenn Smith, president of the Chattanooga Teamsters Union local, had just been completed in Judge Miller's court when *Baker* v. *Carr* was filed. But motions concerning Smith's conviction for income-tax evasion were still before Miller, and he was bothered by them. The government had prosecuted Smith for failure to report $18,500 in income easily traceable to him. But Smith had electrified the court by testifying that he was only a conduit for the money; it could not be considered income because he had passed the cash along to be used as bribes to dismiss criminal cases against a number of Teamsters officials on trial in Judge Raulston Schoolfield's criminal court in Chattanooga. Miller thought that the record strongly supported Smith's testimony, that the government should have prosecuted him for criminal conspiracy, not for tax evasion. In his view, Smith was not guilty of tax evasion, but the jury had convicted him of it. Miller thought Smith "morally unfit to hold the important position entrusted to him," and it was likely the jury had thought that, too. In such circumstances, faced with a motion to reverse the jury, what should a responsible jurist do?

The Smith affair was one of only a dozen or so

matters — motions, appeals, arguments, briefs — in the back of Bill Miller's mind that humid Monday, two days beyond the Fourth of July 1959, when Walter Chandler, Tommy Osborn and Hobart Atkins appeared before him with the State's attorneys, prepared to argue the State's motion to dismiss *Baker* v. *Carr*. All three of the plaintiffs' attorneys argued before Miller that day, but Chandler had written Osborn and Atkins in advance asking that they take the lead. Both had experience in reapportionment law through *Kidd*, while this was Chandler's first day in court with it. Also, the latest word from St. Paul was disquieting. On June 23, replying to Chandler's query, Dan Magraw had informed him that "Frank Farrell . . . feels very strongly that in view of the substantial improvement made by the Minnesota Legislature that your case and the case in Florida stand a much better chance of succeeding in the Federal Court." Attached to this letter was a more precise statement of what had been decided in Minnesota in the form of a carbon copy of a letter written by Magraw to Richard S. Childs, chairman of the executive committee of the National Municipal League in New York:

The consensus of our lawyers is that it might be better for the total legal effort if we do not go back into Federal Court. The bill passed here is still not satisfactory in that there are discrepancies of 4 to 1 in the House and 3 to 1 in the Senate. However, we feel that to jeopardize the progress we have made in the case so far by going back into court and risking an unfavorable opinion would be a serious error. This is particularly true because the Ten-

[153]

nessee and Florida cases are concerned with far worse situations than ours is now. At one point we were in the 37 to 1 ratio, and the Federal Court might take the position that there has been such substantial improvement that the Court would be reluctant to act.

As you probably know, the Tennessee case is based precisely on our case, and we expect that the Florida case is similarly based.

That his case was so precisely patterned was what worried Chandler. He wrote his associates that "my hopes were based largely on the probable outcome of the Minnesota case. Unfortunately, that case probably will be dropped by reason of the action of the Minnesota Legislature in passing a partial reapportionment act." Nevertheless, he suggested that they "rely on the principles enunciated in the Hawaii and *Magraw* v. *Donovan* cases, put in as many favorable three-judge court cases as we can find, and point out that the *Colegrove* case, insofar as jurisdiction is concerned, held by a 5 to 4 decision [this was not the precise count] that jurisdiction was accepted."

In the division of arguments, the plan was followed. Atkins leaned heavily upon the *Colegrove* circumstances: While the Supreme Court split 3–3–1 in rejecting the case itself, four of the seven justices acknowledged the Court's jurisdiction. Osborn attacked the thorny "political question" issue, which all three agreed was their hardest hurdle to surmount. In doing so, he went back to the kings of England and their dealings with Parliament. He did not note it, and may not have known it, but his arguments were based on philosophical grounds not unlike those used by the Levellers, that radical group of seventeenth-century democratic zealots under the leadership of John Lilburne.

In 1959, in Nashville, Tennessee, before Judge William E. Miller, the arguments were more sophisticated, and Osborn was treading a thin line. What is a "political question"? And when is a question involving politics not political to the extent that it might escape being tossed again into Justice Frankfurter's thicket?

When the kings of England contended with Parliament for power, Osborn argued, Parliament won from the kings "the right to judge as to who has been elected to Parliament." That victory, carried over into the American republican form, was "the power within the body to rule on the seating of its members." *That,* Osborn was saying, was a political question. (In the Adam Clayton Powell case, the Court later attacked this one, too.) In the earlier days when the people themselves contended with kings to have a Parliament, the question was different. That, he argued, was *not* a political question but a matter of civil rights. Those rights, Osborn and his colleagues argued that July day, were under the equal protection guarantees of the Fourteenth Amendment.

"The Legislature belongs to the people," he said. "It does not belong to the individuals that comprise the Legislature." The legislature's members might decide who among the elected could be seated; they could not decide who would be elected.

The arguments, begun at 9 A.M. that Monday, were finished by the luncheon break. Hobart Atkins had to leave at once, for he had a commitment back in Knoxville, but the following day he wrote Chandler of his optimism: "I can't help but feel that we made some progress." Chandler replied: "If Judge Miller is the courageous judge that I believe he is, he will not take the easy way out of this case in view of the terrible state of affairs."

Miller had requested briefs to help him in reaching a decision, and Osborn set to work on one. The political question remained the thorn. Osborn filed his brief with Miller July 21, and Chandler was pleased with it: "I feel that your analysis of the *Colegrove* case is unanswerable, and I must say that it is difficult for me to conceive that Judge Miller would undertake to dispose of as vital a case as we have presented without convening a three-judge court." He was right about Miller on all scores: On July 31, the judge rejected the State's plea for a summary dismissal, declaring that "the issues presented are of such character that they should be evaluated and considered by a three-judge court."

Six days earlier, Miller had resolved another dilemma. He had reversed Teamster Glenn Smith's conviction for income tax evasion, thus freeing a man who had confessed to conspiring in the attempted bribery of a criminal court judge. Miller was not happy with the choice, but he thought the law gave him no other alternative. The State had other alternatives, though, and shortly set out on an investigation of the alleged bribery of a state judge. Bob Kennedy was more than happy to join in this undertaking, which established for him lasting contacts in Tennessee — contacts interested in the outcome of *Baker* v. *Carr*.

For some weeks before Judge Miller's decision set the stage for a three-judge hearing, Walter Chandler had been displeased with the way matters were going. The Tennessee case was not following the Minnesota script. There a three-judge trial of the case on its merits had been relatively easy to obtain. In Minnesota, almost as a matter of course, District Judge Edward J. Devitt disposed of the dismissal motion; at once, within six weeks, *Magraw* v. *Donovan* moved to a full trial on the merits. But in Tennessee, the attorney general's office, and more specifically Solicitor General Allison Humphreys, was attacking the case as if it involved a personal stake.

Chandler had grown impatient with Humphreys (who later was elevated to the Tennessee Supreme Court). He felt the Solicitor General's oath of office did not call upon him to reduce this case in equity to a bitter fight — only to present the facts and arguments as one representing the public. However, Humphreys had filed four separate briefs on the simple motion before Judge Miller, and when it came to arguments on this motion, he spent an aggressive hour and a half on his feet. Chandler also did not believe some of the matters contained in the defendants' briefs were entirely ethical, in that they cited as authority cases then on appeal. At one time he threatened to go to Attorney General George McCanless about it. Tom Osborn had dissuaded him.

Now, as the case approached the three-judge panel stage, Chandler and Osborn felt sure Humphreys would resist their claim to "the right to a trial of the case on its merits" and would demand instead that the three jurists rule separately on the State's motion to dismiss. Osborn and Chandler thought the court would possibly hear the motion as a part of the trial; Atkins, even more optimistic, believed that Judge Miller's decision on the motion foreclosed that question before the three judges. Both were wrong; they got no full-scale trial on the merits, as had their counterparts in Minnesota. But they had to be prepared for it anyway. Accordingly, Chandler commissioned State Historian Robert H. White to begin at once a search of the legislative journals from 1870 through the legislative session just ended. Dr. White's meticulous research became vital when *Baker* v. *Carr* reached the high court, for it helped document the argument that Tennessee citizens of the United States could find no remedy at home: Their state legislature, year after year, session after session, had either ignored its constitutional mandate altogether or had openly violated its collective oath by systematically defeating all efforts to redistribute the seats on the basis of shifting population.

Ten days after Judge Miller's ruling, the three-judge

panel was named by the acting chief judge of the Sixth Circuit Court of Appeals in Cincinnati. Joining Bill Miller on the panel were Judge John D. Martin, a justice of the Sixth Circuit Court, and United States District Judge Marion Speed Boyd of the West Tennessee Division. The makeup of that panel was not altogether pleasing to the plaintiffs. Judge Martin and Judge Boyd were both Memphians, and, like Chandler, had once been members of the Crump organization. Martin was a second cousin of the late Boss, and, as a federal district judge, he had once participated in a political battle between Crump and Governor Gordon Browning by issuing a famous injunction against the Governor. If Boyd and Martin had ties and common interests in Memphis, however, both jurists were noted as extremely conservative men; this gave no comfort to reformers seeking to undo the *status quo* by shattering precedents and scaling walls erected between coordinate branches of American government.

The first official word from the panel, on September 15, confirmed somewhat the plaintiffs' discomfort. They were not to get a trial on the merits as in Minnesota but only another hearing "on the defendants' motion to dismiss," which was set for November 23, 1959. Moreover, by this time it was definite that they would have no opinion from the *Magraw* case to bolster their arguments. Frank Farrell had so informed Chandler promptly after the Minnesota plaintiffs, on August 18, filed a plaintiffs' motion for voluntary dismissal of the lawsuit there. In the hasty exchange of letters about these developments, the only optimistic note came from Tom Osborn, who reported to his colleagues that it looked as if Mayor Ben West of Nashville was about to take an active interest in *Baker* v. *Carr*. Osborn also reported that he had discussed procedures with Judge Miller and had been informed, as had the attorney general's office, that all parties should be prepared for an early trial of the case on its merits if the motion to dismiss was denied. The three attorneys therefore decided they needed an immediate strategy session.

Chandler, Atkins and Osborn met for this purpose on Thursday, September 24, in Osborn's Nashville office. Both the pretrial work and the arguments were divided up:

— Atkins was to search the general law of Tennessee for further illustrations of power abuses by the Tennessee legislature. He would have the second argument at the forthcoming hearing; it would deal with the legal authorities relied upon by the State in its expected challenge of the court's jurisdiction.

— Chandler was to rewrite the briefs the plaintiffs had used before Judge Miller. He would have the leadoff argument November 23. It would cover the right of the plaintiffs to be in court, the unconstitutionality of the 1901 act, and the right of the courts to question the validity of acts of apportionment, specifically in view of changing circumstances.

— Osborn was to prepare the plaintiffs' proof and assemble material directed by the district court clerk for distribution to the three jurists. As anchor man in the arguments, he would cover the question of the availability of relief, analyzing the cases in which apportionment lawsuits had met with success and the relief in such cases. His argument would also deal with the violations of the due-process clause that the plaintiffs had alleged in their complaint.

The three attorneys agreed that their proof, should they get a trial, would have two main thrusts. One would be the testimony of Dr. White, supported by his legislative journal research, that the legislature had refused systematically since the turn of the century, despite numerous efforts, to redistrict the seats. The second effort would be to show that the result of this was a pattern of discrimination in the allocation of state tax funds. If this could be established, Osborn felt, it would give strong support to a "due process" argument — that is, that *property* protected by the Fourteenth Amendment was being taken from urban citizens without due process of law. In pursuit of the latter proof, requiring careful statistical analysis, Osborn visited Mayor West a few days after the strategy conference. Ben West promised him the cooperation of Nashville's advance planning staff in preparing whatever data he might need.

Supportive of the proof that discrimination was practiced in dividing state funds, the attorneys believed, would be a taped copy of a speech made by Jim Cummings on the floor of the Tennessee House during the 1959 session. The colorful sage of Cannon County never attempted to disguise his motives; he was intellectually honest and invariably delivered his true feelings about reapportionment anytime the subject arose.

The final two months before the three-judge hearing were occupied in assembling this proof. Dr. White tired of the tedious task of checking page after page of journals grown yellow and dusty. He felt his labors were to be lost, anyway, and wanted to quit when, halfway through, he felt he had enough to prove the point. Chandler diplomatically encouraged him to plug on and finally, on November 12, Dr. White delivered the final page of his research which he had been carrying on "like the cat gnawing away the grindstone. . . . It is done. Am I glad!"

Meanwhile, on November 3, Mayor West definitely committed himself to the cause by asking the Nashville City Council to authorize intervention and help finance the lawsuit. Six days later, Chattanooga's City Attorney Joel Anderson wrote Chandler that his city wanted in, too, and Hobart Atkins reported on November 13 that Knoxville also was interested in intervening. "The more the merrier," Chandler chortled, and he wrote Osborn suggesting that Harris Gilbert, the young attorney Ben West had named to help in the case, be set to putting Dr. White's material, the Nashville planning staff's statistics, and Jim Cummings's recorded speech into proper shape for exhibits.

Two weeks before their big day in court, Chandler suggested a second get-together to map final plans. Atkins could not make the meeting set for Wednesday, November 18, but Chandler and Osborn decided to go ahead. Osborn brought Gilbert along, and Chandler had with him a young attorney from his firm, Carl H. Langschmidt, Jr. They spent the afternoon in review and in seeing that the papers were all in order. They decided that Dr. White's research would enter the official record as a part of Nashville's intervening petition. Chandler and Osborn also met the following Sunday afternoon with Mayor West. The next day, at 9:30 A.M., they were due before the three judges, sitting in Judge Miller's courtroom.

Monday, November 23, 1959, was a bleak and dreary day. Fog and drizzling rain hung over the Cumberland Mountains between Knoxville and Nashville. That and the road construction that seems never to end in the rocky, crumbling passes winding up toward the plateau country delayed Hobart Atkins, who disliked flying. He was late for the brief conference the plaintiffs' attorneys had planned immediately before the convening of court. It mattered little; as usual, the preliminaries occupied the first half-hour. Each side was allocated an hour and a half to present its case. Solicitor General Allison Humphreys offered a mild and rather perfunctory resistance to Nashville's entry into the lawsuit. Harris Gilbert presented the city's brief. Tom Osborn introduced Ellis Meacham, who appeared as counsel for Chattanooga. The proper courtesy nod was accorded the presence of Attorney General George McCanless, who took no further part in the proceedings. And a quarter-hour was spent in unenthusiastic discussion of the State's first, rather technical, ground for its dismissal motion: failure of the plaintiffs to join indispensable parties to the lawsuit. The remaining two grounds were, of course, the heart of the defendants' case: lack of jurisdiction, a ground laid firmly upon the rock of the *Colegrove* case; and the failure of the plaintiffs to state a case upon which relief could be granted.

The judges did not want for full and well-developed arguments that late November day. When it ended, the trio of men who had been preparing the case for almost a year now, felt their arguments had gone well. But they could hardly be certain how the judges would rule. Remarks from the bench, not invariably a good guide to judicial sentiment, had indicated a deep unease about *Baker* v. *Carr* in all of the judges, and in the two older men in particular. That much they understood: *Baker* was simply the toughest of cases. It would not have been easy had it involved the separation-of-powers issue alone. But it also involved states rights, no matter how hard Walter Chandler labored to recast it in terms of another tough issue — that of the individual's fundamental right to meaningful suffrage. It was a classic case of rights — not just two but several — in deadly conflict: legislative, judicial, states, federal, individual. Added to this vexation was the strange and ambiguous guidance of the so-called "controlling" case, *Colegrove* v. *Green*.

Humphreys argued first, and it was perfectly true, as he insisted, that the *Colegrove* "opinion has been followed consistently from that day to this except in two instances," the Hawaiian case and the one from Minnesota. It was equally true that the Hawaiian case involved a territory, not a state, while the Minnesota case "never proceeded to a final adjudication." But it was also true that in both cases jurisdiction over the subject matter had posed no problem to other federal courts, a point underscored quickly by Chandler and Atkins when they came on in that order. It was absolutely true, as Humphreys emphasized, that the *Colegrove* case was rejected. It was just as true, as the Leveller lawyers replied, that four of the seven justices hearing the case in the Supreme Court had acknowledged jurisdiction. But one of the four, Humphreys rejoined, found "the cure is worse than the disease" when time arrived for a remedy.

The second of Humphreys's key grounds for dismissal was that the plaintiffs had failed to state a case upon which relief could be granted. The anchor argument on this point was Osborn's, though Atkins had spent some time on it. The remedy, he insisted, was an at-large election. Just as the Supreme Court had held in a congressional reapportionment case (*Smiley* v. *Holm*) that the absence of an apportionment act required an at-large election, so it would be in Tennessee with the legislature should the judges invalidate the state statute of 1901. If chaos resulted, as some insisted, Osborn said, "chaos is to be preferred to tyranny."

At the end of the day, enough had been said from the bench to assure most spectators that Judge Martin could never be shaken from a states-rights stance so firm that to rule for the plaintiffs would shatter his innermost principles. At one point he had declared: "There are still some of us left who think that the dual system of government established by the Constitution should be preserved and that federalism should not run riot to the deprivation of the fundamental rights of the states. . . . We still have the Tenth Amendment although it has not been alluded to as much as the Fourteenth and the Fifteenth in recent years. It is still there in the Constitution unchanged."

Atkins's argument had almost dissolved into a running debate with the senior judge, whose questioning dominated the panel. "I just have difficulty in getting to the point where we have any fundamental jurisdiction here at all," Judge Martin told Atkins during this sharp colloquy. "Of course, these cases have defined it, but I think it reasonably [sic] is pretty simple that we just have not any jurisdiction at all vested in us about the state officials in connection with the policy of Tennessee." He asked Atkins to respond, and after a bit more give-and-take, the Knoxvillian did, with a question:

"If the State Legislature were down in my pocket taking my money, I could come into court all right, and the Court would stop it; but here, they are not taking my money, they are taking something more valuable to me. Now, do I understand that the Court should look the other way?"

JUDGE MARTIN: No, not look the other way, but not look at all because it is no business of this Federal Court. That is my position. We haven't any right to direct the Legislature of Tennessee to pass any law.

Still later, Atkins who had fought *Kidd-McCanless* through the state courts, argued that "chancery practice or chancery courts originated in conscience. . . . Once conscious of a wrong, then there should be a remedy; and you at once begin to look for that remedy."

JUDGE MARTIN: The remedy is the State Supreme Court.
ATKINS: But the State Supreme Court said in that [*Kidd*] case . . .
JUDGE MARTIN: I am not saying what they said. I am pointing you where the remedy was. Because they did not give you a remedy did not give the Federal Court a right to come in and try to be boss.

Judge Boyd, taller and more reserved than his Memphis colleague, put his finger early on the major problem the plaintiffs had and in doing so indicated strongly that he, too, had doubts about jurisdiction.

JUDGE BOYD: Captain, pardon my interrupting.
CHANDLER: Yes, sir.
JUDGE BOYD: Is not the Oklahoma case really the last word on the subject?
CHANDLER: *Radford* v. *Gary*?
JUDGE BOYD: Yes. A case which incidentally was affirmed by the Supreme Court. It was not just certiorari denied. They affirmed that case on the basis of *Colegrove* and on the basis of *Kidd* v. *McCanless*. That case is pretty much in point on the facts here, is it not?

[167]

They were dealing with a legislature in that case. Let us hear you discuss that briefly if it won't interrupt you.

CHANDLER: That case is in point. There was a divided decision in the three-judge court there in Oklahoma, and the presiding judge, Judge Murrah, said that the Court felt itself bound by the *Colegrove* case.

Chandler then went on to deliver himself of his feeling about the *Colegrove* decision and why he was determined, as his letters many times reflected, to wipe it off the books: "I think that the *Colegrove* case has created more mischief in the jurisprudence of this country than any case that has been decided in a long time, if I may say it with the utmost respect to the Supreme Court of the United States. That case is contrary to us. I want to say that frankly."

JUDGE BOYD: But the Supreme Court has not departed from the *Colegrove* doctrine.

CHANDLER: No. It has not departed from it. . . .

Only Judge Miller, then, left any indication that he might be swayed on the jurisdictional argument. The matter of remedy, however, obviously bothered him.

JUDGE MILLER: Suppose that we ordered an election at large. . . . That has been the only suggestion made as a practical solution to this matter and I think every one will agree that the Constitution of Tennessee has been ignored and violated continuously and systematically over a period of years resulting in aborting the Constitution of Tennessee.

HUMPHREYS: Yes, sir.

[168]

JUDGE MILLER: I do not think there is any doubt about that. But suppose this Court would so declare this law unconstitutional, the Act of 1901, and then direct an election at large, and then suppose that the Legislature so elected would convene. I suppose the theory would be that that Legislature would enact a statute that would meet the requirements of the Constitution. But what assurance would there be that the Legislature would re-map the state or redistrict it? . . . That is the difficulty I am having. My problem in this matter is the problem of a proper remedy. . . . I can see the wrong of the thing, but whether or not a remedy can be worked out . . .

The day had been long and the arguments were dying when Walter Chandler asked for one final word: "One other thing I would like to say that I believe is right: No case is ever decided finally until it is decided right, the *Colegrove* case to the contrary notwithstanding. The right in this matter is what we are trying to get at, the right which we are trying to have prevail here. And the State won't even deny that there is a great wrong. It has already been admitted."

Despite the admissions, the battle was lost before the three-judge panel, and Chandler acknowledged that he suspected this to be so. On December 9, twelve days before the court's decision was released, he wrote Richard Childs of the National Municipal League: "Two of the judges seemed to feel that the case of *Colegrove* v. *Green,* with which we are all familiar, may deprive the Court of jurisdiction of the case, but one of the Judges definitely indicated that he did not believe that this case governed the pending suit."

When the three judges made their decision known December 21, 1959, then, there were no surprises and only one major disappointment: Bill Miller had not dissented. The decision, once again recognizing great evil but declaring that nothing could be done, was unanimous.

3

Mayor Ben West
and Charles S. Rhyne

On the same day the Nashville three-judge panel dismissed *Baker* v. *Carr*, the jurists made a second determination that probably contributed as much to the ultimate success of one man, one vote as a favorable judgment would have. They allowed Nashville Mayor Ben West to remain in the lawsuit and they permitted him further to amend and supplement his intervening petition.

Walter Chandler was bitterly disappointed at the time by the decision, less for the judges' upholding precedent than for their failure to give him a trial on the merits. No case on reapportionment had then advanced to the Supreme Court with the record of proof from a full trial behind it. Always, as Chandler complained, "only one side of the question, to wit, the cold, legal proposition [had] been presented." That was why, as the hearing neared its end on November 23, Tommy Osborn had begged the federal judges to let him put before them evidence of the evils resulting from the failure of the Tennessee legislature to obey its mandate, and how the situation might be rectified.

"Why couldn't Your Honors on this question of remedy permit us to . . . offer proof as to how a statewide election might result?" he had pleaded. "Why would not Your Honors let us offer proof as to why it is that the presently constituted majority of the Legislature is willing to ignore its constitutional duty? We want so much to have Your Honors hear the evidence in the case and to note the abuses and to note *this* in connection with the remedy: That if the financial aspect of it were removed, then what reason would there be for any Tennessean selected by the voters of this State to refuse to obey a patently fair constitutional provision? We would like for you to hear the evidence."

However, Judge Martin had cut Osborn short with a reminder that "just as soon as a court finds that it has no jurisdiction, it does not proceed further." His remarks from the bench also made it quite clear that he considered that a majority of the Supreme Court had refused jurisdiction in *Colegrove* despite the positive holding of only three justices on that point. The matter was closed.

When Ben West entered the case, however, the bare bones of two important documents entered it with him. One was the legislative journal research of the state historian, Dr. Robert White; the other was the statistics hastily put together by the Nashville Planning Commission's advance planning division showing a general pattern of discrimination in the distribution of Tennessee tax revenues funneled through the General Assembly. Neither of these documents was impressive as it then stood. Both had been drawn up in a race against time. Dr. White had had only his spare hours over about two months to devote to the original journal research (for which he refused payment). The Planning Commission staff had had only the twenty days between West's definite commitment to the lawsuit on November 3 and its trial date before the three judges to prepare its exhibit.

These two documents represented potentially wide avenues of proof, however, once the judges permitted West to amend and supplement and refine them. Given that opening, Tennessee's Leveller lawyers took full advantage. Dr. White's research, with the luxury of time, expanded to an impressive, elaborately footnoted "Documented Study of Tennessee Legislative Reapportionment, 1870 through 1957" by the time the case reached the United States Supreme Court. The Planning Commission's work, during the same period, fanned out to examine in more than 180 pages of statistical data every conceivable angle of legislative discrimination, every possible maldistribution of state tax funds. By becoming the vehicle through which this mountain of research was driven into the case record, then, Mayor West's entry was the practical equivalent of producing witnesses and testimony for Walter Chandler's much-sought but never-granted trial on the merits. Indeed, Chandler with a dozen witnesses probably could not have created clearer, more complete or persuasive proof of the historical failings and fiscal evils of Tennessee's legislative situation.

The ultimate impact on the U.S. Supreme Court was considerable. Of Dr. White's contribution, Harris Gilbert, the young attorney Ben West retained as special counsel for Nashville, later said: "I think this was one of the most important documents prepared in the matter. He went back and checked the archives, even the journals of the various Senate and House committees of Tennessee every year that the legislature had met since 1870. . . . He documented the results in great detail. He further investigated the votes — who was voting which way — and documented which counties the legislators came from. The purpose and thrust of all this was to show the utter impossibility of obtaining any relief from the Tennessee legislature. That avenue was closed. Justice Brennan [who wrote the *Baker* majority opinion] referred to this survey twice in his opinion."

For Dr. White, then in his seventies, the survey had been a labor of love and friendship for the man who asked him to do it, "Captain" Chandler. It had also been "one of the most tedious jobs I ever tackled, due to the numerous errors in the legislative journals. From time to time, the numbering of the bills was erroneous, and this factor really gums the works when you attempt to trace a bill through the legislature." But he deeply believed in the cause, as his letters to Chandler made clear. On Thanksgiving Day, 1959, depressed by news accounts which indicated that Judge Martin and Judge Boyd, at least, were going to rule against *Baker*, he wrote Chandler: "If I were not a sort of fool optimist, I would be ready to exclaim that justice and equity have lain down to weep! It seems almost a mockery to allude to some of the maxims of equity, such as 'Equity delights to do justice,' 'Equity suffers not a wrong without a remedy,' et cetera. I have always thought of equity as being the synonym of natural justice of inherent right. Now I wonder."

As for the Planning Commission data, Nashville was still supplementing it right up until the final argument day in the United States Supreme Court. By the time the case was argued a second time, in October 1961, the final results of the 1960 census were in, confirming the growth of the apportionment crisis. To the mound of analytical material covering a full half century, 1900–1950, then, Nashville's planning staff added the final decade, 1950–1960. "They had already covered it from every angle to eliminate the possibility of any argument that there was a rational basis for apportionment in Tennessee," Gilbert said. "They had also worked the tax distribution from as many angles as they could — [per] capita, per county, you know, the various statistical things the lawyer was not able to do."

Such an abundance — even overabundance — of

support from Mayor Ben West was typical of the man. He was a tenacious, aggressive, often hyperdefensive person who had never believed in doing anything by halves. "It don't cost much more to go first class," he was fond of saying, and he lived by the adage. He had been slow coming to the side of Chandler and Osborn, his former city attorney, but once he set his mind to a cause or a project, turning him aside was like resisting a buzzsaw.

Chandler and Osborn had both courted West for months in the hope that he would help them. He had held back, believing, Osborn explained, that the courts held no solution to the problem. But in late September, lingering after a Saturday luncheon at the Colemere Club, the Nashville politicians' hangout, West fell into deep conversation with colleagues about the situation and decided that the time was propitious. At the invitation of friends, he had driven out to the Colemere, once a railroad magnate's antebellum home and now situated on property acquired for the municipal airport. Besides young Harris Gilbert, not long out of the University of Chicago law school, the group included Harris's father, Criminal Court Judge Charles Gilbert, his politically active uncle, Leon Gilbert, and some of their friends.

"After we got through with lunch we talked about this reapportionment problem and the terrible injustice to the city taxpayers," West recalled. The Mayor had just returned from Atlanta where he had had a long conference with Bill Hartsfield, for twenty-four years the mayor of Atlanta. "He had fought this fight down in Georgia. As I remember it, Atlanta had more people and paid more state taxes than the rest of Georgia put together. But they could not get any relief for the taxpayers of Atlanta whatsoever." Hartsfield had attempted to crack the Georgia unit rule system through *Hartsfield* v. *Sloan* the previous year. He had failed. But in the discussions at the Colemere that day, Gilbert remembered, it was mentioned that Hartsfield "came very close to getting a favorable Supreme Court vote on accepting jurisdiction."

Someone remarked the case was a straw in the wind suggesting that the courts might look more favorably toward a solution. Beyond favorable straws, West was also influenced by treatment accorded him — and Nashville — at the last session of the General Assembly. "I've had my last licking from the legislature," he told his luncheon friends. "I went up there this last time and asked them for a better shake. . . . They laughed at me."

The Assembly had done more than laugh when West made that appearance. Some of the members had boiled with rage. The Nashvillian, then completing his term as president of the American Municipal Association, delivered to the Tennessee legislature a refinement of a speech he made all over the nation and even abroad, in Tel Aviv and The Hague, in Rio and San Juan. It also won him praise from Chicago Mayor Richard Daley, who "thanked God for a mayor who put people ahead of pigs and cows." For to prepare for it,

West had sent his assistants to the state Agriculture Department to get the total number of cows and pigs in Moore County. "So I had some diagrams drawn showing the pigs, cows and people," West recalled. "The pigs, cows, and people in Moore County were three times better represented than the people in Davidson County. . . . In 1957, wherever I spoke I referred to the legislative problems that the cities had and always brought up how many pigs and cows there were in Moore County, and always got a chuckle." Inside Tennessee, however, the speech won little friendship from the rural majority on Capitol Hill.

Up until this time, like Walter Chandler earlier, the Nashville mayor had stayed out of this struggle for fear of possible retribution against Nashville. He had taken no part in *Kidd* v. *McCanless*. The Tennessee Municipal League, in which he was a powerful influence as past president, sat out the entire one-man-one-vote revolution in Tennessee for the same reason. But Mayor West's talk with Hartsfield and another with former Mayor Walter Chandler of Memphis sealed his decision. "Walter Chandler came to talk to me about it. He and I had been in the Historical Association together and he came to me and said, 'We need help, Ben. This thing is going to fall by the wayside unless we get help. Things are just that desperate.' Well, I had watched the boys flounder because of lack of money, and I felt the city of Nashville should contribute to the fund to fight this lawsuit," West explained. Conferences with Robert Jennings, West's city attorney, followed, and Gilbert recalled that the Mayor himself went over his intervening brief with great care. He had been a successful attorney before becoming mayor; he not only knew the law involved but also was aware that the procedures would be expensive. In what he thought a proper cause, Mayor West had never been stingy with Nashville's money.

Perhaps most important of all, then, West's entry into *Baker* v. *Carr* was essential from a financial standpoint. Taking the case on to the Supreme Court would be costly, and it was primarily for this reason that Walter Chandler and Tom Osborn had worked so hard to encourage West's participation, which would end their fiscal worries. They understood his personality; once in a thing, he would never pull back. David Harsh and Memphis Mayor Edmund Orgill had given the go-ahead on money, but Chandler thought it unwise to ask the West Tennessee metropolis to foot the bill alone. By the time the three-judge panel was formed, he had already billed Memphis–Shelby County for $6,000, and $2,000 of that had been paid out — $1,100 to Osborn and the rest for necessary expenses. Chandler was going back to ask for more, but West and Nashville would still be needed.

The Nashville City Council, at West's request, authorized his entry into the lawsuit and the hiring of counsel on November 3. The resolution, containing no limitations, amounted to a blank check permitting the Mayor "to take any and all necessary steps in proving the long continued mistreatment of the people of the

City of Nashville at the hands of the unlawfully apportioned General Assemblies of Tennessee convened pursuant to the Apportionment Act of 1901." From then until *Baker* v. *Carr* reached the first argument stage in the Supreme Court in April 1961, West paid legal fees and expenses totaling $35,902.48. The total amount Nashville contributed to the case can only be estimated — perhaps $50,000, possibly even more when staff time is considered. For Planning Commission staffers spent many hours producing the statistical data. To this has to be added staff time put in by the city legal office. Printing and distributing the pounds of exhibit material added further to the expense. And when the case finally was remanded to district court for implementation, the costs soared far beyond the Supreme Court expenses.

Few lawyers would ever argue, however, that a case of such import, involving such complex matters, seeking to overturn such a well-established line, could ever be won without this kind of investment. Such things do happen, perhaps, but poor young idealists seldom make it through the white portals of the Supreme Court building in Washington.

Raphael Benjamin West was literally born and reared on the wrong side of the tracks from anything that could be considered Establishment in American society. He had to claw his way into it. His family was, in his own colloquial terms, "as pore as Job's turkey" and he was proud that, during his boyhood in Lewisburg, Tennessee, they lived next door to the large Negro family of John and Fannie Hill.

West's father was James Wat Wilson, a railroad telegrapher, and the family lived along the tracks near his work. When West was in the fifth grade, the father was transferred for two years to Mattoon, Illinois, then back to the Nashville terminals. The family settled in the Woodbine section, near the Radnor railroad yards, and Ben West, the middle of seven children, channeled his enormous energies and aggressiveness toward scholastic pursuits and hard work. He waited on table through grade school, worked as a newspaper copy boy through high school and as a reporter through college. For eight years following his graduation from Vanderbilt, West was a driving, tough-minded assistant prosecuting attorney in that era of American politics when fighting DA's aspired to higher things. West prosecuted some sensational criminal cases, and he knew from his newspaper experience how to get the best political mileage from all this color. After a stint in the state Senate and as Nashville's vice mayor, his third shot at the mayor's office paid off by fifty-five votes in 1951.

Ben West's City Hall was a stormy one. He kept long hours, scheduled endless night meetings and drove those who worked beneath him. He made his habitual bow tie and short, chubby figure trademarks of the office, which had, during his tenure, an aura of Fiorello La Guardia about it. Tom Osborn began as West's city attorney, as we have seen, but that did not last

long. There were wounds on both when Osborn resigned. Four years later, in 1955, West won with ease
his first reelection, and one of the opponents he defeated was a candidate Tom Osborn almost personally
sponsored against him. (That was the year Osborn
also inaugurated the *Kidd* lawsuit with the Miller
brothers and encouraged Mac Davis, Jr., in his legislative joust with Jim Cummings.) The rift between Osborn and West had been such, in fact, that Osborn expressed uncertainty in his letters to Chandler as to
whether West would include his name among attorneys to be paid legal fees by Nashville for the *Baker*
case.

If West bore grudges, however, they had disap-
peared in the 1959 spring election that handily gave
him his third term. The Mayor was flushed with easy
victory, then, when he decided to support the cause
Osborn had championed for four years. Besides, West
was now a recognized statesman in the municipal
field; as a reward for the kind of grinding work on
which he had thrived since boyhood, in tribute to the
truly exceptional record of achievement he had at-
tained, the American Municipal Association had made
him the Nation's number one mayor in 1957–1958 by
elevating him to its national presidency. The position
had once been held by Atlanta's Hartsfield, Ben West's
idol. It was the pinnacle of West's career.

The Mayor's personality itself, therefore, was one of
the key factors that must be considered in any appraisal of the one-man-one-vote victory. Besides the re-

searched record he poured into the case, besides the money, besides himself, he still had one more contribution to make: Shortly after the three-judge panel entered its final order dismissing *Baker* v. *Carr* on February 4, 1960, as a last step before appeal, Ben West flew to Washington determined to retain a specialist in Supreme Court matters to handle the appeal of a lawsuit his aggressive personality was about to take over from its originators.

In his search for the right man, West began where one might expect of a recent past president — at the national headquarters of the American Municipal Association. He talked over his problem with its secretary, Pat Healy. "Healy, a Republican from Utah, suggested Charlie Rhyne," West said. "Rhyne was a Republican and there were a number of Republicans in the Supreme Court at that time." West, the politician, was also much aware at the time that Rhyne was a good friend and former classmate of Vice President Richard M. Nixon, and that he was well acquainted with President Eisenhower and with Attorney General William P. Rogers.

Charles Sylvanus Rhyne would agree little with the political implications suggested there. "You can talk politics all you want to," was his rejoinder to questions about it, "but my relationship with Nixon is entirely personal. I'm a Democrat from North Carolina, if I'm anything, and my participation in two national campaigns for him [Nixon] is my only participation in partisan politics in my life. Both times I took leave of absence from my public position, so politics in my judgment had nothing whatsoever to do with this lawsuit."

From Rhyne's end, indeed, there may have been no politics. He did not seek the assignment but was sought out, and his first thoughts of involvement occurred when Healy called him one mid-February day in 1960 and asked if he might bring Ben West to Rhyne's office. "They came over and said that their interest was in getting me to handle this reapportionment case in the Supreme Court of the United States. Healy knew that . . . oh, I have handled a hundred or so cases up in the Supreme Court, and I was of course familiar with the reapportionment picture. . . . So I told Mayor West that this was an enormously difficult task in the light of the history of these cases, and it would require an enormous amount of work, but if they were willing to at least underwrite our basic fees and expenses for that work we would do it. . . . I told him he had to get the consent and the permission of all the lawyers involved in Tennessee for my participation, because when I participated I had to be in complete charge of the case."

Charlie Rhyne had been a take-charge type from early manhood, possessed of the sort of personality that had led him to the command of an entire floor full of lawyers in Washington's Hill Building. His ratings in the legal directories were "a" and "v" — the very best awarded. The day of West's visit, Walter Chandler called Rhyne to assure him how pleased he was to have him in the case. (Rhyne had known Chandler for years.) Hobart Atkins also called, and later Rhyne got the same assurances from Tom Osborn. (Osborn was reluctant, as we shall see.) Ben West paid Rhyne an initial retainer of five thousand dollars on February 18, 1960. Rhyne set to work at once.

The first task he undertook, in the Supreme Court library, was to personally "review the records and briefs of these fourteen or fifteen — I forget precisely how many it was — cases that had come up to the Supreme Court, and which the Court had declined to review," in an attempt to find the holes that had to be plugged. To get the Supreme Court to take jurisdiction was the big hurdle, and Rhyne was laying the groundwork for the all-important jurisdictional statement, the document on which the Court bases its decision to hear or refuse a case.

"I spent about two weeks in studying those cases, which was quite a chore for me to perform at this stage in my career, but I did it because I realized that would be the only way we'd ever have a chance in the *Baker* case. In each one of those cases I could see that there were three or four things that the Court could turn down the case on. You see, the Court will decline jurisdiction in every case that they can. In every one of these cases there were certain obvious reasons. [But] they never tell you why: they just say, 'Certiorari denied,' or 'No substantial federal question,' or 'Jurisdiction denied,' two or three words. So I figured out in each of these fourteen or fifteen cases what it was that the Court had — or could have — based its decision on. The Court never said.

"A lot of lawyers and lower courts thought it was this 'political thicket' idea. But in studying that I could see pretty quickly that Mr. Frankfurter only had two other justices who agreed with him on that cliché. So that was not the real decision of the Supreme Court." Rhyne had discovered what Leveller lawyers from the beginning of *Kidd* had been insisting: the "thicket doctrine" was *not* the law of the land. On a yellow pad he summarized the reasons, as he saw them, that the Court had turned down all the other cases. Then he set lawyers in his office to researching — far back into the beginnings of the nation on down to the present — to shape his petition for a writ of certiorari. Through it, he hoped to convince the Court to accept the case.

Into this intensive research, Rhyne threw partners, associates and legal assistants from his firm. "I've now been practicing law fifteen years," Harris Gilbert said later, "and I can say I never saw anything worked over as hard as that jurisdictional statement was. I can't begin to tell you the number of lawyers or the amount of time that went into it." There were five or six meetings in Washington with the young attorney from Rhyne's firm assigned the basic draftsmanship — Herzel H. E. Plaine — who had experience with the Justice Department. It was all a matter of "getting on base," Gilbert said. "The Supreme Court does not have to hear appeals of this nature. The main thing was getting a hearing. If we didn't get on base, the ball game was over." That was the first of two key reasons Rhyne had been hired.

The other reason, Rhyne's disclaimers to the contrary, was to try to influence the Republican Administration to enter the lawsuit as *amicus curiae* — "friend of the court" — on behalf of the plaintiffs. Nor was Rhyne unready to acknowledge, some years later, that "I was the one that brought the government in because Lee Rankin is a very close friend of mine, so I talked to him about the case, and I also talked to Bill Rogers about the case, both of them. . . . Rogers was Attorney General and Lee Rankin was Solicitor General, and they were the ones who made the decision that the government would file a brief as friend of the Court."

Rhyne *almost* brought the government in, but not quite. The reason was closely associated with his first venture into partisan politics.

Charles S. Rhyne first met Richard Milhous Nixon during Rhyne's second stint at Duke University in Durham, North Carolina. Rhyne was only twenty and married when he returned to Duke for the fall term of 1932 after a two-year working odyssey through the West. With his bride, the former Sue M. Cotton of Denver, Rhyne had come back to Duke to pursue an interest in the law that began with watching jury trials in a North Carolina courtroom when he was a lad of eleven or twelve. Nixon was a law school classmate. Charles Rhyne's first pursuit of the prerequisite college education, however, had been cut short by poverty. He had been born into a poor family, on September 23, 1912, one of three sons of Sydneyham S. and Mary Wilson Rhyne. His father was a cotton farmer in the Catawba River country of Mecklenburg County, near Charlotte. The man who was later to become a municipal legal expert, and a key contributor to urban victory in *Baker*, was himself an individual with a totally rural upbringing.

"I started to school in a one-room schoolhouse where the teacher taught all eleven grades," Rhyne said. He graduated from high school at the precocious age of fourteen. That was too young to go off to college, so he stayed out a year before, at sixteen, he enrolled at Duke University in the autumn of 1928. Rhyne had worked as a Western Union messenger boy to earn and save three hundred dollars; at Duke, he carried an early-morning newspaper route and trudged the back roads of West Virginia selling Bibles in the summer in a futile effort to remain in school.

"In 1929, the Depression was so bad that I couldn't either borrow or earn money to stay in Duke," Rhyne said, "and you could stay in for about a hundred dollars a year then. Through a classmate at Duke, I had a job working out in Colorado." He hitchhiked out to take it. He drove a truck on Highway 40 and a team of three horses, moving dirt for the storm sewers of Denver. For extra money he hired out as a sparring partner in a local gymnasium and after that landed a job as a ranch hand in Wyoming's Jackson Hole country. It was still more work when Rhyne and his wife returned to Duke, where he completed his undergraduate course before entering law school. Again he carried papers before school hours, and after classes he worked for a contractor repairing tobacco barns. His carpenter work almost cost Rhyne his right arm. A huge splinter was driven into his right hand on one of the jobs and physicians considered amputation. The hand was impaired and Rhyne thereafter wrote awkwardly, his stiffened little finger curled upward. The injury contributed to his leaving Duke before obtaining his law degree. For his final two years of study, Rhyne moved to Washington where he could get a government job requiring little use of the injured hand. His wife worked as a department store clerk while he completed the degree at George Washington University. When he received it, in 1937, Rhyne was twenty-five.

It was "pure accident" that steered Charlie Rhyne into a specialty in municipal law. He had taken no courses in the subject but while finishing up at George Washington he had worked for a law firm that "took part in some . . . highly important lawsuits" in the field. One of his law professors had just been retained by several cities fighting the price-fixing edicts of the National Bituminous Coal Commission. "Well, [the professor] had never been to court so he couldn't do it." Rhyne explained, "and he thought because of all the litigation that my firm had been involved in that I would know just what to do. Just being out of law school, I had all the assurance in the world that I could do it so I told him yes." On the day he was admitted to the bar, in October 1937, then, Rhyne became counsel "for the cities of New York, St. Louis, Atlanta, Detroit and a whole raft of large cities" in the price-fixing action.

Within the year, he argued his first case in the Supreme Court of the United States for the City of Atlanta; he had to be specially admitted because he had not been a member of the bar for the required three years. Rhyne argued this case against Robert Jackson, then United States Attorney General, and later a Supreme Court justice. He lost, but his career as a specialist in municipal matters was launched, if not already established.

When Rhyne turned a portion of his attention to internal professional matters, his supreme confidence, drive, intellect, and willingness to endure long hours of work at breakneck pace shoved him quickly up the achievement ladder of the American Bar Association. He became its youngest president ever at the age of forty-four. Such success, for a young man up from the cotton patches of Mecklenburg County, called for a celebration back in Charlotte, North Carolina. On August 19, 1957, a month after his return from his London installation, a civic dinner honored him in his hometown. The dinner testified strongly to the racing, single-generation change in America from the days of Rhyne's one-room schoolhouse boyhood to the era of urban sprawl: "That was the day my father's farm was taken into the city limits," recalled Rhyne "and my father was so mad . . . so angry about it, that he wouldn't speak to the mayor of Charlotte at this banquet that the mayor and some others were giving in my honor."

Immediately after his election to the ABA presidency, Rhyne also had been honored by a short note: "If they don't stop electing these 44-year-olds to positions of responsibility, I don't know what will happen to the country," it said. It was signed by Richard M. Nixon. The Vice President, just past his own forty-fourth birthday, had been reelected three months earlier.

With this background, Charles S. Rhyne obviously was an excellent choice not only to lead the *Baker* appeal in court, but to impress its import upon Solicitor General Rankin, as well. Rankin's office was already interested, as it turned out; at about the time Rhyne was being retained, the Solicitor General had written Nashville for a complete file of the *Baker* case. Walter Chandler had been ecstatic:

"It is rather significant to me that the Solicitor General . . . would be interested in our case," he wrote Osborn on February 17. "Let us hope and pray that the United States Supreme Court will hear one of the apportionment cases or consolidate them all and that ours will be among those to be considered. This news seems to me almost too good to be true." Osborn promptly called Rhyne. Rhyne, in turn, phoned Rankin and confirmed the Solicitor General's interest. Osborn and Chandler immediately began to fan this interest through their Republican allies, Hobart Atkins and Guy Smith. Congressman Reece, the former GOP national chairman, they suggested, might be just the right person to inform Attorney General Rogers how important the case was to national, not to mention Tennessee, GOP interests.

Formal notice of the *Baker* appeal was given March 29, 1960. The appeal had been regarded as a matter of course, in one sense, but the language of the three-judge panel's decision reinforced the plaintiffs' determination. "There were three or four plain, unequivocal sentences of that opinion that spurred us on," Harris Gilbert explained. Meanwhile, work on the jurisdictional statement progressed. After four months in the shaping, it was ready for the finishing touches on May 20. Rhyne, Osborn and Gilbert attended to this during another of the Washington caucuses. A week later, on May 27, 1960, the *Baker* v. *Carr* jurisdictional statement was filed with the Supreme Court. Rhyne estimated that thirteen hundred man-hours of work had gone into it.

From that point it was sit and sweat for Atkins, Chandler and Osborn, waiting to learn whether the high court would hear their case or whether this trio's months of work and research — even years — would be wasted. No one else seemed to care very much. National attention suddenly was riveted on the intensity of the presidential battle between Charlie Rhyne's law school classmate and his Democratic challenger from

Massachusetts, United States Senator John F. Kennedy. Rhyne enlisted in his friend's campaign:

WASHINGTON, Aug. 21 (UPI) — Vice President Nixon today named a former head of the American Bar Association as chairman of the "volunteer" organization he hopes will woo independent voters to the Republican ticket in the November election.

Chosen by Nixon as national chairman of the "Volunteers for Nixon-Lodge" was Charles S. Rhyne, a Washington, D.C., attorney who headed the bar association and the American Bar Foundation in 1957–58.

The arrival of this news in Nashville pleased Tom Osborn. His antennae were constantly alert to political signals and he wrote Rhyne on September 2, that he felt "the role you are to play in the campaign should somehow serve to further impress the Solicitor General with the fact that the Tennessee reapportionment case is, indeed, distinguishable from *Colegrove* v. *Green*." But that is not the way it worked out, of course. The Tennessee Levellers were still awaiting word from the Court on November 8, when John Fitzgerald Kennedy was elected thirty-fifth President of the United States. Thirteen days later, on November 21, 1960, the United States Supreme Court noted probable jurisdiction of *Baker* v. *Carr*.

So the justices would hear the case. The Tennesseans were, in Gilbert's metaphor, "on base." There would be a ball game. Charlie Rhyne's fine team of lawyers, under his expert and skilled direction, had performed the key legal task assigned it. However,

Rhyne's value as a possible influence at the Justice Department was gone. Considering his campaign role, it might even prove negative. Lee Rankin had given Rhyne informal assurance that, should the Court agree to hear *Baker*, the Solicitor General's office would take up a bat for the plaintiffs. But Rankin was no longer in office. It was necessary now to look toward the New Frontier.

4

The Kennedy Brothers and Solicitor General Archibald Cox

The older men who had surrounded Dwight David Eisenhower for eight years passed the torch, as President Kennedy's Inaugural Address put it, to "a new generation of Americans — born in this century, tempered by war, disciplined by a cold and bitter peace, proud of our heritage." In many of the traditionally Democratic states, however, the old-line Democrats as well had no connections, tangible or spiritual, with the New Frontiersmen mustering on the Potomac. Indeed, they had done little or nothing to install Jack Kennedy in the White House, and some had contributed only their hostility. Tennessee was such a state.

For a number of years the Democrats in Tennessee had been split between two forces and neither had much incentive for helping a New England Roman Catholic millionaire to 1600 Pennsylvania Avenue.

The populist-progressive followers of Senator Estes Kefauver had not forgotten the senator from Massachusetts who almost undid Kefauver's vice presidential hopes in 1956, when Adlai Stevenson had jarred the convention by throwing the number two party spot open for untraditional jousting. The more conservative wing, at the time headed by Governor Buford Ellington, went to the 1960 convention committed head-to-heel to Ellington's personal friend and idol, Senate Majority Leader Lyndon B. Johnson. LBJ's accepting the vice presidential spot kept Ellington from bolting altogether, no doubt, but there was much hand-sitting among Dixie Democrats in Tennessee during the late summer and autumn of 1960. One result was a victory for Nixon in Tennessee that November.

It would have been difficult, therefore, for the Democratic sponsors of *Baker* v. *Carr,* to establish rapport with the new Justice Department under the President's brother and thus replenish their hopes for intervention, had it not been for one slender entree. That single tie existed by virtue of the circumstance that on appeal in Judge William E. Miller's court, when the Tennessee reapportionment case was first put before him, was the Chattanooga Teamster official Glenn Smith's conviction in the $18,500 income tax case.

Attorney General Robert F. Kennedy brought to the Justice Department a deep commitment against the Teamsters Union. His work as chief counsel for the labor rackets subcommittee headed by Senator John McClellan, convinced him that the union's chieftains

— first Dave Beck and later James R. Hoffa — were a corrupting influence, with the cynicism that would make them capable of using the union's power to paralyze the nation. He set out to dilute that power and destroy its corruptions. In early 1957, he met a young Tennessee investigative reporter, John Seigenthaler of the Nashville *Tennessean,* who shared his beliefs and commitments. In time, their acquaintance ripened into friendship of the closest sort. When Bob Kennedy was assassinated in Los Angeles in June 1968, while seeking the presidential nomination through the primary route, Seigenthaler was in San Francisco organizing for him; when he was buried beside his brother in Arlington National Cemetery a few days later, Seigenthaler was among the closest friends who bore his body to its grave.

The association did not begin with such admiration. John Seigenthaler, the eldest son of a large Catholic family reared in Nashville in modest circumstances, considered Bob Kennedy "a rich little snob" the first time he met him. He had been futilely trying for weeks to meet Kennedy, not so much for himself as for his editor and one of the directors of his newspaper who very much wanted Seigenthaler to put before Kennedy his findings about Teamster activities in Tennessee. Since the middle of 1956, Seigenthaler had been reporting a pattern of violence — bombings, shootings, vandalism, window-breakings and beatings — involving the Teamsters. There was a paralleling pattern of laxity and downright blindness in the official investigations of these incidents which Seigenthaler thought indicated a thread of collusion leading into the law enforcement establishment. The Glenn Smith bribery case was a part of it.

Seigenthaler finally met Bob Kennedy through press connections. While attending a seminar for journalists at Columbia University, he met Clark Mollenhoff, Washington correspondent for Cowles Publications, one of the seminar's discussion leaders. Mollenhoff was a Teamster-watcher himself, and well acquainted with Robert Kennedy. Knowing that Kennedy was in New York on business that very day, Mollenhoff arranged for Seigenthaler to meet the future Attorney General at once. Seigenthaler was not favorably impressed, mainly because Kennedy did not appear very interested in his material.

"I made about two or three trips to Washington between April and June. Whenever I got to see Kennedy I'd get the same sort of brushoff," Seigenthaler remembered. But a month later, Kennedy phoned to inform him that McClellan's committee was sending two of its top investigators, Laverne Duffy and James P. McShane, to look into the Tennessee situation. Kennedy asked Seigenthaler to meet the pair in Chattanooga; they were going to dig into the Glenn Smith–Judge Raulston Schoolfield bribery affair.

In November of that year, 1957, the findings of Duffy and McShane concerning Tennessee were the subject of widely publicized hearings in Washington before the McClellan group. "I think it shook Tennessee to its very foundation," said Seigenthaler. "I think it embarrassed the state administration, the Nashville district attorney and sheriff, the Tennessee Bureau of Investigation, Judge Schoolfield certainly, and the district attorney in Chattanooga as well as some of the city officials in Knoxville. The hearings had statewide implications and really demonstrated a pattern of violence and corruption all across the state that reached not only from labor to business offices, but from labor into higher-ranking offices of the government."

The evidence suggested, for example, that the bribe money originated with the late Robert Crichton, then president of a large Nashville motor freight line and a leading financial angel of Governor Frank Clement. Though Crichton later denied this, the Governor was sufficiently moved by the disclosures to name a prominent Nashville criminal lawyer, Jack Norman, to make yet another investigation with a view to seeking the impeachment of Judge Schoolfield. As his assistant, Norman appointed a young attorney just out of Vanderbilt University law school, John Jay Hooker, Jr., the son of Norman's friendly rival in the Nashville criminal law field.

Through the first three months of 1958, the probe continued. Seigenthaler, assigned to cover it for his newspaper, became extremely friendly with young Hooker, whom he had never met before. By this time, through Duffy and McShane, he had also established warm relations with Bob Kennedy and "had pretty much free access to what the committee was doing."

Out of the Norman-Hooker probe came twenty-four articles of impeachment against Schoolfield. The historic proceedings took place in the Tennessee legislature during the spring and summer of 1958. After the House impeached the Chattanooga judge in May, the Senate trial, ending July 11, resulted in his conviction on three counts, though none of these involved the bribes. Robert F. Kennedy flew to Nashville to testify in the impeachment proceedings. There he met Hooker.

John Seigenthaler's reporting achievements won him a Nieman Fellowship for a year's study at Harvard University that fall. He came to Massachusetts at a time when John Kennedy was positioning himself to enter the presidential race the following year. It was an open secret that JFK had such ambitions after his vice presidential bid in 1956. In an effort to embarrass his prospects, the Massachusetts GOP concentrated its efforts that fall on trying to deny him a wide margin in his U.S. Senate reelection race against obscure opposition. The contest was just getting under way when Seigenthaler arrived in Cambridge, and he became a camp follower of John F. Kennedy's campaign. Seigenthaler visited the Kennedys in their Hyannisport compound on Cape Cod several times that fall, and at Christmas break, he and his family drove down from Boston to spend a week with Bob and Ethel Kennedy at Hickory Hill, their Virginia home outside Washington. Bob Kennedy asked Seigenthaler during this visit to help edit a book he had in mind about his experience with the McClellan committee.

Working with the assistance of two secretaries, sandwiching their editing and writing and rewriting between long walks, swims and touch football sessions, Bob Kennedy and Seigenthaler finished the book in ten weeks — May, June and most of July 1959 — after Bob resigned his McClellan post and before taking up duties in his brother's behalf. Robert Kennedy's best-selling book, *The Enemy Within*, was published in early 1960, a timing that would bring the Kennedy name to public view when brother John was about to open his drive on the primaries in his bid for the presidency. Seigenthaler, having received an extension of his Nieman leave, lived with Kennedy at Hickory Hill during that time.

It was during such periods of close association that the friendship of Robert F. Kennedy and John Lawrence Seigenthaler was sealed. They had many interests and many traits in common. Both were fascinated by the game of politics; both played it rough-and-tumble with the reckless, free style of touch football, but with the game's good humor, too. Both had a deep sense of serious moral indignation that appeared at times to run against the grain of the surface Irish politician's joyous irreverence. The humor and irreverence were deceiving; the indignation was genuine and it could be ruthless in its pursuit of what it deemed to be an evil in society. For both, the Teamsters Union as personified by James Riddle Hoffa deserved such pursuit. The book their minds had produced together, Kennedy writing, Seigenthaler editing, was a map of those convictions, suggesting where they thought the Justice Department ought to be working.

As the presidential campaign got set to begin in 1960, Seigenthaler's editors were not surprised that he asked for a leave of absence to join what was, for him, a crusade to put moral fire and progressive action back in the White House. He took with him, from Tennessee, John Jay Hooker, Jr. They moved into the makeshift Constitution Avenue headquarters, sharing a partitioned-off corner which Seigenthaler used when he was in town and trom which Hooker organized, largely by long-distance telephone, a group known as Professional Men, Lawyers, Doctors, Scientists, Military Leaders and Mental Health Leaders for Kennedy-Johnson. Another young Tennessee lawyer recruited to the Kennedy cause was E. William Henry, a law school classmate of Hooker's at Vanderbilt, who was later to become chairman of the Federal Communications Commision. Bill Henry had been associated in Memphis with the law firm of Walter Chandler.

All these young men met the criteria laid down by Robert Kennedy for New Frontiersmen. Suddenly, with the hairline victory of John Kennedy, the upstarts became the Tennessee brokers of a new administration in charge of the United States government. They were the new avenues to the White House, the Justice Department, and the myriad government alphabet agencies. When the Kennedy administration set up house after that cold, breath-congealing inaugural, John Seigenthaler, a non-lawyer, was installed in Attorney General Robert F. Kennedy's outer office as his trouble-shooter, administrative aide and good right arm.

John Jay Hooker, Jr., was offered the reward of a spot at Justice, too, but he chose to return to Nashville. Before Hooker left Washington, he was led outside Kennedy's Georgetown home and interviewed in the biting wind alongside the new President while press and television clamored for the meaning of his presence. It was that famous scene where the President-elect shaped up his cabinet. This was, as the saying goes, like the aspiring young banker being photographed with John D. Rockefeller's arm around him. The people back home got the message: Young Hooker's political credit was good in the proper quarters. Those interested in having the Solicitor General intervene in *Baker* v. *Carr* went calling on Mr. Hooker. Accordingly, Tom Osborn and Harris Gilbert, in the company of Hooker, appeared in the new Solicitor General's office shortly after noon February 3, 1961, with an appointment arranged by Hooker.

There had been no large public outcry when John F. Kennedy named his brother Attorney General, but the appointment was sharply debated in legal circles and on the nation's editorial pages. Aside from nepotism, there was Bobby's inexperience. His law diploma was a perfectly respectable document from the University of Virginia, but the only real use to which he had put it was in the pursuit, before the McClellan committee, of Beck, Hoffa and assorted labor racketeers. Indeed, he had been chasing some of those engaged in the Jersey garbage rackets on the day he and John Seigenthaler first met.

Jack Kennedy answered critics of Bobby's appointment with disarming humor; a more practical evidence of his good intentions was the quality of the men the new President installed in the number two and number three posts of the Justice Department. As Deputy Attorney General, Bob Kennedy's first legal assistant, the President had named Byron (Whizzer) White, a highly respected Rhodes scholar whose legal luster was enhanced by a gleam the most lowbrow American could not fail to respect: He had been an All-American football halfback from Colorado University. As Solicitor General, the President had chosen Archibald Cox, without much question one of the more astute scholars of labor law in the nation, and certainly not identifiable as the left-leaning Harvard ideologue so unpopular in mid-America's mythology.

Cox was, in fact, a nonpartisan type who had acknowledged voting for Henry Cabot Lodge over Kennedy for United States senator in 1952. He had also once resigned in protest from the chairmanship of the Wage Stabilization Board when President Harry S. Truman overruled the board's decision, an act that Republican publishers found "courageous." Cox returned to the Harvard faculty from which he had taken leave to serve the Truman administration during the Korean War.

Labor reform legislation first brought Archibald Cox to Senator John Kennedy's side. Kennedy was a member of the McClellan group when his younger brother served as chief counsel of the subcommittee, and Cox had made suggestions for the revision of the Taft-Hartley Act. He had worked with the Massachusetts senator on the Kennedy-Ives labor reform bill, and later the Kennedy-Ervin bill. When the House rejected this legislation, Kennedy became chairman of the conference committee that reconciled it with the tougher House version, and Cox stayed close by.

"That Kennedy escaped treacherous obstacles on his announced run for the presidency is due in large measure to his top adviser on labor matters, Archibald Cox, professor of labor law at Harvard University," Washington correspondent Fletcher Knebel wrote that year. When Kennedy entered the presidential race, then, Archibald Cox joined his campaign team of brain-trusters. He was head of Kennedy's speechwriters and organized Educators for Kennedy while John Hooker organized the other professional people. The contact they maintained was logically close.

Cox was approaching his forty-ninth birthday when he became Solicitor General, the thirty-second person to hold that post, and it is doubtful if many could have brought to the office a better set of credentials. Law was his father's business, too: Cox was one of four sons and two daughters of a New York patent attorney. Out of Harvard Law *magna cum laude* in 1937, he served for a year as law clerk to the famous Judge Learned Hand, then three years with a distinguished Boston firm. Following a brief time with the National Defense Mediation Board in Washington, he worked in the Solicitor General's office. After a bit more of wartime Washington (special assistant to the Secretary of State; associate solicitor for the Department of Labor) Cox went back to Harvard as a lecturer. In 1946, at the age of thirty-four, he became a full professor. He remained at Harvard for fifteen years, frequently arbitrating wage disputes during that time. (His leave to return to Truman's Washington ended abruptly in a protest resignation, as noted, and he resumed his Harvard post.)

To appreciate fully why the sponsors of *Baker* v. *Carr* were anxious to have Cox in the case, one must first understand both the nature of his office and the role of the *amicus curiae* petitioner in modern American jurisprudence. The *amicus curiae* procedure, departing from the traditional American adversary system, permits third parties a voice in issues of such broad interest that more than two points of view are needed. Originally, the idea was to provide the court with additional information it might need to reach its decision. That notion evolved into one of greater advocacy on the part of the parties permitted into the lawsuit and more frequent entry to the point of abuse. In the view of many legal authorities, the *amicus* procedure tended to turn the Court into a legislative body — one reaching decisions from many points of view — rather than a judicial tribunal. Accordingly, the Court in 1949 restricted the privilege by requiring the consent of both parties to a lawsuit before an *amicus* entry can be made. The *amicus* brief appears most often when great social or political issues affecting large masses of people are present. Before *Baker*, the procedure had perhaps been put to most effective use in *Brown* v. *Board of Education*, the school desegregation case. Similar broad interests were at play in the apportionment issue, and other *amicus* briefs were filed by citizen groups in Mississippi; Nassau County, New York; and Kansas; by August Scholle of Michigan, lead plaintiff in a lawsuit there; by the Louisville suburban city of St. Matthews, Kentucky; and by Governor J. Howard Edmondson of Oklahoma. These briefs, far better than the eyewitnesses sought by Chandler in his trial on the merits, testified to the depth of the issue and the breadth of American interest in it.

Solicitor General is an office of far greater import than the protocol charts indicate. The Solicitor General does not so much as rate a government limousine, for example, but as his parsimonious employer's appointed representative in the United States Supreme Court, its justices listen attentively when he enters a case. Fully half of the high court's work, perhaps more, is government business, which puts him before the justices often enough to learn their idiosyncrasies.

The Solicitor General is empowered to argue any case in which the United States has an interest in any court in the land. And no appeal can be taken by the government to an appellate court or to the Supreme Court without his authorization. His office supervises all government briefs — almost one thousand a year — filed in the Court. When Cox occupied the office, a staff of nine shared this task and the less time-consuming but more visible chore of arguing before the Supreme Court. By tradition, the Solicitor General also keeps a wary eye on any unfairness in government cases. If he thinks there is unfairness, he files what is called a "confession of error" in the Supreme Court, asking it to set aside a victory won by the government in the lower court. Indeed, Archibald Cox's first appearance before the Supreme Court for the Solicitor General's office, as a young lawyer in 1942, had been in such a case.

Cox brought to his office, because of this earlier service, a better knowledge of the Court and its justices than most of his predecessors (who included William Howard Taft and Charles Evans Hughes). Some of the justices he had known during his earlier term were still on the bench in 1960. And, at Harvard, he had been a favorite student of Mr. Justice Felix Frankfurter, who had once referred to his protégé by name in one of his opinions.

Cox also contributed his own style, charm and philosophy concerning the nature of his duties. Archibald Cox never considered the office one of policy-making:

"We will handle our cases as we go along," he said, shortly after his appointment was announced, "and I'll bear in mind that I have had some very distinguished predecessors to follow." At Harvard, he had been considered one of the "nice-guy" professors with a sense of humor and a Socratic method, a long, lanky type who lolled in his chair and fired questions that probed deeply. His neighbors in suburban Wayland, where he was a selectman, called him "the Perfesser," and he drove a half-ton pickup truck to work.

Cox considered it his duty, unlike that of a district attorney, "not to wade into cases trying to win everything in sight. I like to think my argument and very existence are aimed at helping the Court. I believe a Solicitor General must achieve a delicate balance between thinking like a justice and thinking like an advocate. And if my opponent should miss a valid argument, even though it opposes my own, I will myself point it out to the Court."

The Tennessee lawyers who had come to see Cox about joining their cause knew how well he personified the legal weight of the federal government and were aware what that could mean to their side. They knew that his entry automatically would extend the length of time they would have in which to argue their case before the Court. They knew it might well add points, perhaps fresh ideas and approaches that had not occurred to them. With the Solicitor General along, they would go before the Court with the support of two experts in its procedures instead of one — both with an understanding of the Court's personalities as well. Most of all, the Solicitor General's participation would testify that theirs was not simply a lawsuit from Tennessee, but a perplexing problem in which many states and millions of citizens and the American republic itself had enormous stakes.

The practical Tom Osborn also knew on the day he arrived in Cox's office that timing was critical. The imminent change of administrations just as the Supreme Court decided to hear the case had created another time bind. The Democrats had ousted the Republicans. Nixon and Lee Rankin were out, the Kennedys and Cox were in. On November 21, 1960, the Supreme Court had expressed its willingness to hear *Baker* v. *Carr*. That was two full months before John F. Kennedy's inaugural, and it would take at least another month before official Washington could begin to settle down after a change of administrations. Any change in national administrations is unsettling, but the change that replaces one political party with another is particularly so. Just cleaning the desk drawers and filing cabinets of some predecessor's useless accumulation is a chore of magnitude when multiplied throughout the bureaucracy. If the Solicitor General's staff was to make a meaningful contribution, it would need time. And as of that moment, there was not even a commitment about the matter. Cox was not fully informed about the case and not especially sensitive to the issue of reapportionment. Like other New Englanders a resident of a tiny, long-urbanized state, any view of the question that he might have was more academic than practical. In Massachusetts and Connecticut, malapportionment had constituted little or no problem; a decade after the *Baker* case was decided, voters in those states could see little difference it had made.

"My recollection is that I didn't know the case to any appreciable extent before John Hooker and Z. T. Osborn and Harris Gilbert came in," Cox recalled later. "Probably Bruce Terris, on our staff, had told me a little about it in the few minutes before they came in or maybe earlier that morning."

If the relatively stably settled New England states had little interest in reapportionment, though, there were already ample *amicus curiae* briefs on file to indicate the wide interest elsewhere. On July 22, 1960, the National Institute of Municipal Law Offices had filed the first of two such briefs. NIMLO is composed of more than twelve hundred municipalities in the fifty states and the District of Columbia. Member cities act through their chief legal officers, and counsel on the NIMLO briefs included the legal officers from Los Angeles, New York, Dallas, Richmond, Portland, Maine, and Portland, Oregon, Minneapolis, Detroit and Cleveland.

"The Institute briefs especially emphasized the glaring malapportionments existing in the upper houses of the various states," wrote Professor Lucius J. Barker in the *Journal of Politics*. "In California, for example,

NIMLO said Los Angeles County with a population of 4,151,687 had but one senator while three counties with a combined population of 14,014 had the same representation." Its brief also underpinned the Tennesseans' arguments about practical effects, detailing a number of examples: for instance, that the Colorado legislature so divided state school money that Denver got only $2.3 million a year for 90,000 school pupils as against Jefferson County's $2.4 million for only 18,000 pupils.

The Tennesseans came for their conference with Cox armed with the expressed interest of another rather important citizen: President John F. Kennedy. They had gathered a couple of speeches Kennedy had made on the subject during his presidential campaign, in which the votes of urban citizens had been a most crucial target. Also in a packet of materials they handed to Cox was a copy of an article written by Kennedy in the May 18, 1958, number of the *New York Times Magazine*. It was titled, after Lincoln Steffens, "The Shame of the States." Its language might have been drawn from one of *Baker*'s more literate *amicus curiae* briefs:

"The shame of our cities today is not political; it is social and economic," the President-to-be had written. "Blight and decay in urban government have been replaced by blight and decay in the cities themselves. They suffer from overcrowded and hazardous schools, undermanned with underpaid teachers — halfway ed-

[212]

ucation in halfway sessions. They suffer from urban housing, congested traffic, juvenile delinquency, overcrowded health and penal institutions and inadequate parking. They lack parks and recreational facilities, too often crowded out and ignored in the hasty, haphazard growth of the metropolitan areas."

The cities were unable to cope with all these problems, Kennedy argued, because "these local governments receive all too little help and cooperation from Washington and the state legislatures. They are refused adequate Federal and state funds for the programs they need so badly, and for which they have paid so heavily. They contribute the lion's share of Federal and state taxes, but an equitable share is rarely returned to them. They have been pre-empted by the Federal and state governments from the best sources of tax revenue." Kennedy found the taproot of this problem to be "that the urban majority is, politically, a minority and the rural minority dominates the polls. Of all the discriminations against the urban areas, the most fundamental and the most blatant is political: the apportionment of representation in our Legislatures and (to a lesser extent) in Congress has been either deliberately rigged or shamefully ignored. . . . The failure of our governments to respond to the problems of the cities reflects this basic political discrimination." Making a point often missed by others, Kennedy added: "Even in Congress, America's urban majority is not equitably represented. The same malapportioned state legislatures, after all, apportion Congressional seats."

Kennedy had offered no specific solution to this "shame of the states," noting that "the Supreme Court has made clear its belief that such changes depend basically upon political, not judicial, processes." But his concluding paragraph suggested who he believed had to assume responsibility here: "One hundred million citizens — constituting a majority of the nation — will not forever accept this modern day taxation without representation. If there is a 'shame of the cities' today, it is the failure of our urban dwellers and their spokesmen to be aware of these discriminations — and to press more vigorously for their elimination." And now, a bit less than three years later, some urban dwellers and their spokesmen were meeting with the Solicitor General of Kennedy's own administration, pressing for help in bringing about that elimination.

Archibald Cox, recollecting the meeting some years later, thought it "quite possible" that he was aware when Osborn, Gilbert and Hooker arrived that his predecessor "had authorized the Civil Rights Division to prepare a brief which would be revised in the office of the Solicitor General and filed. On the other hand, I certainly hadn't studied it. I think it is safe to say that I gave them a noncommittal answer."

The Tennesseans had hardly expected a formal declaration from the meeting, considering its informal beginnings. Hooker always operated in a casual, breezy style, which he later maintained through two hard-fought but unsuccessful campaigns for the governorship of Tennessee. He had come to know Cox quite well during the hectic days of the campaign headquarters with its jangling telephones, untidy desks, pastepots, shears, and littered floors. "Archie, this is a far cry from that little office you had during the campaign," Hooker had greeted Cox the moment the Solicitor General strode into the room.

"By this time," Gilbert recalled with amusement, "John Jay had his feet on the Solicitor General's desk. And of course the offices in the Justice Department are very beautiful . . . Oriental rugs and very large, spacious, high-ceilinged, from those days when they didn't have air conditioning. And John Jay had his feet right up in front of him."

It was snowing that February day in Washington, though the weather had been clear in Nashville when the Leveller lawyers left home. Four or five inches of snow lay on the ground by midmorning. The afternoon brought threats of a storm as bad as the one that almost paralyzed Jack Kennedy's inaugural. The Tennesseans, that morning, had dropped by the Attorney General's office, chatted with John Seigenthaler, and met First Deputy Byron White; but Bob Kennedy had been tied up when they arrived that morning. When the session with Cox was over, Kennedy had left for the day to avoid the prospect of being snowbound overnight in his office. Their inability to lay their case before the Attorney General personally was a mild disappointment, but the Tennesseans felt good about the

Cox conference. He, after all, would be the key man in deciding. They left reasonably confident that an *amicus curiae* petition would be soon forthcoming. Nonetheless, the Justice Department mail in the next two days contained letters to Attorney General Kennedy from Chandler's young associate, E. William Henry, and White got another copy of "The Shame of the States" from Osborn.

"It appears to be widely recognized that our case involves a question of extreme importance to a number of states, and that similar cases from such other states are now pending in the Federal Courts," Henry wrote Kennedy. "Undoubtedly our case will receive the closest attention and the most thorough consideration by the Court if your Department will file a brief *amicus curiae*, and I will appreciate your looking into the matter as a favor to me."

Having pulled every string they knew with the new administration, the reapportionment lawyers from Tennessee might have been a bit disappointed had they known the undramatic fashion in which the decision finally was made. "Within the next day or two," said Cox, "I was in the Attorney General's office and remarked to him that his friend John Jay Hooker had been in and sent his regards. The Attorney General asked what he wanted, and I told him that he wanted us to file a brief in *Baker-Carr*. The Attorney General asked whether I was going to do it, and I said, well, I thought I would unless he saw some strong objection. The Attorney General said, 'Well, are you going to win?' I said, 'No, I don't think so, but it would be a lot of fun anyway.' On the strength of that we went ahead and filed a brief."

Cox was not being entirely facetious about his appraisal of *Baker*'s chances, nor was the decision quite as casual as it might seem. "Even then," he explained, "I had gotten to know the Attorney General's mind pretty well. The President's position on this was perfectly well known to me and to the Attorney General. So behind the apparently casual conversation went an awareness all the way around of our concern with the problem and interest in doing what we could to correct the malapportionment." As for the prospects before the Supreme Court: "Anyone who was presenting the issue of justiciability of an apportionment case to the Supreme Court would have to figure he had an upstream route."

On April 19, 1961, the American Levellers — now including Charles S. Rhyne and Archibald Cox — would start on that journey against the odds. The Supreme Court had set initial arguments for that date. But thanks to many circumstances, no apportionment case in history had ever gone before that august body so complete in every detail of proof, so bolstered by the support of so many interests, including that of the United States government itself.

5

Mr. Justice Frankfurter's Thicket Cleared

Solicitor General Archibald Cox had been before the Supreme Court many times. Yet he went to bed nervous the evening of April 18, 1961. By midnight, two hours after retiring, he was still wide awake. He tossed the rest of the night, and finally drove his bad case of butterflies into his Justice Department office at 6 A.M.

"A lawyer never loses his awe and respect for the Supreme Court," he later said. "You can never escape the awesomeness of their responsibilities."

Z. T. Osborn, Jr., at the age of forty-two, had never been there, and the thrill was a high one, dulled at the edges by the gnaw of resentment. He had brought his wife, Dottie, and their daughters along to hear him argue before the highest court in the land an issue he had fought longer than any other lawyer in the case. He alone had started with the first petition in *Kidd* v.

McCanless, six years before, and now, at the moment of climax, a newcomer to the battle had tried to cut him out of the arguments. Only an angry insistence on his rights had salvaged for Tom Osborn the concession of a scant five minutes of rebuttal.

Ben West, the mayor of Nashville, Tennessee, was likewise excited. He was to be introduced to the Supreme Court as a practicing lawyer on this day, an honor accorded a tiny minority in his profession. West was much impressed with the scene, with Archibald Cox, "a very suave gentleman in his cutaway coat and striped pants," with the kindness and consideration Chief Justice Warren extended to the young lawyer applicants also being introduced to the Court for the first time. The man he had hired as Washington counsel for the *Baker* plaintiffs, Charles S. Rhyne, presented West to the nine robed justices. At that awe-filled moment it is doubtful if the Nashville mayor felt quite confident of the statement he had made in a final strategy conference of the Leveller lawyers the day before: "These judges are just like any other men," he had told Rhyne. "They get in their britches one leg at a time, they don't jump in them. If you will make the argument that we've done everything that we could — in the courts and in the legislature — and now if they don't do something, it won't be done, somewhere we're going to reach those justices."

And Charlie Rhyne, poised and confident before the Court, was thoroughly prepared. But attuned to the ways of this great court and acquainted with its members and their eccentricities, he knew he would have scant chance to get all the complex issues before them before their questions began to rain down on him. He knew the weaknesses of divided arguments, and it had been, for this reason, he who had angered Tom Osborn by his effort to claim for himself all the plaintiffs' arguing time. Reluctantly, at the intervention of Walter Chandler and Harris Gilbert, he had yielded to Osborn and granted the Tennessean five minutes.

On the other side of the bench, Associate Justice Potter Stewart was unaware, when the *Baker* arguments opened at 2:55 P.M., that the plaintiffs' side was keyed directly to him. Many hours of conferences, research and debate among the lawyers led to that strategic decision. In their preparation of the jurisdictional statement, every word written or uttered by the nine justices in past cases that touched on reapportionment had been researched. In drafting it, Rhyne's team had attempted to answer all questions raised by each of the justices in these past cases, and to touch the possible prejudices each had expressed. A careful analysis of these past views led the team to believe there was a possible 5-to-4 victory here, but Potter Stewart, then forty-six, on the bench but a scant two years, was their question mark. He was the Levellers' "swing man."

"We felt that Harlan and Frankfurter would definitely be against us," explained Harris Gilbert. Associate Justice John M. Harlan, an earlier Eisenhower appointee, and Associate Justice Felix Frankfurter, the

[220]

veteran, both had records clearly indicating hostility to the plaintiffs' cause. "We felt that Whittaker and Clark probably would be against us." Associate Justice Charles Evans Whittaker, an Eisenhower Republican from Kansas City, was considered a bit too conservative to overturn such a long-standing precedent; Associate Justice Tom Clark's voting record with Frankfurter over the years was a circumstance the Levellers considered more than a statistical accident. They felt he probably would stick with Frankfurter on this one, too. Four votes against the Levellers. On the other hand, the plaintiffs counted Associate Justice Hugo L. Black and Associate Justice William O. Douglas "definitely on our side." They put down Chief Justice Earl Warren and Associate Justice William J. Brennan, Jr., as "probables."

Justice Stewart was thus the key man. He was, in Gilbert's view, "the most underrated Justice of this era . . . a man of towering legal abilities with a brilliant background. If he could be persuaded to come to our side, we felt we could maybe get the 5-to-4." Stewart, they thought, might help bring Brennan and the Chief Justice — the "probables" — with him.

In this enigmatic but electric atmosphere that Wednesday April afternoon, Charles S. Rhyne stepped to the lectern to open the oral arguments in Supreme Court case No. 103, October term of 1960. He had before him a black looseleaf notebook headed:

[221]

PRELIMINARY STATEMENT
ORIGIN

This is a voting rights case:
1. THIS CASE IS HERE VIA DIRECT APPEAL FROM A THREE-JUDGE Federal Court dismissing a complaint *seeking protection and enforcement of voting rights* conferred upon plaintiffs . . ."

Like the jurisdictional statement, Rhyne's prepared argument was a team job. "You must know," he later explained, "that we lawyers spent some time in determining just what I was going to say up there. This is not just a great extemporaneous business. I advised Captain Chandler and Hobart Atkins exactly what I was going to say. . . . I went over the argument in detail with them."

On the very first page of the typed preliminary statement, indeed, Rhyne had renumbered the points to be made, in order to pencil in a notation that anyone who had followed the case closely knew must be Walter Chandler's contribution: "4. Our Position no judicial 'no man's land' exists insofar as guaranteed indiv. Constit. rights are concerned." Chandler, the Argonne Forest captain, had used the same World War I metaphor in his own argument before the three-judge panel in Nashville; Rhyne would twice employ it in the first *Baker* v. *Carr* arguments conducted that day and the next. And before those arguments were finished at 1:50 P.M. the following day, every one of the nine justices would pepper the plaintiffs' attorneys with questions — a rare occurrence.

[222]

Rhyne was not far into his argument, in fact, before he encountered the first query from the bench. It was from Justice Douglas: "This is not an inequality based upon racial discrimination, is it?" Advised that it was not, Douglas promptly remarked that "unlike the Tuskegee case, then, this is straight across the board."

Douglas's first question and comment appeared to be needling Frankfurter, with whom he had sharply differed on this matter since the days of *Colegrove*. For the Tuskegee case, *Gomillion* v. *Lightfoot*, revealed a vulnerable spot in Mr. Justice Frankfurter's "political thicket." *Gomillion*, involving the gerrymander of the Tuskegee, Alabama, city limits by the Alabama state legislature to exclude Negroes from voting, had been argued in the Supreme Court only a few days before the Court noted probable jurisdiction in *Baker*. It had been decided November 14, six days after Kennedy's election. Justice Frankfurter, an invariable foe of the slightest hint of racial discrimination, wrote the Court's opinion.

As Justice Douglas well knew, the Tuskegee case had put his colleague in a most distressing philosophical quandary. As a case involving districting by a state legislature in a voting situation, it ran across the grain of Frankfurter's *Colegrove* labeling of such cases as political and beyond judicial remedy. But to deny remedy in this instance was to permit blatant racial discrimination of the sort that Frankfurter had never been willing to tolerate. To escape this dilemma, Frankfurter shrewdly had led counsel for the *Gomil-*

lion plaintiffs into allegation of a Fifteenth Amendment violation during the arguments, and when he wrote the majority opinion he disappointed the Tennessee Levellers by thus skirting the Fourteenth Amendment and leaving intact his "political" taboo enunciated in the *Colegrove* case.

This was fancy footwork in view of the defense put up by the State of Alabama. Defending the gerrymander, Alabama had based its case squarely on *Colegrove;* it insisted that the Tuskegee districting was a political matter in which the Court had no business, just as Frankfurter had always claimed. But the wily Mr. Frankfurter handled that one. In *Gomillion,* he wrote: "When a legislature . . . singles out a readily isolated segment of a racial majority for special discriminatory treatment, it violates the Fifteenth Amendment. In no case involving unequal weight in voting distribution that has come before this Court did the decision sanction a differentiation on racial lines whereby approval was given to unequivocal withdrawal of the vote solely from colored citizens," Frankfurter added. "Apart from all else, these considerations lift this controversy out of the so-called 'political' arena and into the conventional sphere of constitutional litigation. . . . The inescapable human effect of this essay in geometry and geography is to despoil colored citizens, and only colored citizens, of their theretofore enjoyed voting rights. That was not *Colegrove* v. *Green.*"

Justice Douglas, concurring in *Gomillion,* noted

that he had taken the opposite view from Frankfurter in *Colegrove;* his first question during the *Baker* arguments, then, gave evidence that he considered the cases similar and could still be counted upon by the plaintiffs.

If Douglas was needling with his opening query, however, Frankfurter was not long in firing back. Rhyne had scarcely made mention of the Tennessee constitution before the Justice wanted to know: "Mr. Rhyne, what is the bearing of these provisions in the Tennessee constitution on the federal Constitution?"

Frankfurter had landed squarely upon the most vulnerable point in the Leveller strategy, and Rhyne was hard put to give him a suitable answer. For a violation by a state of its own constitution does not make it a federal case, and this is a legal principle so well established that Archibald Cox had puzzled why the plaintiffs would bring it up. During an interview some years later the Solicitor General mentioned this aspect of the approach to *Baker:* "The complainants had some theory which I have never fully understood to the effect that the violation of Tennessee's own constitution helped them make out a case that there was a violation of the Constitution of the United States. And we thought there was no merit to that argument, and indeed they had a very rough time trying to present that argument to the Supreme Court because there was a Supreme Court case by Justice Frankfurter that was squarely opposed to it . . . not one on which there had been any dissent."

In fact, it was Walter Chandler, the former Memphis mayor and best-loved of the Leveller lawyers, who was responsible for this argument and another based upon violations of the state constitution. When all was said, Chandler remained a basic states-righter, and his reluctance at entering the federal arena in the first instance now prompted him to urge that the Tennessee constitution was the "polestar" of the *Baker* case. "He couldn't get it out of his head," said Gilbert. "He abhorred the idea that the Tennessee legislature would violate its own oath of office and its own constitution. Even when the case was remanded to the district court, Mr. Chandler was still insisting that this was the 'polestar' of our case."

The matter greatly bothered Rhyne. He deeply respected Chandler, had known him from their mutual association with the Municipal League and later when both were high in the organizational structure of the American Bar Association; Chandler was once considered for the ABA presidency that Rhyne later won. Rhyne also thought of Chandler as a client in this case and wanted to adhere to his wishes, but the argument Chandler was insisting upon was one he considered extremely hazardous. Besides the state constitutional violation, Chandler also urged that the practical effect of that violation — the inequitable division of state tax dollars that had prompted his own entry into this crusade — be made a major point of emphasis in the oral arguments.

"I told them Mr. Chief Justice Warren, as a former

governor, wouldn't like that analogy," said Rhyne. "I told them he would say, 'What's that got to do with the constitutional issue?' — that this is a matter of legislative judgment. He'd jump right down my throat if I started talking about that, because as a governor, he knew these people back in the rural areas had to have a little more support than the urban areas.

"So Captain Chandler just insisted that I mention it," Rhyne continued, "and I told him exactly what was going to happen. I put that down in my outline. And bingo! when I mentioned it, Chief Justice Warren said to me: 'What has that got to do with the constitutional issue?' I said, 'Nothing. That's just part of the background.' And I skipped it quickly because I could see that if I pegged anything on that, we might lose his vote." (As it turned out, Rhyne was correct in his concern about the relevance of the Tennessee constitution, but wrong in his assessment of Warren's reaction to the dollar-division figures. During an interview some years later, when the Chief Justice was told there had been concern on the part of some of the attorneys about the legal relevance of dollar-division figures, he asserted that in his own mind these matters had been very important to the case.)

After the opening salvo of questions from Douglas and Frankfurter, Rhyne had no chance to get back to the line of his main argument before Justice Stewart jumped in with a line of questioning. But the Associate Justice to whom the Leveller lawyers had keyed their argument gave them no clues that day or the next as to

[227]

where he might stand. As Harris Gilbert put it, "Stewart was heavy with the questioning but you could hardly see where he was going." About this time came the first break — and a most surprising one — "Justice Whittaker came on very strong for us. He took a very active part and asked some very astute questions. His questions were really from our standpoint the most helpful in the first argument," said Gilbert.

JUSTICE WHITTAKER: You do not contend, I would suppose, then, that there has to be an exact equality?

MR. RHYNE: Oh, no. The Constitution itself says as near as may be practicable. No, no — we do not contend that you have to have exact mathematical equality at all — but as near as may be practicable. And certainly the picture that is presented there now, Mr. Justice Whittaker, is not as near as may be practicable, according to the enumeration of qualified voters.

JUSTICE WHITTAKER: As I understand, it is not disputed, that this matter is here upon a three-man court judgment that it is without power to do anything about it. Is that right?

MR. RHYNE: That is true. That was a decision of the three-judge court, that it had no power to enforce or protect the voting rights of these individual complainants.

JUSTICE WHITTAKER: So these facts stand admitted, do they?

MR. RHYNE: Yes, they do, by the motion to dismiss.

Justice Whittaker had opened the door for Rhyne's entry into the facts of the case. He moved in quickly: "Now just to show how it is practically impossible to expect this state legislature, after sixty years of doing

[228]

nothing, to act now, they set forth in the complaint, these plaintiffs do, many facts showing how the legislature, controlled by the rural areas, favor themselves. They will adopt a general statute and then exempt favorite counties out. So that as a result, you have a situation where, with respect to state allocation of school funds, on an average, the favored counties get $152, the unfavored get $107. And these are all set forth in rather voluminous exhibits attached to the complaint. You have things like this: Pickett County gets $226 per pupil; Shelby County gets $95."

Shortly thereafter, questions by Justice Clark and Chief Justice Warren offered another opportunity to get back to the prepared argument and show how the avenues of relief were closed. "I have referred to the state legislature," Rhyne said. "We have set forth here, in an exhibition pages 126 to 160, the record of every proposal for reapportionment in the Tennessee legislature [this was Dr. White's research] that shows that over and over again every bill for reapportionment since 1901 has been voted down. It shows that in the Senate no such bill has ever received more than 13 of the 33 votes. In the House, no bill has ever received more than 36 of the 99 votes. So I think that it is almost beyond question that the legislature itself is not going to change this situation.

"Now with respect to the Tennessee courts, the state courts, the supreme court has held that it will not grant any relief here, because to do so, according to their views, would destroy the legislature and destroy the government of Tennessee. Without discussing the merits of that at this point, I say that that demonstrates that relief through the state courts is absolutely impossible in the state of Tennessee.

"Now how about the governors?" Rhyne asked. "The governors, I should say, have repeatedly in their messages to the legislature called attention to this shocking situation and asked the legislature to reapportion itself. . . . The governor can do nothing about it but call it to the attention of the legislature, and they have done that over and over again, as this exhibit attached to the complaint shows, without results.

"Now as for the people themselves, there is no initiative and referendum in Tennessee. So the people can do nothing.

"What about constitutional amendment? A constitutional amendment requires this: It requires that an amendment pass the state legislature once, and then be advertised six months before the next meeting of the legislature, passing the first time by majority vote, but the second time it must pass by two-thirds vote. And of course these legislators obviously are not going to vote any constitutional amendment that will take care of the situation, because they control the legislature."

Whittaker came in to help again:

JUSTICE WHITTAKER: But even if they did, wouldn't you then have just what you have now?
MR. RHYNE: I would say if they did it, we would have just what we have now, Mr. Justice Whittaker.

JUSTICE WHITTAKER: How would that help?

MR. RHYNE: It would not help. I am merely illustrating it to show it is no avenue of relief for us; that we have no way to turn under the state government. I would also point out that a constitutional convention would not help us, because the constitutional convention is selected the same way as the legislature. So there is no way, no action that we can get on the state level that will do anything about this inequity of giving us on an average of about one-tenth of a vote.

Rhyne quoted District Judge William E. Miller, and then the three-judge court, in their holdings that rights under the state constitution had been violated, and that no remedy was available at all without federal judicial assistance.

"I think it is a fair summary of the facts to say, as Mr. Chandler has said so many times, that the real question here is whether or not you are going to have two classes of citizenship in Tennessee, half slave and half free, or at least one-third free and two-thirds slave, because there is no way that you can get out of this illegal straitjacket without some federal assistance."

Rhyne then turned to *Colegrove*'s barring of that door, but strongly objected to lower court notions that the 3–3–1 decision somehow had ended the prospect of jurisdiction over such cases. "Our interpretation of *Colegrove* simply is that it is not a decision against us on jurisdiction, but it is for us on jurisdiction; that the decision of this Court was not against jurisdiction, but for jurisdiction. . . . We say that the lower court here, and the other courts that have cited it as holding that no jurisdiction exists are in error." The direct challenge brought the unusually quiet Frankfurter to life again:

JUSTICE FRANKFURTER: Does that imply, Mr. Rhyne, that the Congress has said that as to Federal voting rights, it would not be constitutional to have what you call second-class citizens — there is greater constitutional protection for states and state voting?

MR. RHYNE: No. I am not trying to distinguish between a Federal voting right and a state voting right, because we have a state voting right here. I am merely saying . . .

JUSTICE FRANKFURTER: You are suggesting that there is exclusive remedy in Congress. [This is what Frankfurter had held in *Colegrove*.] Does that mean that Congress can establish second-rate voters with reference to national interests?

MR. RHYNE: I am not agreeing with your [*Colegrove*] opinion. I am merely distinguishing it from this case, Mr. Justice Frankfurter.

JUSTICE FRANKFURTER: I am merely suggesting the implication of your distinguishing it.

MR. RHYNE: I would say that I do not intend to distinguish it on that basis. I think that all voters should be equal in Federal elections and in state elections.

JUSTICE FRANKFURTER: I can understand your saying the [*Colegrove*] decision is wrong and you would object to it. I cannot understand the distinction you made, because it would not lead to that conclusion — that under the United States Constitution Congress would have the power to differentiate on voting rights, but that state voters have greater rights than anybody has under the Federal Constitution with regard to Federal rights.

[232]

MR. RHYNE: I do not come to that conclusion.

JUSTICE BLACK, interjecting: You distinguished on the grounds that only three members of the Court agreed to it.

MR. RHYNE: That is right.

JUSTICE BLACK: Four members thought there was jurisdiction — but one of the four thought that relief should not be granted on equitable grounds.

MR. RHYNE: That is true.

JUSTICE FRANKFURTER: You say that. But you also said I relied — the [*Colegrove*] opinion relied on the specific congressional power.

MR. RHYNE: And it did. I would say insofar as *Colegrove* is concerned, I will just make the one distinction that it did vote four-to-three for jurisdiction.

JUSTICE FRANKFURTER: That I can understand.

And had that declaration of understanding ever before been frankly and publicly made, in such a way that lawyers and lower courts might understand as clearly, the sixteen years of frustration between *Colegrove* and *Baker* might never have elapsed.

Charles Rhyne had five more minutes, which he devoted to possible remedies the Court might find to the Tennessee malapportionment, and once again Justice Whittaker came in with sympathetic questions. Pressed by Justice Harlan with a "what-if?" question, Rhyne was in the process of giving such answer as hypothetical situations permit when Whittaker rescued him with "What about the suggestion that it will be time enough to meet that situation when it arises?"

"I like that suggestion, Mr. Justice Whittaker,"

Rhyne replied, and promptly the friendly Justice Black added more assistance: "Why do we have to anticipate what steps they [the Tennessee legislature] take at all?"

"I don't think you do, Mr. Justice Black," the pleased plaintiffs' lawyer answered, and shortly he sat down, feeling his argument had gone very well, indeed. So did Ben West and Harris Gilbert; both were already optimistic when the Solicitor General of the United States began:

"The United States appears in this case as *amicus curiae*, partly because it involves constitutional rights of a large number of citizens, both in Tennessee and elsewhere — but also because it raises issues that lie very closely to the heart of our system of government."

With measured calm Cox now laid forth the three propositions on which the government would base its support of the Leveller's cause: that there *was* a question under the Fourteenth Amendment; that a justiciable controversy, and hence jurisdiction *did* exist; and that "the court below, sitting as a court of equity, could find some administerable form of relief."

There was but a hairline difference in emphasis, but Cox's argument was more narrowly laid than Rhyne's. Cox saw no reason to decide whether the Fourteenth had been violated: "The court below had jurisdiction if the complaint states a claim under the Fourteenth Amendment, whether the complaint is well founded or not . . . at least if it is not patently frivolous. We think the point is involved at least to the extent that we should show that this isn't a futile, silly fact. But it does not seem necessary or, indeed, even appropriate for the Court to rule now whether there has or has not been a violation of the Fourteenth if it decides that there is a substantial claim. Then there *was* jurisdiction and there ought to be a ruling by the lower court."

Justice Stewart, the legal scholar toward whom Rhyne's tack had been directed, promptly responded to Cox's approach. And once again Justice Whittaker came in with a helpful query: "Mr. Solicitor, if we should take your view, need we do more than hold that the complaint states a cause of action and the district court must exercise it?"

"I think all you need hold," replied Archibald Cox, "is that the case is within the jurisdiction of the federal courts and that the court below must go on and determine whether this complaint states a cause of action; in other words, adjudicate the merits of the claim that there is a violation under the Fourteenth Amendment."

The tenor of Cox's argument was one of casual acceptance, as a matter of fact, of the most bitterly contested point: jurisdiction. His argument took for granted that *Colegrove* v. *Green* was a 4-to-3 decision on that point, and that Rhyne had already established the fact. He moved on to lay his main emphasis on the irrationality of voter discrimination as practiced in Tennessee.

"The right to be free from hostile or capricious discrimination by a state in defining the class of people entitled to vote or in the exercise of the franchise is a federal right protected by the Fourteenth Amendment," he declared. "It is also a right enforceable by the courts. Both points have been adjudicated on many occasions in cases such as *Nixon* v. *Herndon*, the *Texas Jaybird* case and others of that type. The closest precedents do involve racial discrimination, but I suggest the Fourteenth Amendment proscribes other arbitrary and capricious distinctions affecting the right to vote.

"Certainly a statute that said that redheaded women could not be permitted to vote, or no one who had ever visited the British Commonwealth should be permitted to vote would be a violation of the Fourteenth Amendment, and I take it we would also agree with the illustration that Mr. Justice Black used in dissenting opinions, that if the statute gave the voters in the west half of the state twenty-five votes, and the voters in the east half of the state only one vote, that there would be a violation of the Fourteenth Amendment." The situation in Tennessee, he hinted, was not much different: "Now where the apportionment statute has this same effect as allowing the voters in the sparsely settled west half to elect five representatives for every one that the populous counties in the east can elect, there, too, it would seem the result is the same and there must, equally, be a violation of the Fourteenth Amendment."

Mr. Justice Frankfurter took on his former pupil just once during Cox's argument, but he was citing a previous Tennessee railroad case with which Cox was not familiar. Their colloquy presently broke down in an argument over the distinction between "rational" and "irrational." Cox made so much of irrational discrimination that Justice Whittaker wanted to know if he was arguing "due process" violations under the Fourteenth instead of "equal protection." Cox replied that he had not intended to distinguish between the Fourteenth's most famous provisions, though he felt if discriminations were sufficiently irrational one might, indeed, make a "due process" argument. But he and Rhyne were not apart on the basic "equal protection" approach, he asserted.

James M. Glasgow, Assistant Attorney General for Tennessee, had just opened the defense case, laying out the basic framework, when Chief Justice Warren recessed the Court at 4:30 P.M. Glasgow took up there at noon the following day, April 20, and the State's arguments, as in the past, were much the same: reliance upon the *Colegrove* case and particularly upon Justice Frankfurter's reasoning that this was a political question unsuited to Court settlements. Glasgow and his associate, Jack Wilson, likewise relied heavily upon the fact that as late as 1956 the Supreme Court had declined to review *Kidd* v. *McCanless*.

Raising that case, however, gave Justice Whittaker, who seemed to take a dim view of the Tennessee Supreme Court's notions about the *de facto* doctrine, an opportunity to question Glasgow about it in a most penetrating manner. Justice Frankfurter also entered the debate about the *de facto* holding — that decision by the Tennessee Supreme Court that the legislature, its laws and even the state government itself would be wiped out by their ruling for the plaintiffs in *Kidd*. And it was a major thrust of Glasgow's colleague, Wilson, who a few moments later was asking the high court what would happen in Tennessee if a federal court ruled that the state legislature was illegally constituted: "If the [Tennessee] government is operating unconstitutionally, may it continue to sentence defendants in criminal courts? May it continue to pay its schoolteachers? It is an unconstitutional government at that time. May it pay its judges? May it maintain its hospitals for the mentally ill? . . . Suppose the State of Tennessee had planned to execute a defendant in a capital case on the day following the declaration [of] the three-judge district court. What would the Attorney General of Tennessee advise the warden of the state penitentiary as to carrying out that execution?"

A number of observers felt the State gained no points, however, when Wilson closed by informing the justices: "If I may be permitted to go outside the record momentarily, the legislature of Tennessee, which adjourned the seventeenth day of March, did take some action. It has not reapportioned. Whether the legislature of Tennessee will reapportion within the next few years I do not know. But it did pass a resolution to require an enumeration of qualified voters under the constitution. It did pass a resolution to study the subject. That fact will have no bearing. It is not persuasive to this Court. But I simply mention it as a matter of information."

It was as good as Tom Osborn, whose five minutes was coming up next, could have asked. He landed on Wilson's outside-the-record comments with fire: "Mr. Chief Justice, may it please the Court. This honorable Court, in light of the closing made, might well be alerted to this: That for the first time in sixty years a state legislature in Tennessee agreed to have an enumeration, and then only after this honorable Court noted probable jurisdiction in this case. Had it not been for that, the allegations made would have been just as literally true as they were following the 1959 legislature!"

It was of course true: The Tennessee General Assembly had been urged in 1959 — and by the strategy of Walter Chandler — to act. To his silent amusement, as we have seen, the body refused even to authorize a study of the subject, a circumstance in which Chandler rejoiced for the oversight of Cummings. Now, with *Baker* v. *Carr* in the Supreme Court's bosom, the "study" and "enumeration" resolutions, a month before the oral arguments, were all too transparent.

Tom Osborn had not proceeded far with his ached-for argument, however, before he was in a tangle with Mr. Justice Frankfurter. The little man behind the bench seemed to love a grappler, and in the long-legged, bushy-haired Osborn he had found one. Later, they would have yet another verbal tussle before this bench, but now Osborn, his time rather short, was hoping Justice Frankfurter would give him a bit more leeway to develop his chain of thought. He got into his argument deeply enough, however, to agree with Whittaker and score a few points on the *de facto* doctrine, something that had galled him from the day the Tennessee Supreme Court laid Chancellor Tom Steele's decision on it aside and later voted to disbar Osborn for disputing the passage too loudly in public.

"You never have to reach the *de facto* doctrine with respect to any prior act of the legislature," Tom Osborn argued that day before the Supreme Court. "The *de facto* doctrine would not be applied by this Court or by the court of Tennessee or any other courts of the United States to the question of a seating in the legislature or the question of whether there were ten invalid votes in the legislature or a dozen people that were not entitled to be there.

"Commencing with the apology of the Parliament of King James," said Osborn (and now he was hastening along somewhere beyond the English Leveller period), "the legislatures have consistently been held to be the exclusive judge of the qualifications of their members, and *de facto* was never applied to anyone except some [specific] official elected to some [specific] office, and the question then of whether he is properly elected or whether his office is properly created.

"The courts *do* pass upon that, but they do not pass upon the question of a seating of the legislature," Osborn continued. "So, if General Wilson should be

[240]

asked whether to go ahead and execute this prisoner, and he is smart enough — I know him well enough — he would say at once, 'Go ahead and execute the prisoner. We had a law against murder long before the illegal act of 1901 unlawfully apportioned Tennessee,' and he would, secondly, say that the courts have always rejected any attack upon an act of the legislature based upon its membership.

"So he sets up . . . he puts the ox in the ditch in order to try to help him get out," stormed this stormy son of the Presbyterian preacher, "but he would not be concerned with any of those things that he argued."

In five more minutes, Charlie Rhyne summed up and closed. It was 1:50 P.M. April 20, 1961, and the arguments of *Baker* v. *Carr* were ended. The last words recorded were those of the strong-willed, fiery justice whose pen had planted the political thicket this lawsuit was destined to clear.

"Thank you very much," said Mr. Justice Frankfurter.

Tommy Osborn was still stewing, when the Court adjourned, about the short time that he had been allotted. Otherwise, the Leveller lawyers felt very good about the way their days in court had turned out. Ben West thought Rhyne had done "a marvelous job," particularly in view of the many questions he had been forced to field. And the Nashville mayor was so enthusiastic about Cox's performance that he had spontaneously jabbed his elbow into the ribs of the spectator seated next to him in the filled courtroom and whispered loudly, "That's it! That's exactly the way it is!" when Cox scored a particularly telling point. Harris Gilbert was much encouraged by the way Justice Whittaker had entered the fray, and Cox, too, thought this was a significant turn of events.

"Through the first argument, on the whole, we thought the odds were against us," Cox said. "At the end of the first argument, we were very optimistic. The argument went very well. I mean, it seemed during the argument that Justice Whittaker was persuaded to our point of view. Justice Frankfurter, as I remember it, had been very quiet during the argument, and since we figured from previous opinions that he would be most strongly against us, we took his silence to mean that he didn't have the votes — that would be one way to put it — knew he was licked. Justice Whittaker was regarded as one of the more conservative members of the Court. The fact that he seemed on oral argument to be following our position, our reasoning . . . it was very encouraging to us."

Justice Frankfurter had hardly remained entirely silent during the arguments, of course. But those who were most familiar with his bench personality, and with his exceptionally strong feelings on this particular subject, thought he had exercised more restraint than was usual for him. The personality nonetheless had been heard enough so that Charles Rhyne felt the Court was "listening to a lot of these questions from

Mr. Justice Frankfurter, and the justices were a little puzzled as to whether they really wanted to do this."

That was Rhyne's explanation for why the Court shortly thereafter shocked its followers with a rare order to reargue *Baker*. When Chief Justice Warren was asked some years later why the rearguments were ordered, he replied with a single word: "Division." The justices had been simply unable the first time around to agree on what Warren called the most important case of his tenure and Rhyne considers today "one of the important constitutional cases of all time."

To his former pupil, Archibald Cox, Mr. Justice Frankfurter offered a somewhat different explanation of the reargument order on the day it was handed down. By chance, the order came down on the same Monday on which the American Bar Association gave its annual spring dinner for the Supreme Court in Washington's lavish Anderson House, home of the Society of the Cincinnati. "This dinner was a very formal affair — white tie, tails, justices, leading law officers of the government — in a splendid old mansion," Cox recalled. "Indeed, my wife told me that the then Deputy Attorney General, now Justice White, who escorted her down the stairway to the dining room, stopped about halfway down, looked down at the glass and silver and candles, then up at the ceiling and said to her, 'My God, this is a long way from where I was born in Buffalo, Wyoming!'

"Well, we went to dinner. I was seated next to Mrs. Potter Stewart and during dinner she made some pleasant and complimentary remarks about my argument in *Baker* v. *Carr*. In an effort to be witty, which was not wholly successful, I referred to the fact that an order had come down that morning and said to her, 'I wish you'd speak to your husband about that case.' I went on and said, 'After all, look what happened. We filed very long briefs. We went up in April and argued the case to the best of our ability. And now, this morning, the Court says: "Come back and do it all over again next October." What kind of way is that to run a Court? Why don't they decide their cases one way or another?'

"Justice Frankfurter, who had been my professor some years before, apparently overheard some of this, and he cut through the conversation: 'Archie! Archie!'

"The whole table — and to me, I might say, it seemed as if the whole room — fell silent.

" 'Archie! I'll tell you why the case was sent down for reargument. We heard the first argument. We went into our conference that Friday, and when we reached *Baker* v. *Carr* on our docket, one of my brethren said, "You know, the new Solicitor General didn't argue very well last April. Let's have him come back and see if he can do better in October." ' "

So on Monday, October 9, 1961, at ten o'clock in the morning, Archibald Cox and all the rest came back to give *Baker* a second go-round.

Even the hour seemed to forebode change. Ten o'clock in the morning! Unheard of!

[244]

Baker v. *Carr* was "the first case ever argued at ten o'clock in the morning in the Supreme Court of the United States," said Charles S. Rhyne, "and all of the old retainers and others were enormously upset by the change from twelve o'clock to ten o'clock."

For any other organization, business or governmental, such a routine change might be effected by a quick memo from a top echelon executive, the adjustments would be made, and the organization would go smoothly on about its business. But the Supreme Court is not just "any other organization"; it is a court steeped in tradition and ritual and precedent. Even a two-hour procedural change, therefore, was enough to create a considerable stir. On this particular precedent-shattering October day, there were other tensions seething beneath the surface which were not so readily discernible.

Specifically, there were bruised feelings and raw nerves among the lawyers preparing on the Supreme Court floor to begin the reargument of this extraordinary case, which bore such significance that it had the galleries packed — and with some very important people. There were senators, congressmen and highly influential municipal officials interspersed with the Supreme Court and Justice Department wives on hand for what all knew was a historic occasion. In such circumstances, there is no lawyer who would not surrender a fee or two for a share of the credit and a piece of the argument action. There had been some spats about this among the Leveller lawyers.

Still another element of rivalry existed between Rhyne's office and the Solicitor General's. From the beginning of the Supreme Court phase of *Baker,* there had been no open rift, but something less than excellent rapport between these camps; there had been little coordination between their staffs. Each approached the issues with a slightly differing emphasis and theory. Perhaps the coolness was to be expected, considering the partisan differences that had prompted Rhyne and Cox actively to work on opposite sides of the very strongly contested and extremely close presidential campaign that had preceded the original arguments in the case. To this day, Nixon and Kennedy partisans are inclined to dispute whether it was Rhyne or Cox who actually brought the government into the *Baker* case, whose argument *really* carried the day with the Court. At the time of the reargument, the passage of almost a year had dulled this rivalry somewhat, but it was still present.

The other conflict was of an angrier and more dangerous type. Approaching the first argument, there had been some disagreement among the Tennessee Levellers concerning who among them should argue the case. Tom Osborn had dealt with the subject longer, but Walter Chandler, a much older and more experienced lawyer with far more prestige, was the team captain and was, in effect, paying Osborn's fee. Hobart Atkins, the third member of the original team, thought Chandler should have the honor. Before this matter was entirely settled, however, Rhyne had rendered the difference moot by letting it be known he would consume the entire time himself. Ben West had put Rhyne in total charge of the case, and the Tennesseans had agreed to those terms. The situation was awkward, for the Tennesseans were together on one point: All of them felt it would be unseemly to put their case before the high court with no one from the state itself involved in the oral arguments. For his part, Osborn was openly angered by Rhyne's proposal. He had never favored Rhyne's taking charge of the case, but there was little he could say; his role in the lawsuit was totally dependent on West and Chandler. At that point, Chandler had graciously waived his own rights, then intervened with Rhyne to assure Osborn the five-minute rebuttal spot.

The personality conflict between Rhyne and Osborn, both strong-willed men, was set, however. When rearguments were ordered, Osborn was determined not to be cut out again. Accordingly, he and Rhyne each filed the required written notice with the Supreme Court clerk, each thereby indicating that he would argue the plaintiffs' case. The clerk, caught in the middle, made discreet inquiries concerning how the plaintiffs intended straightening out this conflict. Ben West stepped in. "We can't afford a lawyers' fight at this stage," he told Harris Gilbert and Walter Chandler, and asked them to see if they couldn't arbitrate the dispute. Gilbert, the good friend and junior law associate of Osborn, and Chandler, the longtime respected friend of Rhyne, managed to damp the sparks with

Rhyne's agreement to let Osborn have "three to five minutes." The threatened explosion within Leveller ranks was averted, but the animosity between these two contributors to *Baker*'s success endured.

The *Baker* partisans had no monopoly on conflicts the day the reargument took place, though, and Charles Rhyne could sense it the moment the justices marched in. So could Archibald Cox. Disputes and strong feelings had surged through the Court already over this complex issue, and one look at the face of Mr. Justice Frankfurter told these two experienced observers of the Court as much.

"The Solicitor General said he was sure that Justice Frankfurter had spent all summer getting ready to tear him apart," Rhyne recalled. "I said, 'Remember he has me for an hour and a half before he gets to you, and I don't think he'll be able to hold it within him.'

"I'll bet," Rhyne had added, "that I can't even get out the usual ritual." Sure enough, "I said, 'Mr. Chief Justice . . .' and before I could get out the other part — 'May it please the Court' — he [Frankfurter] leveled his finger at me and said: 'Mr. Rhyne, when we interpret the Constitution of the United States, we take into consideration *history!*' and he slammed his brief down on the bench."

Justice Frankfurter then "proceeded to name a number of criteria which he thought the Court should take into consideration in interpreting the Constitution. . . . I had no opportunity to say anything because the Justice was obviously very, very worked up.

He finally finished ticking off these things, and then he said, 'Mr. Rhyne, I've asked you a number of questions; you've answered none. I assume you can't.'

"And I said, 'Mr. Justice, I thought you were making statements rather than asking questions but if you'll give me an opportunity, I'll answer them and I'll answer them with one word.'

"He said, 'Preposterous!'

"And I said, 'The word is *equality,* and it's your duty to give it.' This was the substance of what took place.

"And he said, 'Don't tell me what my duty is!'

"I said, 'Well, I think that's a lawyer's responsibility, too.' But he proceeded, then, to cross-examine me to his heart's content for the next hour and a half. The intensity of Mr. Justice Frankfurter, both times, is almost impossible to describe in words."

Solicitor General Cox remembered the second argument as "a lively workout. I mentioned before that Frankfurter had been very silent (for him) on the initial argument. He was in strong form on the reargument, very much opposed to the Court's taking jurisdiction . . . very vocal in his philosophy and reasons. I had some recollection of leaving the Court feeling that we had made the best case we could and that the Court was not unsympathetic, but with no feelings on how the case was going to come out."

There had not been much new to add, actually, to the full arguments made before the Court in April. As Archibald Cox had remarked to "Andy" Stewart, the Associate Justice's wife, at the ABA dinner back in the spring, the briefs had been long and the arguments full. And with *amicus* galore, there was a sufficiency of both; no argument in *Baker* went unexplored. The prepared arguments of both Rhyne and Cox suggested, indeed, that neither had much else to say beyond what had already been said. There were, nonetheless, a few fresh ingredients in the reargument session.

For one thing, the 1960 census results were complete now, and there was some discussion among the Leveller lawyers about how they might be gotten into the record. Someone suggested that census records are by nature matters of which courts are always able to take judicial notice. Accordingly, the Nashville planners had been put back to work in the five months between arguments. When he returned to Washington, then, for the second argument, Harrison Gilbert took aboard the plane with him seventy-five pounds of updated statistics for distribution. A package for each of the justices was simply brought into the courtroom and, without comment, laid on the bench for the Court's attention.

For the first hour, while the arguments droned (and sometimes raged) on, the robed jurists thumbed through their packets, passed notes to each other about them, whispered questions down the bench, and at times appeared to Harris Gilbert to be not much listening to anything else going on in the courtroom. "They really got into it like a bunch of kids with toys," said Gilbert. "I just can't begin to tell you how more interested they were at this point in the statistical data than they seemed to be in the legal principles. Of course this has been the key aspect of Fourteenth Amendment litigation. You can have differentiations and discriminations and distinctions, but there must be a rational basis for it." The statistical evidence was intended, therefore, to convince the jurists that there existed in Tennessee what Archibald Cox was calling invidious (for which read "irrational") discrimination.

Cox, too, added something of a new ingredient by providing, through his "irrational" argument, a clear relationship between the Tuskegee case and *Baker*. It was a problem that had bothered the plaintiffs: How to get around Mr. Justice Frankfurter's clever distinction between them. But with the weight of the government and an administration deeply committed to racial justice behind him, Cox argued the point he had made in his reargument brief: "We recognize the breadth and importance of the state's political power to apportion representation in its legislature, but we submit that to exalt this power into an absolute is to misconceive the reach and meaning of the Fourteenth Amendment. It is unsound to distinguish *Gomillion* [the Tuskegee case] from the present case on the ground that it arose under the Fifteenth Amendment. The Fourteenth Amendment protects the right to vote . . . and arbitrary geographical distinctions are scarcely less invidious than discriminations based upon race."

In his prepared argument, Cox asserted that "*Gomillion* v. *Lightfoot,* which was decided only last term, makes it plain that a case is not removed from the domain of judicial review merely because the unconstitutional discrimination is accomplished by an exercise of the state's power to lay out political subdivisions — in one sense this is the very question at issue here. . . .

"In *Gomillion*," Cox added, "the Court distinguished *Colegrove* on the ground that *Colegrove* involved legislative inaction because of dilution in voting strength in contrast to affirmative legislation depriving Negroes of a right to vote. The distinction, I submit, goes not to the power of the federal courts to deal with the subject matter but to the possibility of devising an appropriate remedy. . . . If one puts *Gomillion* and *Colegrove* side by side, the comparison establishes the very point which I seek to make — there are cases dealing with the composition of political subdivisions such as municipalities and legislative districts with which the courts can and do deal; there are other situations, like *Colegrove*, in which the problem of devising a remedy seems so insoluble that equity should decline to act; the propriety of judicial intervention is therefore to be approached case by case, not by a rule denying jurisdiction but in the exercise of the traditional discretion of an equity court."

The pupil had speared the master with his own weapon. Mr. Justice Frankfurter, whose brain had composed both *Colegrove* and *Gomillion*, had used both cases to argue against *Baker*. His pupil stood each on its head to prove the opposite point.

Tom Osborn considered Cox's argument on this Tuskegee case, which had confronted the plaintiffs with such problems, as the high point of the reargument session. "All of us benefited a great, great deal from Solicitor General Cox," he said. "He was the man of sophistication and erudition. He was the scholar in the crew. Archibald Cox made an enormous contribution to this lawsuit."

Osborn himself finally got satisfaction during the reargument. Mr. Justice Frankfurter's back was against the wall when Osborn's scheduled five minutes arrived, but he was not through fighting. The sort of skirmish he had with Osborn during the first argument was this time extended; it roared on for thirty or forty minutes as Frankfurter clung to the colloquy in a last effort to sway his colleagues. The Court extended its time for arguments in this case, forgot the clock and kept going. It was a role in which Tommy Osborn excelled; extemporaneous exchange was his meat, and after six years of battling, he knew this case and all its precedents cold.

"The rebuttal is often very important," explained Harris Gilbert. "In a rebuttal, in just a few minutes, you can destroy the other guy with two or three well-chosen sentences. And this was a perfect opportunity for Tom. He knew the case well, he was a capable man. . . . In fact, Tommy was probably a little better at arguing in a courtroom — very bright, quick — than in brief-writing. Tommy didn't go for all the constant, word-changing nit-picking that goes into brief-writing. But he was about as good a lawyer as I ever saw recoiling from the punch."

Such an occasion arose with Justice Frankfurter in that final rebuttal, and both Ben West and Gilbert recalled it with glee. "He made one of the finest replies I ever saw to a very adroit and astute question Frankfurter had asked him," says Gilbert. "Frankfurter said, 'You're telling us today that 33 per cent of the Tennessee electorate elects 66⅔ of the legislature, and we should agree with your position that some way or another — with a magic wand probably — there will be some remedy worked out. So the Court will agree to some alleviation. And the next year 40 per cent will be electing 60 per cent of the legislature. You'll be right back up here complaining about that, won't you?' Tommy looked at him just as square and said, 'Yessir. For a fee.' And the whole courtroom just fell apart, Frankfurter did, everybody did. They just recognized that this was the basic lawyer coming out. It was the perfect lawyer's answer."

West, too, became the butt of laughter in the final argument session. Jack Wilson, with the final argument for the defense, reminded the Court: "In the city of Nashville, whose honorable Mayor is a party to this lawsuit, citizens are clamoring for equal representation on the City Council. And what does the honorable Mayor say? He says, 'We're working on it.'" The audience broke into laughter and several of the justices joined in. What Wilson had said was true enough — the Council districts in Nashville ranged in population from 1,200 to 14,000 — and the Mayor's inconsistencies had been pointed out by the press. But in fact, the demands in Nashville for equity were a certain fallout from all the *Baker* publicity, simply more evidence of the rising consciousness concerning the problem and the growing insistence upon its correction. A new form of metropolitan government, consolidating city and county governments, ultimately balanced the councilmanic districts in Nashville.

Another difference in the second *Baker* argument was a change in the plaintiffs' strategy. The first argument had been beamed toward Associate Justice Potter Stewart, as we have seen, but Stewart's questions during that argument had failed to offer much clue as to his feelings. Meanwhile, it had appeared from other questions that two justices the plaintiffs had counted on losing — Whittaker and Clark — were surprisingly sympathetic. On reargument, then, the Levellers switched their principal emphasis to Chief Justice Warren, one of their earlier "probables." The Chief Justice, who had been very quiet during the first argument, now had to be counted a doubtful and he, after all, would assign the case and the task of writing it. In such important cases, indeed, the Chief Justice frequently wrote the opinion himself; it was his prerogative to take for himself those cases he wished to write.

Rhyne kept Chandler at his side to help him plan possible changes in strategy and to advise him during the course of both *Baker* arguments. In such a position, the Captain served as a conduit for notes to Rhyne from other counsel, and even from one expert layman, Anthony Lewis, of the New York *Times*. Rhyne declared: "I think that Tony is the only newspaper reporter I know who had a direct participation in the Supreme Court of the United States." Lewis had already contributed much to the preparation of the *Baker* case through his careful research into the background of the subject of reapportionment. This research went into a major article in the *Harvard Law Review* following Lewis's year at Harvard as a Nieman Fellow. And in doing his own research, Rhyne had found Lewis's work "one of the most helpful articles that I used in preparing our Supreme Court brief." Rhyne also discussed the case at length with the reporter during its preparation. Lewis's article was among the material that had been presented to Cox by Osborn, Gilbert and John Jay Hooker, Jr., when they sought the Solicitor General's participation in the case. The article was mentioned by Justice Douglas in his concurring opinion in *Baker*.

The subject, then, was one into which Tony Lewis had poured much of himself, and now, said Rhyne, "During the course of this argument, Tony kept — he was sitting right across from me — kept handing me notes. Before I got up to make my argument, and after I was up there, he handed notes to Captain Chandler, which Captain Chandler handed to me. And one of the notes Tony handed me said I should refer to this district court case in Hawaii.

"He was writing out answers to a lot of Frankfurter's questions, too, and this was real cute because he was so personally involved in this thing he really didn't realize what he was doing. There were a lot of people watching Tony — watching what he was doing. I think it would almost embarrass him to have him reminded of this, although he's got to admit he did it. I once had the notes. Maybe I still have them."

Newspaper reporter Tony Lewis, then, became another of those many, many Americans whose efforts came to a head in the Supreme Court of the United States of America in *Baker* v. *Carr* that day. Hundreds, even thousands of Americans contributed indirectly to the success of the lawsuit, and thus to the eradication of America's "rotten borough" system. The popular tide running toward this reform constituted by this time a movement — as powerful and broad in scope as the earlier tides of people surging into the nation's cities and suburbs from its agricultural past. Such social change cannot forever be denied politically. The pressures eventually become too great, and now there were bearing down upon the Court just such pressures, visible in all those *amicus curiae* petitions and audible in the rising swell of eloquence from aspiring young politicians who were discovering where the voters were situated.

As the pressures built, it sometimes appeared in those final days of *Baker* that the tiny figure and towering intellect of Felix Frankfurter stood there in solitary defiance against it all — an old man, not a boy, at

[257]

the dike, stubbornly trying to preserve not an idea but a phrase. The dike had Tennessee's low parallelogram profile, but the crest of a national flood was now surging against it, a flood of sentiment swelled by the United States government itself.

As Ben West had suggested and as Charles Rhyne had argued, the last possible remedy was gone in Tennessee — judicial, legislative, executive, initiative, referendum, even the hope of a constitutional amendment. If the complainant citizens of Tennessee, representing many more beyond their borders, had no recourse but to the Supreme Court, then, its nine justices of ordinary men seemed to have little recourse but to offer relief. That the Court did on March 26, 1962, after five more months of debate and study. The justices voted — one vote each — 6 to 2 for the American Levellers. Justice Harlan dissented, but it was Mr. Justice Frankfurter who was the more visible of the two dissenters. For his "political thicket" had not been simply uprooted. Before a virtual floodtide, it was washed away forever.

6

What the Levellers Wrought

"The rush through the door unlocked by *Baker* v. *Carr* has been staggering," Arthur J. Goldberg wrote, before the decision was a year old. By the first anniversary, March 26, 1963, no fewer than thirty-six states had become involved in reapportionment lawsuits. By the end of that year, forty-two of the fifty states had been subjected to court suits, referendums or actual reapportionments.

It was a surprising reaction in view of the narrow terms of the *Baker* opinion, drawn by Justice Brennan. The decision, as Brennan wrote it and as Justice Stewart underscored in his separate opinion, did no more than hold "(a) that the court possessed jurisdiction of the subject matter; (b) that a justiciable cause of action is stated upon which appellants would be entitled to appropriate relief; and (c) . . . that the appellants have standing to challenge the Tennessee apportionment statutes." The case was sent back to district court in Nashville for trial.

The Supreme Court's holding therefore was along almost the identical lines suggested by Archibald Cox in his argument. The Solicitor General had seen no reason why the Court was required either to find a specific Fourteenth Amendment violation or to chart a remedy. And Justice Brennan's opinion, after laying down its trio of conclusions, added, "[Since] we have no cause at this stage to doubt the District Court will be able to fashion relief if violations of constitutional rights are found, it is improper now to consider what remedy would be most appropriate."

Walter Chandler did not miss the significance of this language. Passing around plaudits to all his colleagues, he wrote Cox three days after the decision: "You are entitled to congratulations and thanks of all the counsel for the plaintiffs in the case of *Baker* v. *Carr*, as well as the gratitude of the people of Tennessee who have striven for years without success to obtain equal voting rights in the Tennessee legislature. The case seems to have been decided along the lines of your argument, and we hope that we can take up from this point and carry the cause to successful completion."

The narrow opinion on which the justices managed consensus was by no means pleasing to all of them, however, and the flurry of dissenting and concurring opinions — five of them altogether — gave telling evi-

[260]

dence that intense debate occurred behind the traditional veil drawn down over Supreme Court delibera-
tions.

Asked some years later if any consideration had
been given to an eventual remedy during these sessions, Chief Justice Warren replied, with a chuckle:
"We were lucky to get the Court to go where it went." It
went there without one of the Levellers' most helpful
questioners, Justice Whittaker. The Kansas Citian did
not participate in the decision, despite having heard
both arguments in *Baker*. After only five years on the
Court, he announced his retirement just before the
case was decided, explaining that the "great volume
and continuous stresses" of the Court's work had
brought him to the "point of physical exhaustion."
Charles S. Rhyne, who had known Whittaker quite
well, felt certain his vote would have made the decision 7 to 2 had he remained on the bench. The dissenters were, of course, the justices the Leveller lawyers had felt from the beginning could be counted definitely against them — Frankfurter and Harlan. The
rest went with *Baker:* Black and Douglas, the votes
that had been considered certain all along; Stewart,
the swing man in the first argument; Warren, the key
target of the reargument; Brennan, one of the hoped-
for "probables"; and Tom Clark, the great admirer of
Frankfurter who broke with him sharply on this occasion.

Indeed, all the opinions were a pattern-breaking
round robin of sharp criticisms. Clark characterized

Frankfurter's sixty-four-page dissenting opinion as one "bursting with words that go through so much and conclude with so little." Frankfurter called the majority opinion, in turn, "a massive repudiation of our whole past" and a decision which "may well impair the Court's position." Justice Harlan attacked Clark's opinion, particularly that part containing statistical tables designed to show discriminations among various rural districts, as well as rural advantages over urban voters. "Certainly, with all due respect, the facile arithmetical argument contained in . . . my Brother Clark's separate opinion provides no tenable basis for considering that there has been such a breach [of rationality] in this instance," wrote Harlan.

Harlan's dissent also illuminated the dispute raging within the Court at that time, and in society even today, concerning the proper scope of judicial power:

Those observers of the Court who see it primarily as the last refuge for the correction of all inequality or injustice, no matter what its nature or source, will no doubt applaud this decision and its break with the past. Those who consider that continuing national respect for the Court's authority depends in large measure upon its wise exercise of self-restraint and discipline in constitutional adjudication, will view the decision with deep concern.

Clark replied:

As John Rutledge said 175 years ago in the course of the Constitutional Convention, a chief function of the Court is to secure the national rights. Its decision today supports the proposition for which our forebears fought and many died, namely, that "to be fully conformable to the principle of right, the form of government must be representative." That is the keystone upon which our Government was founded and lacking which no republic can survive.

It is well for this Court to practice self-restraint and discipline in constitutional adjudication, but never in its history have those principles received sanction where the national rights of so many have been so clearly infringed for so long a time. National respect for the courts is more enhanced through the forthright enforcement of those rights rather than by rendering them nugatory through the interposition of subterfuges. In my view, the ultimate decision today is in the greatest tradition of this Court.

Justice Douglas argued the basic philosophy question in his opinion, too, quoting the language of Judge McLaughlin in the Hawaii case, *Dyer* v. *Kazuhisa Abe:*

The whole thrust of today's legal climate is to end unconstitutional discrimination. It is ludicrous to preclude judicial relief when a mainspring of representative government is impaired. Legislators have no immunity from the Constitution. The legislatures of our land should be made as responsive to the Constitution of the United States as are the citizens who elect the legislators.

With the exceptions of *Colegrove* v. *Green, MacDougall* v. *Green,* and *South* v. *Peters,* and the decisions they spawned, the Court has never thought that protection of voting rights was beyond judicial cognizance. Today's treatment of those cases removes the only impediment to judicial cognizance of the claims stated in the present complaint.

Opinions written by members of the Court were in such conflict, in fact, that Justice Stewart tried, in his own brief opinion, to straighten them all out:

The separate writings of my dissenting and concurring Brothers stray so far from the subject of today's decision as to convey, I think, a distressingly inaccurate impression of what the Court decides.

Contrary to the suggestion of my Brother Harlan, the Court does not say or imply that "state legislatures must be so structured as to reflect with approximate equality the voice of every voter." The Court does not say or imply that there is anything in the Federal Constitution "to prevent a State, acting not irrationally, from choosing any electoral legislative structure it thinks best suited to the interests, temper and customs of its people." And contrary to to the suggestion of my Brother Douglas, the Court most assuredly does not decide the question, "may a State weight the vote of one county or one district more heavily than it weighs the vote in another?" . . .

My Brother Clark has made a convincing prima facie showing that Tennessee's system of apportionment is in fact utterly arbitrary — without any possible justification in rationality. My Brother Harlan has, with imagination and ingenuity, hypothesized possibly rational bases for Tennessee's system. But the merits of this case are not before us now. The defendants have not yet had an opportunity to be heard in defense of the State's system of apportionment; indeed, they have not yet even filed an answer to the complaint. As in other cases, the proper place for the trial is in the trial court, not here.

From a strictly legal point of view, the legal intellect of Stewart had stated the decision precisely. But both Justices Clark and Frankfurter, while differing, were nearer the practical implications. Clark, at the outset of his opinion, had complained that the Court "refuses to award relief here — although the facts are undisputed — and fails to give the District Court any guidance whatever." And Frankfurter, chiding his former pupil, Archibald Cox, along the way, landed upon the decision's same basic weakness:

We were soothingly told at the bar of this Court that we need not worry about the kind of remedy a court could effectively fashion once the abstract constitutional right to have courts pass on a state-wide system of electoral districting is recognized as a matter of judicial rhetoric, because legislatures would heed the Court's admonition. This is not only an euphoric hope. It implies a sorry confession of judicial impotence in place of a frank acknowledgment that there is not under our Constitution a judicial remedy for every political mischief, for every undesirable exercise of legislative power.

Baker v. *Carr*, however narrowly drawn, thus foreshadowed an eventual Court answer to two questions it left unsettled: What sort of remedy could the Court provide to correct this obvious injustice? Where are the metes and bounds of voter equity — the guidelines — in matters of representation? The most naïve did not suppose that the narrowness of the *Baker* decision would end this dispute; but perhaps not even the most reformist spirit expected the turn of subsequent cases toward a political upheaval of such great breadth and depth as eventually occurred.

Certainly, the man who helped begin this suit and

took it all the way through did not expect such results. "I would have settled for the federal plan," said Tom Osborn. "I felt that if we could have accomplished the federal plan and had one house absolutely representative of the population of Tennessee, of the people wherever the people lived, then . . . everything we had spent on it, all the time we had spent on it would have been well worth while. I really felt that that would be about the maximum we could achieve."

That view was in line with the feelings of Solicitor General Cox. Speaking before the Tennessee Bar Association June 8, 1962, with the decision not three months behind him, Cox made it plain that he did not consider the outcome as narrow as his arguments before the Court had suggested:

"Strictly speaking, the Court has not yet decided that the Fourteenth Amendment imposes any limit upon the legislature's freedom of choice, but this technically accurate view of the decision seems a little unrealistic. The majority would hardly have labored to sustain the Court's jurisdiction if it believed that no apportionment, however discriminatory or capricious, would violate the Fourteenth Amendment. The more pressing question is, what standards will the courts evolve in the traditional, pragmatic process of adjudication. I think we can hazard a few very tentative guesses." His most important guess was wrong: "I do not mean to suggest how the question should be decided, but it would not surprise me greatly if the Supreme Court were ultimately to hold that if seats in one branch of the legislature are apportioned in direct ratio to population, the allocation of seats in the upper branch may recognize historical, political and geographical subdivisions provided that the departure from equal representation in proportion to the population is not too extreme."

Before it was to jump to the critical question of both houses of a legislature, however, the Supreme Court took the necessary hop and skip through two related precedents, both in cases from Georgia. The year after the *Baker* decision, on March 18, 1963, it struck down Georgia's unique county unit system of voting in statewide and congressional primary elections. In *Gray* v. *Sanders*, the Court declared: "The concept of political equality from the Declaration of Independence to Lincoln's Gettysburg Address, to the Fifteenth, Seventeenth and Nineteenth Amendments can mean only one thing — one person, one vote."

And the following year, on February 17, 1964, it decided in *Westberry* v. *Sanders* that its authority over apportionment matters, as established by *Baker*, extended as well to congressional districts. This was the final reversal of *Colegrove* v. *Green*, which had itself been a congressional case. The Court based its decision on Article I, Section 2 of the Constitution, which states that representatives "shall be apportioned among the several states . . . according to their respective numbers" and "chosen . . . by the people of the several states." This language, the Court said, means that "as nearly as practicable one man's vote in a congressional election is to be worth as much as another's."

One man, one vote was now spelled out as the standard in national and state legislative races, but one step remained in the latter: It had not been made clear whether the rule applied to both houses of a state legislature. That came on June 15, 1964, in cases handed down in a six-state bundle: Alabama, Colorado, Delaware, Maryland, New York, Virginia. They are often referred to, together, as *Reynolds* v. *Sims*, one of a trio of Alabama cases decided that day. The opinion, written by Chief Justice Warren, held that representation in both houses of a bicameral legislature must be "based substantially on population," although it might not be possible to draw district lines with "mathematical exactness of precision." The Court held that the one-man-one-vote principle had to apply in both houses even when the voters of a state — in this case Colorado — had approved by popular referendum an apportionment based on factors other than population.

"A citizen's constitutional rights can hardly be infringed upon," wrote Warren in *Lucas* v. *Colorado*, "because a majority of the people choose to do so." Seven days later, on June 22, 1964, the Supreme Court underscored its outlawing of the "little federal system" in state legislatures by disposing of cases from nine more states — Connecticut, Florida, Idaho, Illinois, Iowa, Michigan, Ohio, Oklahoma and Washington.

Even then, the peaceful revolution wrought by the

Tennessee Levellers was not ended. In December 1966, the Supreme Court agreed to hear three reapportionment cases brought by groups seeking to extend the one-man-one-vote doctrine to local governing bodies and school boards. In two of these cases — involving the Kent County, Michigan, School Board and the Houston County, Alabama, Governing Board — three-judge federal courts had refused to order reapportionment on grounds that the Court had not yet ruled the doctrine applicable to such subdivisions of a state. In the third case, affecting the Suffolk County, New York, Board of Supervisors, a three-judge panel had ordered a weighted reapportionment plan and directed that a permanent plan be submitted to the county's voters.

Before the Supreme Court reached its decision on the local government issue, in 1968, a three-judge panel back in Tennessee had declared the one-man-one-vote principle applicable to county governing bodies, however. On February 13, 1968, a panel which included District Judge William E. Miller ordered the Shelby County governing body, headed by Charles W. Baker, and the one in Miller's native Washington County, of which Ella Ross was now an elected member, to reapportion. She was pleased; reapportioning the Washington County Quarterly Court (the county legislative body in Tennessee) had been one of her ultimate aims in originating *Kidd* v. *McCanless* years before. When the Supreme Court handed down its own ruling on local government, the opinion contained some uncertainties; it implied, for example, that only those units of government that exercised broad legislative powers — such as county governing bodies and city councils — would be affected. But on February 25, 1970, the Court declared that the election of school boards and most if not all other local officials had to adhere to the one-man-one-vote standard. Its 5-to-3 opinion, which grew out of a dispute over the election of the six trustees of the junior college district that operated three junior colleges in the Kansas City, Missouri, area, laid down this general rule:

Whenever a state or local government decides to select persons by popular election to perform government functions, the Equal Protection clause of the Fourteenth Amendment requires that each qualified voter must be given an equal opportunity to participate in that election.
When members of an elected body are chosen from separate districts, each district must be established on a basis which will insure, as far as is practicable, that equal numbers of voters can vote for proportionally equal numbers of officials.

Fred P. Graham, interpreting the rule in the New York *Times,* wrote: "By using this broad language, the Court let it be known that those governmental officials who are elected from geographical districts, such as many board members of sewer and water districts, administrative and regulatory officials, and perhaps even judges, will apparently have to be elected from districts of nearly even population."

On June 23, the Court further extended the one-man-one-vote doctrine to hold that persons who do not pay real estate taxes cannot be barred from voting on proposed general obligation bond issues. Fourteen states had laws excluding such citizens from the franchise in bonding referenda — Alaska, Arizona, Colorado, Florida, Idaho, Louisiana, Michigan, Montana, New Mexico, New York, Oklahoma, Rhode Island, Texas and Utah. Again the decision was 5 to 3. In the same month, however, the Court may have signaled the revolution's end: On June 15, 1970, it affirmed a lower court's ruling in *Bergerman* v. *Lindsay* that the Board of Estimate of the City of New York was not affected by the one-man-one-vote doctrine and did not have to be apportioned on an equal basis because it did not exercise general governmental powers. The fine line, it appears, was drawn at that point.

Seldom has a revolution moved more rapidly or been more widely accepted. "In the space of five years reapportionment virtually remade the political map of America," wrote the political scientist Robert G. Dixon, Jr. "By the election of 1966, the equal population rule had affected virtually every legislative seat and congressional district in the nation."

Since the 1970 census, city councils and county governing bodies, by that time also subject to the rule, have also readjusted membership; indeed, many already had done so before the law of the land caught up with them. In Nashville, Tennessee, with a minimum of wrangling, the Metropolitan Council redistricted within weeks of publication in early 1971 of the final census results; however, a few blocks away, up Tennessee's Capitol Hill, the General Assembly struggled in vain in an effort to solve its congressional redistricting problem before its May 31 adjournment. The state lost a seat in Congress, dropping from nine to eight. But the legislature, unable to break a stalemate between House and Senate versions of a Democratic redistricting plan, put off until its second session in early 1972 both the congressional matter and the reapportionment of its own seats. The stalemate came not so much from Democratic-Republican infighting over rival plans as from the inability of Democrats to stand solidly behind their own caucus scheme. But such a deadlock would have been unthinkable in the days before *Baker*, when Democratic margins in both Tennessee houses were of such overpowering weight that both the GOP and Democratic mavericks would have been crushed with ease.

In the case of Tennessee and other Southern and border states, then, the predictions that reapportionment would serve up gains for the Republican party have been generally accurate. Not so accurate were predictions that the Democrats would gain somewhat in the growing cities of the North. Here, too, the short-term edge seems likely to favor the Republicans, primarily because large voting blocs in the center cities, traditionally Democratic, have been broken up and scattered by urban renewal and interstate highway building. The movement to the suburbs by core-city groups, moreover, has created great tension in the Northern urban centers, intensifying the tendency of well-to-do suburbanites to vote Republican. As the new decade began, in fact, the Republican National Committee was so confident of gains by reason of reapportionment that it announced a major goal of winning state legislative elections because congressional districts are redrawn by state legislatures.

"The combination of significant population shifts and redrawn congressional district lines gives us a golden opportunity to pick up nearly 50 congressional seats in 1972 and thereby gain control of the House," declared a GOP party organ published in early 1970. Not in the previous fifty years, it is likely, had either national party given such attention to state races.

Without question, one of the major contributions of the American Levellers was to rejuvenate state government, which political scientists considered of lowly estate and which many had advocated abolishing altogether. "The biggest thing it [*Baker*] has done," said Charles S. Rhyne, "is take the shackles off state government. I believe that state governments for the first time in all history are responsive to urban needs. Up until this time, because the rural elements controlled state legislatures, the legislatures paid very little attention to cities . . . and of course I've lived through this whole thing of cities having to come to Washington hat in hand to get anything. I wasn't in on the beginning of what I would call the city trek to Washington, which started really in 1932, but I knew quite intimately Frank Murphy, Mayor La Guardia, and all of those who really took part in that — where cities began to look toward Washington instead of the state capital to help solve their problems, for money, for all the things they needed because the state legislatures wouldn't respond. Already you can see the state governments are doing things for cities they never did before."

Tom Osborn saw an improvement in the quality of the legislature: "There is, I think, a reawakened interest in state legislatures all over the United States. The state legislatures are no longer cut-and-dried. I don't believe that in any state they are any longer dominated by a small clique. There is more interest in the type of man that goes to the legislature than formerly. I'm speaking now as far as the majority of the people are concerned; the country people always sent good men to the legislature, you know; their big men in the community would vie for the place in the legislature. You'd have men like Haynes and Cummings from the country, whereas in Davidson County, in the metropolitan centers, it was something the young lawyers or a few of the young businessmen might be interested in."

Osborn also believed that "a part of the disruption that we have is attributable to the lack of a meaningful vote. I don't think there is any question but that the Negroes' dissatisfaction with the ordinary democratic processes is attributable to the fact that the democratic processes simply didn't work. They didn't work even for white people, let alone for colored people. I think had *Baker* v. *Carr* come, let's say, at the time of *Colegrove* v. *Green,* had the same decision been made at that time [1946], there would have been far less of the disruption and riots and civil disobedience that we have had to see.

"If, immediately after the war, it had been ruled by the courts that people . . . You see, the courts were already ruling that people had a right to vote. Every voting-rights case was going in favor of the man who wasn't being permitted to vote. They had ruled that Negroes could not be excluded from primaries. . . . Now if *Colegrove* v. *Green* had followed in that pattern, then the processes of democracy as we know them in the United States would have been able, with a good conscience, to face the returning Negro veteran. Negroes had worked side-by-side with whites in the war effort and in the factories . . . and said to him, 'If there is something you want to change, you have a right to elect a representative just like I have, both to the Congress and to your legislature.' But in Tennessee, for example, and all over the United States, truthfully, that could not be held out to the Negroes. You could not have said to a Negro in Nashville in 1946, or really until *Baker* v. *Carr,* that you have any possibility of electing yourself or the most respected member of your community to the legislature. It simply could not have been done."

Earl Warren had once called *Baker* the most important case considered while he was on the bench. When asked to elaborate, the Chief Justice replied that he deeply believed in representative government and had all of his life. A cardinal principle of his political philosophy, he said, had always been great confidence in the popular will of the people as expressed through the ballot. But before the *Baker* decision, he said, the ballot-box expression had ceased to be truly representative due to the years of failure on the part of many state and local governments to adjust to shifting and growing population.

It was not so much that a minority had absolute rule in the legislature as a result of this, Chief Justice Warren explained, as it was that they had sufficient power to block essential and progressive legislation. Some time after the *Baker* decision, he related by way of illustration, he was discussing this matter with an industry representative who told him it was possible in a small Eastern state to line up just nine men and block any legislation he wanted. "Think of that," the Chief Justice said. "Only nine men could block something the people of an entire state needed. That's too much negative power in the hands of too few." Nothing could have been of greater importance, he added, than restoring the basic ingredient of representation to the American political system.

There were those, of course, who felt the nine men of the Supreme Court had too much power, positive or negative, and the reapportionment decisions sparked a couple of concerted drives to limit that power. One of these efforts originated in the Council of State Governments, which proposed in December 1962 that state legislatures petition Congress to call a constitutional convention to consider three amendments dealing with limitations on federal control, and particularly that of the Court, over state matters. The second effort, mounted when the first floundered, was spearheaded by United States Senator Everett McKinley Dirksen, of Illinois, and likewise centered on the proposed amending of the federal Constitution, by state initiatives, so as to reverse the effect of *Reynolds* v. *Sims* and permit state legislatures to apportion at least one house on bases other than population.

The key amendment proposed by the Council of State Governments would have created a "Court of the Union" composed of the chief justices of the state supreme courts to review decisions of the United States Supreme Court "relating to the rights reserved to the states or the people." As chance had it, the proposal was offered at a General Assembly of the States attended by George McCanless, who had given his name as defendant to *Kidd* v. *McCanless* and who directed defense efforts against *Baker* v. *Carr,* in which he was also listed defendant. Representing Tennessee at the General Assembly with him was Harold Miller, the state's director of planning. Miller recalled:

"This thing was brought up toward the end when a lot of the delegates had left and George and I were the only Tennesseans still present. When they brought up this super-court thing, I looked at George and said, 'That would be a bad thing, wouldn't it?' He agreed.

"So when the roll call got to Tennessee, we voted 'No!' loud and clear. A lot of the delegates turned around and stared; I guess they couldn't believe that representatives of the state that produced *Baker* v. *Carr* would vote to defend the Supreme Court of the United States." The delegates, in the main state legislators, would have been the more surprised, undoubtedly, had they known that one of those casting Tennessee's negative vote had defended the case through its last hearing before the Court they sought to curb.

Dirksen's drive, of course, died with the Senator. In view of public response to reapportionment, it is doubtful it could have succeeded in any event. The Dirksen proposal, at its peak, was also caught in a tangle of legal questions. He had succeeded in obtaining resolutions calling for the constitutional convention from thirty-three of the thirty-four required state legislatures. But many of these resolutions were adopted by malapportioned "old" legislatures which had voted as might have been expected. Some of these assemblies later bowed to court orders while the Dirksen convention's prospects hung in the balance, and thereafter some of the "new" legislatures (or at least one house) repealed the resolutions calling for the convention. Whether, in such circumstances, these states could have been counted among the needed thirty-four was never resolved, but the issue certainly would have been adjudicated. Among these states, by the way, was Senator Dirksen's own Illinois, where United States Senator Paul Douglas took the opposite view.

Douglas had been one of the original behind-the-scenes sponsors of *Colegrove* v. *Green,* and his views were unchanged. "In my opinion, and that of other observers, there is little real expectation that the Congress will call a convention even if two-thirds of the state legislatures pass the applications," Douglas commented during the Dirksen amendment campaigns. "It cannot, I believe, be forced to do so."

History could be cited to that effect. As Professor John Lowenthal of the Rutgers University law department noted:

The Constitution requires Congress to call a constitutional convention on the application of two-thirds of the states' legislatures, but Congress has nevertheless several times ignored that constitutional mandate.

The last time was in 1963 when Colorado became the 34th state to file a petition for a constitutional convention to limit or abolish the Federal income tax.

To be sure, there were possible defects in the petitions that could have justified or explained Congress' inaction: Some petitions had been purportedly rescinded; others had been vetoed by governors; several were vulnerable in form or content. But many of the present petitions on reapportionment are just as vulnerable for similar reasons, and, in addition, were passed by malapportioned legislatures.

In short, Congress can readily find reasons either to call a constitutional convention or not, and its decision will probably be a sounder expression of the present national political temper than would the petitions of 34 state legislatures over the past seven years.

The evidence of public acceptance, if not support of reapportionment was substantial by the time the Dirksen proposals reached the critical stages in the summer of 1969. A Gallup poll released at about that time showed only 23 per cent of the public in support of the Illinois Senator's proposal and 52 per cent favoring the one-man-one-vote concept. As Professor Robert B. McKay, associate dean of law at New York University, had written earlier:

"Popular support for the Supreme Court [reapportionment] decision was scarcely surprising. These decisions promised relief from the worsening underrepresentation suffered by the majority of American voters, those living in the more populous areas. This popular reaction was at first, however, largely nonvocal. For a time the anguished protests of legislators who saw in the decisions an immediate threat to their source of power were the most audible response." The most telling evidence of popular acceptance, however, was the manner in which compliance with the one-man-one-vote doctrine moved. Professor McKay found this speed and apparent good faith "nothing short of remarkable in a matter as complex and emotion-ridden as the fixing of state legislative election districts. These were auspicious omens for a relatively prompt acceptance and smooth accommodation to what many had honestly thought would be a severely disruptive process."

In the state where *Baker* began, compliance went much as George McCanless had predicted to Archibald Cox immediately after the decision was announced. The Attorney General of Tennessee told the Solicitor General of the United States: "I'll tell you what's going to happen. The legislature will get around to it now that there is a court order, and they'll reapportion the legislature a little bit. And then that will go back to court, and the court will throw that out — just like it did this time. And then the legislature will make another little change. Then it'll go back to court, and that one will be thrown out. Then pretty soon it will get back to the legislature and they'll do a pretty good one, finally."

Just such a cat-and-mouse game occurred between the General Assembly and the United States District Court in Tennessee. But to give both participants justice, they were making the rules of this game, and in the midst of it the Supreme Court was changing those rules. Until June 1964, for example, no one knew that both houses would have to be apportioned by population. The Tennessee constitution provided for this, it's true, but the Assembly discussed the possibility of substituting a "little federal plan" and the solons kept waiting around for the high court to lay down some guidelines. It was also true that the legislature tried, in the absence of such guidelines, to get by with as little change as it could. It was not until 1965, therefore, that the Tennessee legislature finally drafted a plan that met the court's approval. And in an effort to block what it feared would be urban domination of the Assembly, the rural bloc led by Jim Cummings in that final malapportioned body split the urban delegations apart by providing that urban state senators and representatives had to be elected from districts instead of from the county at large, which had been custom and law in Tennessee.

This provision, however, opened the Assembly door to blacks from the center cities of Memphis, Nashville and Knoxville. It also carved from the suburbs affluent districts where Republicans, suddenly, were winning local elections in Dixie. What happened in Tennessee was typical of *Baker*'s effect throughout the South.

"Seven years after the Supreme Court's one-man, one-vote decision," wrote Bruce Galphin of Atlanta in the summer of 1969, "reapportionment is gradually reshaping southern legislative politics. Although rural and small town legislators still hold the speakerships and important committee chairmanships, the cities are beginning to make themselves heard on such gut issues as who pays the taxes and who receives how much state aid." In Tennessee, the historic speakership bastions began to fall from traditional hands in 1969 as a result of *Baker*. The first Republican House speaker since Reconstruction was elected and the Senate chose an urban senator from Nashville, Frank Gorrell, for speaker and lieutenant governor. In 1971,

Rep. James McKinney, another Nashvillian, became the first urban House speaker since 1919.

"The most dramatic visible change," wrote Galphin, "is the appearance of a few black faces on the floors of halls that in the early days of this decade [1960's] still maintained segregated public galleries. Racially, the alteration has been more extensive than the relatively few Negro lawmakers would indicate. For reapportionment, combined with the Voting Rights Act of 1964, has made the black vote a potent factor in hundreds of legislative districts still represented by white officials."

The same effect was true in congressional districts, once the *Baker* revolution moved from the state to national levels. Rural West Tennessee congressional districts, their population bases shriveled by years of migration but their basic geographic boundaries unchanged for decades, suddenly contained vocal black voting blocs from Shelby County when the court split Shelby three ways in equalizing the population in congressional districts. At the same time, however, the court indulged itself in an horrendous gerrymander of the main Memphis congressional district, an unusual carving that one could easily argue was designed to keep a black man from representing Memphis in Congress. The gerrymander, which some Memphians referred to as a "sitting duck" because it physically resembled one, took unusual twists and turns to include within its boundaries the more affluent sections and suburbs. The upshot was election of the first Republican to represent that district in Congress.

Throughout Dixie, then, of which Tennessee was an excellent prototype, and in the Southwest, massive gains were made by urban areas through reapportionment (Atlanta's Georgia House delegation rose dramatically from three members to twenty-four), as well as by black voters and Republicans.

In the state where *Colegrove* v. *Green* began and where Senator Dirksen and Senator Douglas debated the issues mightily, where a lawyer once was shot to death and a judge was fired upon because of this matter of voter equity, the problems were a bit more bizarre. But they were solved.

Illinois might be said to be typical of a Northern industrial state, though one in which a single metropolitan center dominates. What happened in Illinois, therefore, served reasonably well to demonstrate reapportionment's effect on the vast Midwest and that tier of states beneath the Great Lakes.

Illinois is a house divided almost evenly between the major parties, between the urban Douglases and the Downstate Dirksens. It had done more than most states about reapportionment before *Baker* v. *Carr,* and because of its cleavages, the battles had always been bitter and characterized by necessary compromise. A constitutional amendment providing a modified "little federal plan" (the original federal legislative plan was itself, of course, the Great Compromise) was ratified by the state's voters in 1954. For the Illinois Senate it set up 58 districts and assigned them to three recognized divisions of the state as follows: the city of Chicago, 18; suburban Cook County, 6; the remaining 101 counties, popularly known as "Downstate" in Illinois, 34. The Illinois House was to be elected primarily on the basis of population from 59 districts with three representatives each, a total of 177 representatives.

Under the unique cumulative voting system of Illinois, each voter receives three votes — one for each of his district's three representatives — but he is permitted to cast his votes in one of four ways: (1) all three for a single candidate; (2) split between two candidates — one and one-half votes for each; (3) the traditional pattern, one vote for each of his choices; (4) two votes for a single candidate and the remaining one for his second choice. The system was designed to produce minority-party representation for every House district, even if that district was overwhelmingly populated by the members of one political party; the split-vote system normally enabled members of the minority party residing in such a district to "triple-shot" at least one minority-party House candidate into the legislature.

The system took on critical importance for the Republicans in 1963–1964 when the Republican-dominated legislature and a Democratic governor deadlocked the state over reapportionment. The legislature enacted on June 27, 1963, a reapportionment bill favoring the Republicans in a party-line vote which saw only one Lake County solon fail to follow his party's official plan. Two days after the General Assembly adjourned, Governor Otto Kerner, a Democrat, vetoed the bill. On August 14, 1963, as provided by the constitutional amendment, the Governor appointed a ten-member bipartisan commission whose job it was to reapportion the legislature when such stalemates arose. The commission, by law, was made up of five Democrats and five Republicans; agreement from seven was required to redistrict. On December 14, 1963, however, the four-month deadline provided by the constitution passed — with the commission, like the government itself, deadlocked over the issue. Thereafter the Illinois constitution had no further instructions. A political impasse without guidelines for solution had thus arisen; the inevitable turn was to the courts.

On January 4, 1964, the Illinois Supreme Court ruled that the state's House members had to be elected at large, but permitted senators to be elected from existing Senate districts. Two days later the legislature met in special session to set forth the procedure for nominating candidates for the House and providing election machinery for the only such at-large election in the nation's history. Under this procedure, enacted January 28, 1964, each political party was to nominate by convention no more than 118 candidates — equal to two-thirds of the 177 House seats. (This limitation recognized the grand design behind cumulative voting

— that each House district have at least one of its three representatives from the minority party.)

Party delegates to these state nominating conventions to name House candidates were chosen in a special election April 4, 1964, and in June both conventions — Democratic and Republican — convened in Springfield to name at-large candidates. In an effort to attract the largest possible vote for its slate of nominees, each party selected a so-called "blue ribbon" panel of "name" candidates. This produced in Illinois yet another Eisenhower-Stevenson political contest. Heading the Republican "blue ribboners" was Earl Eisenhower, brother of the former President, then living in La Grange, Illinois, where he directed public relations for Suburban Life Newspapers, a chain serving twenty-six Chicago suburbs. Leading the Democratic blue-ribbon list was Adlai E. Stevenson III, then a Chicago lawyer, whose first step into state politics with the panel led to his later election as Illinois state treasurer, and thence to the United States Senate.

As it happened, the "blue-ribboners" had less to do with the outcome that November 3 than the presidential contest held along with the legislative election. President Lyndon B. Johnson, having succeeded the assassinated Kennedy, outpolled United States Senator Barry Goldwater of Arizona by more than 900,000 votes in normally pivotal Illinois. LBJ's coattails, plus an outpouring of straight-ticket votes prompted by the confusing orange bedsheet ballot and a spate of unknown at-large candidates, produced an Illinois House made up of the maximum number of Democrats, 118, and the minimum of Republicans, 59. In the unprecedented sweep, the Democrats' weakest candidate outpolled the strongest Republican. But the Illinois Senate, elected by traditional patterns, remained under the control of the GOP. Kerner remained as governor, so once again the ingredients for deadlock were present.

Illinois's reapportionment ordeal, therefore, was not yet ended. In the midst of it, on June 15, 1964, *Reynolds* v. *Sims* had complicated matters by intimating that in all likelihood the state's new constitutionally provided "little federal plan" was out the window. Both houses, said the Court, had to be apportioned on the basis of population alone; a week later, the rule was made explicit for Illinois when its own lawsuit, *Germano* v. *Kerner,* was decided among the nine-state cluster of cases handed down June 22. The Illinois lawsuit had been brought by Joseph Germano, district representative for the United Steelworkers Union, in a deliberate attack on the geographic provisions of the Illinois Senate apportionment provided by the constitutional amendment of 1954. The suit was brought, according to Germano's attorney, Bernard Kleiman, then of Chicago, "because progressive legislation which Mr. Germano felt was in the public interest, as well as the union's, was continually blocked in the Illinois Senate. The legislation would go through the Illinois House with ease — the pattern was much the same — and be blocked in the Senate, which was controlled by the rural Downstate."

Despite the arrival of the *Germano* v. *Kerner* decision ahead of the 1964 elections, those elections were permitted to proceed under the old apportionment. The upshot was the lopsided Democratic House margin already mentioned, but solid Republican Senate control. When this unique legislature convened on January 6, 1965, for its regular session, Governor Kerner was waiting with his plan for reapportionment, which favored the Democrats. Expectedly, the Republican Senate did not find the Democrats' plan acceptable, though the bill predictably won easy approval from the two-thirds Democratic House. On January 22, while the General Assembly wrestled with its built-in deadlock, the three-judge court to which *Germano* had been remanded held Illinois's "little federal plan" invalid, enjoined the holding of further elections under it, and threatened another at-large election for the 58 Senate seats if the fatally divided legislature failed again to produce a valid reapportionment. In February, the state supreme court, in a separate proceeding, also held invalid the composition of the state Senate, and retained jurisdiction. The federal court, with the state courts now in the arena, was asked to vacate its January order. It declined. But the United States Supreme Court, on appeal, vacated the three-judge order. Subsequently, in another history-making proceeding, the state and federal courts agreed, in August 1965, on a Senate apportionment formula, recognizing only population and not area. The formula gave the city of Chicago 21 state senators, suburban Cook County 9, and the rest of the state — Downstate — 28. Urban-suburban Chicago had thus gained 6 state senators at the expense of Downstate. But Downstate Illinois, by 1970, was becoming as urban-suburban as it was rural.

In 1968, behind the Supreme Court's application of one man, one vote to local governments, Sherman Skolnick, a Chicago legal researcher, instituted a series of lawsuits designed to force compliance with the doctrine across the governmental board. He won a U.S. district court lawsuit ordering the redistricting of Chicago's fifty wards before the 1971 city elections. In another of Skolnick's suits, decided in January 1970, the Illinois state election board was ordered to present to federal court an acceptable plan for redistricting congressional seats by July 1, 1971. That deadline was given to enable the board to use statistics from the 1970 census. Another three-judge panel had ordered, in December 1969, the remapping of both houses of the Illinois General Assembly after Skolnick filed suit. And still another legal action was brought by Skolnick against Cook County Board and ward committeemen. With the 1970 census results, then, the one-man-one-vote revolution appeared to be ending in the state that had tried, in 1946, to set it in motion. In Tennessee, the state which first succeeded, it was likewise all over but the adjustments. Indeed, the same could be said for the nation.

My own view is that the census of 1970 can safely be used to date the beginning of the end of the massive reform the American Levellers wrought. And by the tenth anniversary of *Baker* v. *Carr* — March 26, 1972 — one could say with confidence, "It is finished."

To be sure, other lawsuits will be brought, perhaps halfway through the 1970's, to force compliance with the restructure of the American legislative branch — top to bottom, city council to Congress. But no one now doubts that defense against such a lawsuit would be a futile expenditure of both time and money. With the last line drawn by the Supreme Court in 1970, it was reasonably clear that every elected body exercising legislative powers over any segment of the public in America must be elected on the basis of population, and that in portions "as equal as practicable." Even the guidelines for this ambiguous phrase are laid out in fairly precise percentage-point terms. There will be no more political convulsions such as the one which unsettled Illinois public life for many years. Never again will Tennessee need to undergo the ordeal of trying, under court compulsion, to right wrongs accumulated over a period of six or seven decades. Even if the trends of migration reverse, as "new city" planners hopefully predict, democracy's representative system will remain abreast of its time. Illinois and Tennessee may not be the perfect prototype cases; each American state confronted its own unique problems in dealing with the mandates that flowed out of *Baker* v. *Carr*. But it will not happen again, ever. Tom Osborn, I believe, was correct when he predicted: "At the end of each ten years I think that the state legislatures without any lawsuits will promptly reapportion themselves. It will be simply habit with them. I do not believe we will ever get back into that situation again."

Too much has been made of the legislatures, perhaps because *Baker* began there. The congressional districts will be thus adjusted, too, and they have not in the past remained balanced. It is my own view that *Westberry* v. *Sanders*, the congressional case from Georgia, will in the long run produce more impact upon American politics than the more celebrated *Reynolds* v. *Sims*. It was more sensational, possibly, to declare, as *Reynolds* did, that members of both houses of a state legislature must be elected on a population-only basis. But not even the great rejuvenation of state government produced by the *Baker* series will ever elevate the several states to the import of the national Congress. Our problems today flow too swiftly across state borders; transport and communications lash us ever more closely together. Neither racism nor pollution can be contained by geography, and national policies will always take precedence in such matters.

That is, indeed, one of the real political lessons to be drawn from the reapportionment revolution: John Marshall's centrist federalism is still atop the heap; states rights remains mostly a myth. It may be true, as Chief Justice Warren once suggested, that the reapportionment cases returned a certain amount of viability to state legislatures. But it was still done by repeated trips through the Fourteenth Amendment to the federal Constitution. Each trip cost a bit of the myth; by the time the reapportionment revolution was ended, one could see little of value left in a state constitution that could not be handled in statutory law. The form of state government was largely established by court construction of the federal Constitution; election rules were set there; the Fourteenth had activated for all the states almost every clause of the American Bill of Rights. So what was left of states rights?

I do not deplore the loss. Most American citizens had not the slightest notion that before this Fourteenth Amendment revolution began, the Bill of Rights was not necessarily a shield they could count on. At the same time, most of the public commotion over *Reynolds,* I fancy, sprang from the mistaken notion of many individuals that their own state legislatures were somehow properly structured after a model they had come to respect — the United States Congress. The rest of the noise over *Reynolds* was a politicians' rebellion, and it was both a surprise and grave disappointment to most of them that they could not effectively mount it, or even keep it alive in the public mind. That, too, was because nobody unfortunately gave much of a shrug before *Baker* what the Statehouse boys were up to. Today, they care a bit more.

They care a bit more for good reason. For all their shortcomings and limitations, state legislatures are still in charge of some important matters in American life and their powers for levying and dividing tax revenues remain considerable. The same can be said for local governments, and if one of these days either level of government is to share revenue from the federal treasury, the best string attached continues to be the necessity for those elected to answer at the polls to people. Despite sophisticated refinements of the self-governing process, it remains subject to doubt whether a more equitable way has yet been found in theory. In fact, of course, one man, one vote has never been tried. It is as old an idea, at least, as the English Levellers of the seventeenth century; but it is new in practice, beginning right now.

To predict what will happen in the longer range of American politics by reason of *Baker* is a bit more hazardous, therefore. It takes no expert — or even the surveys that have already been run — to see that the American suburbs have gained much political power, and likely will gain even more when the newest census is fully applied. But what does that mean? Liberal ideologues, applying the measure of the past to the suburbs, are inclined to wail that all has been lost to conservatism. This is a particular disappointment to those who had expected the ghetto-dweller and the laboring man to come out on top as a result of reapportionment.

A more reasonable interpretation, it seems to me, is that more ghetto-dwellers and laboring men are moving into the middle classes and out to the suburbs. As Richard M. Scammon, former director of the Census Bureau, has written: "The 'suburban vote' in America, while still more Republican [in 1964] than that of the whole country, seems to be tending more and more toward the national average — because the national average is becoming more and more suburban."

Whether this is good or bad politically is often in the mind of the beholder. Most "refinements" of straight poll voting, it can be argued, come at the hands of special pleaders more interested in grafting their personal political ideologies to a self-governing system which would not otherwise yield to their notions. Put another way, should the people or the elite rule? Many of these refinements and concessions to history were clearly in the mind of Mr. Justice Frankfurter when he wrote his eloquent dissent to *Baker*. "But when the Court concluded that election of Congressmen 'by the people' does require equality 'as nearly as is practicable' and that state election districts must also satisfy a population test, the underlying premise of the Frankfurter opinion was largely cut away," wrote Professor McKay. "While problems of interpretation and judgment remain, they are not at all of the order anticipated by Frankfurter. Once equality is defined to mean equality, the hardest questions disappear, and the remaining issues are seen to be entirely manageable within the accustomed competence of the judicial experience."

The American Levellers finally defined equality to mean equality, not some sophistry of substitute rhetoric. In the 1640's, one of the earlier Levellers had defined it that way:

Really I think that the poorest he that is in England has a right to live as the greatest he; and therefore truly, Sir, I think it's clear, that every man that is to live under a government ought first by his own consent to put himself under that government; and I do think that the poorest man in England is not at all bound in a strict sense to that government that he hath not had a voice to put himself under.

In pursuit of that doctrine, one draft of the English Levellers' proposed Agreement of the People specified a detailed mathematical legislative apportionment based on population.

"Legislators represent people, not trees or acres," wrote Earl Warren in *Reynolds* v. *Sims*, some 325 years later. "Legislators are elected by voters, not farms or cities or economic interests. . . . To the extent that a citizen's right to vote is debased, he is that much less a citizen."

Learned political scientists have said the Chief Justice's solution to a complicated problem in a complex society was far too simple; learned scholars of the law have declared that his legal opinions, straightforward and clear, were too simplistic. I do not agree in this instance. Beginning with the tenth anniversary of *Baker* v. *Carr*, with the one-man-one-vote revolution completed, its wisdom will be confirmed. History will pay its tribute to the American Levellers.

Their contributions were various, but in the last analysis, the most important might well prove to be their diligent use of the judicial branch to salvage the legislative. Some fear the central power of the federal government, others a too-powerful Supreme Court, and these concerns were deeply imbedded in *Baker* v. *Carr*. But it is my own observation that neither contains the danger to the American system inherent in the rising level of executive power and the enormous bureaucracy around it. Behind this rise is not the evil design of a would-be dictator but the extraordinary acceleration of technology and numbers, twin threats which have prompted some scholars to suggest that only a super-executive will be able to supply the speed and efficiency necessary to govern the automated industrial society and its confusing, conflicting array of priorities.

Perhaps. But when that happens, self-determination is no more than a catchphrase, and one man as expendable as one vote is useless. The legislative branch will require deep reforms to speed its decision-making process, to remove its timeworn roadblocks. It will have to reassert itself, strip away the curtain of secrecy behind which the executive branch demonstrably has taken to working, and declare full confidence in the electorate's ability to judge intelligently among complicated issues. Thomas Jefferson reminded his countrymen a long while ago that self-governance presumes an informed public. There is no other choice. The rejuvenated legislative branch will have to believe that truism if it is to remain a viable servant of democracy for even the second decade beyond *Baker-Carr*. But at least the Levellers have given it that excellent chance, which may be its last.

EPILOGUE

Mist' Jim Cummings eased himself slowly out of his bed and set about preparing for opening day again up on Capitol Hill. There was much to do in the five hours before State Representative James H. Cummings, Democrat, Woodbury, Cannon County, would raise his hand, trembling just a bit now, for his eighteenth oath of office as a state legislator. It was a record of tenure unmatched in Tennessee history. Since his first term he had not missed an opening day.

Getting there would be a little bit different this time, though. Normally, he would stay in Nashville the night before opening day, but he had a case set in Chancery Court this morning and had to be present. That attended, he would make the hour-long drive to Nashville, stop off in his room at the Noel Hotel, then walk up the Hill, arriving about an hour before the speaker's gavel swung down at high noon on the Eighty-seventh General Assembly.

On this biting fifth day of January 1971, he was two months beyond his eightieth birthday, the oldest man in the legislature and venerated by this body as it came to order. Outside there was the sound of jackhammers. One could hardly hear the preacher's prayer for the noise, but everyone was pleased by what it meant. Workmen were rushing to complete in the War Memorial building across the street from the Capitol a renovation which would provide individual offices for each of the thirty-three senators and ninety-nine representatives sworn in today. Before the session was over, the new office wing would be dedicated to honor the name of James Cummings.

Individual offices, secretaries, permanent Capitol offices for both speakers, new committee rooms, increased compensations, annual sessions — all these were said in Tennessee to be results of the new prestige owned by state legislatures all over the nation as the 1970's began with the balance of power restored in these bodies. If that is so, it is not altogether irony to find Cummings so honored. He survived reapportionment by his own wits and service and ability to adjust to the times. And the times had changed some.

Pete Haynes and I. D. Beasley were both long dead, and Walter Chandler was also gone. Joe Carr was still in office on the floor below. Four years after the famous lawsuit that bore his name was decided, he had gone over to Memphis to meet for the first time that other party litigant, Quarterly Court Chairman Charles W. Baker, and Baker was still in office. Mac Davis, that scion of Democratic aristocracy, had become a "new Republican." Ben West was defeated for mayor of Nashville. Archibald Cox was back at Harvard after assassinations took both of the Kennedy brothers he had served. Thomas Wardlaw Steele, long since retired from the bench, had a lucrative private practice from his law firm's offices high in the Life & Casualty Tower. District Judge William E. Miller was advanced to the United States Sixth Circuit Court of Appeals. Charles Rhyne had been mentioned as a prominent Nixon candidate for the United States Supreme Court itself. Still and all, as Cummings so often said, one should "go to the head of the spring."

Mayne Miller

It was his idea. Not the idea of reapportionment itself, of course, since that was not new, nor even the idea of trying to bring it about by court action. That had been tried before. But it was Mayne Miller's idea, borrowed from his old Vanderbilt University Caucus Club of law school cronies, to bring a lawsuit in Tennessee and thus try again to do what others had failed to accomplish. He conceived legal action for reapportionment in Tennessee.

Mayne Miller did not see it through. The eldest of the brothers Miller had returned to his native Johnson City, in the first place, with a view to pursuing his life-long ambition of serving in Congress. In the summer of 1958, he thought the time had arrived to make his bid. *Kidd* v. *McCanless,* the reapportionment lawsuit he and his brother commenced, was one of the key factors that influenced him to do something he felt sure his father would have done had he lived: He announced his candidacy for congressman, as a Democrat, in the solidly Republican Upper East Tennessee congressional district.

Kidd v. *McCanless* had given the Miller brothers a great deal of favorable publicity. Given that and the adverse consequences of Sputnik to the Republicans' prestige, Mayne Miller felt there would never be a better chance than 1958 for an underdog Democrat to take on Tennessee's "Mr. Republican" himself, U.S. Representative B. Carroll Reece.

Mayne and Mariko Tenasaki Miller were quick to encounter in their 1958 congressional campaign the traditional Democrat–East Tennessee Republican trade-out that he had learned to despise. Miller was led to believe he would get his party's support and felt he had been betrayed when opposition for the nomination forced him to make two campaigns, thus depleting his thin resources. Nonetheless, Miller smashed his opponent, Arthur Bright, by 22,170 to 12,473 in the August 7 primary and won his party's official endorsement to carry the conflict to Congressman Reece that fall.

Mayne Miller, however, found himself *persona non grata* in his own party. When the organization Democrats had their annual fall fund-raising bash before the November 1958 election, Miller not only received no funds from the Nashville rally, but got no invitation to attend, even. When he went anyway, Miller and his Japanese-American wife were given a chilly reception.

It was a surprisingly good race in the circumstances. "Mako" Miller, who had lived in this country only nine years at the time, took quickly to American campaign methods. Mako Miller's father was Hidenori Tenasati, a member of the Japanese "Peace Delegation" to this country at the time of Pearl Harbor. Her American mother was a native of Johnson City, Tennessee. She was perhaps even more of a crusading spirit than her husband, and she worked endless hours among the poverty-laden hill counties and desperate mountain neighborhoods surrounding the relative affluence in the clean and neat cities of Upper East Tennessee. But the efforts of both were far from enough to overcome the traditional Republican voting pattern of the First District. Reece defeated Miller 42,615 to 29,999. Though he hadn't really expected to win, Miller was nevertheless crushed by defeat; in more euphoric moments he had nurtured his hopes. The election experience, primarily, prompted Miller's move to Wyoming. He lost in November 1958; he and Mako took up residence in Casper the following April.

When Mayne and Mako Miller moved to Wyoming, both plunged promptly into public affairs. Mayne went to work at once in Democratic party matters, and again it was an underdog cause. By the spring of 1966, he had managed to stir within him the old ambitions and announced his candidacy for the single seat Wyoming was allotted in Congress. It meant a statewide campaign over a vast area. Once again, he worked at it long and hard, lashing away at Wyoming's "establishment," particularly the Union Pacific Railway, which he accused of dominating the state's industrial development. Once again Mako worked beside him, and this time the two oldest boys pitched in, too. But once again he lost, this time in the Democratic primary by a paper-thin margin of about a hundred votes. Miller blamed a combination of labor votes and the activity of U.S. Senator Gale McGee for his undoing; his opponent, Al Christian, had been an executive director for COPE in Wyoming.

Mayne Miller had long since adopted the Platonic philosophy that "the penalty good men pay for not being interested in politics is to be governed by people worse than themselves." His interest in the reapportionment battle did not flag when he moved; he kept close tabs on the progress of *Baker* v. *Carr*, and at the request of lawyers involved in the issue in Wyoming, he offered counsel but he did not participate actively in the Wyoming redistricting case, *Whitehead* v. *Gage*, that followed *Baker*. His law practice thrived, but whenever an important political race arose he was there with his time and his talent and whatever portions of his fortune he felt the family purse could afford. In 1960, Miller worked actively at the Democratic National Convention for the ill-starred candidacy of Adlai Stevenson. In 1964, Lyndon Johnson's nomination was assured, but Miller was on hand in a futile effort to nudge the vice presidential nomination toward that Minnesotan who had eloquently nominated Stevenson four years before — U.S. Senator Eugene McCarthy. In 1968, he was firmly rooted in the McCarthy camp, and while his fellow Tennessean, John Seigenthaler, labored along the West Coast for Bob Kennedy in the surviving brother's Oregon and California primary contests with McCarthy, Mayne Miller worked the opposite side of the street.

Haynes Miller

He took the idea and drove it. Unlike his brother Mayne, Haynes Miller had intended from the outset to take his case to the highest court; he had no scruples about states rights and such. But the younger Miller was not around when his lawsuit finally made it there. On almost the same day that Tommy Osborn and Hobart Atkins filed the *Kidd* v. *McCanless* jurisdictional statement with the U.S. Supreme Court clerk, Miller arrived in Bangkok, Thailand, all set for high adventure and another and broader joust for justice.

Haynes Miller had long coveted a diplomatic career, and to this end Tom Osborn's diplomat brother, David, a talented linguist later assigned to Japan and Hong Kong, had opened some doors for him. But the contact that finally sent Haynes Miller abroad resulted from his continuing crusade for tax equity in Johnson City, the matter that had upset his businessmen uncles and brother Mayne.

"While I was in the course of doing that work," he later said, "I worked with the University of Tennessee Law School [and its] Municipal Technical Advisory Service made up largely of lawyers and tax experts or [experts in] various fields of public administration." It was there that a recruiter for the Government Administration Section of the International Cooperative Administration (ICA) learned of Miller's qualifications. "He was looking for a lawyer who had some notion of French law and who spoke French well," and Haynes Miller was Sorbonne-trained and had spent two years in law in Paris. Haynes accordingly entered the ICA service August 26, 1956, and following two weeks of Washington indoctrination, was designated an end-use auditor and assigned to the year-old United States Operations Mission in Laos (USOM/Laos).

In a fashion altogether typical of him, Haynes Miller threw himself into his new challenge, but early on he incurred the dislike of some of the American colony by living outside the American compound and making friends with the natives. His fluent French gave him an ever-widening circle of contacts and before long some of these, inside and outside the Lao government, began to funnel to him ugly reports about the use of American foreign aid, presumably the matter he had come to audit and investigate.

Haynes Miller was a hunter; he loved guns and collected them. From the days when Uncle Haynes gave him his first skeet lesson, he had been skilled in their use and had been dismayed when the armed forces rejected him because of his asthma. Now, making friends with the gentle Lao woodsmen, Miller went on frequent hunting trips with them, and far in the backwoods he met Buddhist monks and French Catholic priests working on land and people reforms. All this formed with young Miller, in a rather strange way, a link with home. Back in East Tennessee, he also took long hunting trips high into the rugged mountains of Johnson County, the northernmost tip of Tennessee, and he had urged economic development of the bean and cannery interests there.

His was a brilliant, if eccentric mind, capable of quickly grasping complex matters of international exchange, trained in the language and law of contracts, wedded to a conscience that accepted, perhaps at naive face value, the official Code of Ethics for Government Service which suggested, in its ninth point, that one should "expose corruption wherever discovered." In Vientiane, he began to make discoveries at once. One of these was a disgraceful racket in phony export-import orders clearing through Bangkok and cleverly designed to take advantage of a favorable currency exchange rate. The United States was pumping in dollars to finance a Laotian army the size of which the State Department had decreed against the recommendations of the Joint Chiefs of Staff. Oriental speculators and some Americans were rolling in enormous profits on phantom orders underwritten by the taxpayers back home. One of Miller's most bizarre discoveries was the "importation" of a boxcar-load of badminton shuttlecocks for this primitive land of mountain farm people.

All these matters Miller dutifully noted, but these were matters of basic policy, made in Washington, which he suspected he could not change. He did not encounter real trouble, then, until he began in the middle of 1957 looking into construction contracts for American technical-assistance projects, and particularly the road construction program with its infamous and ill-starred Road to Luang Prabang. At once, it became obvious that he was treading on some rather large toes; Haynes Miller was called off by the mission controller, Harry Harting, and "told to stay home, that I had rocked the boat enough and that I wouldn't need to come to work." But Miller had already sought out the records of the prime road contractor involved, Universal Construction Co., Ltd. of Bangkok, a firm headed by two Americans. He was then ordered to omit from his report any information he had concerning these contracts. Miller refused and, feeling harassed, resigned. He also threatened to go directly to Washington. Mission officials denied him access to a mission secretary to make his report. When he persisted, they took away his typewriter. The stubborn Miller promptly began writing longhand a Final End-Use Report which ultimately filled fourteen pages of tiny type in the minutes of the U.S. House Committee on Government Operations, Subcommittee on Foreign Operations and Monetary Affairs, then headed by Representative Porter Hardy, Jr., of Virginia.

All this did not come to light at once, however. Miller resigned, but he was also fired: "Mr. Harting told me that he didn't want me to resign but if I did . . . I would have to leave the first of October. I told him that was fine with me, that in that case I would be leaving at the government's convenience and he would have to pay my way home. He said he would not pay my way home. I told him that that was a violation of ICA regulations, at least as I read the regulations, and that I would sue ICA as soon as I got home, that that [the law] was my business and it shouldn't cause me much trouble.

"I made my plans to leave on October 1, and got a private passport and bought my ticket and sold my library, or a good part of it, and my guns to get money to buy my ticket. Then, three days before I was to leave I was told that I was fired, that they would pay my way, and that I would not be able to make the hunting trip which I had planned before I left; that the Ambassador would see that I got out of the country one way or another. . . . They fired me," said Haynes Miller, "for inability to adjust to overseas life."

Following a full investigation of USOM/Laos, in which Haynes Miller was called to testify, the Hardy Subcommittee didn't see it that way: "Miller's removal from the mission was based upon an undefined catchphrase, 'unable to adjust.' It appears to the subcommittee that, if this refers to Miller's inability to adjust to the environment in Laos, it is grossly inaccurate. He was one of the few qualified French linguists at the mission, probably the most linguistically competent of the American employees. He was also, on the testimony of a number of witnesses, the one who most sought out on a social basis, in a real wish to 'adjust,' Lao and French nationals."

The treatment of Haynes Miller was a bit more brutal than that. In conjunction with his removal, Ambassador J. Graham Parsons had sent a telegram to the State Department declaring that he was invited to resign by USOM Director Carl Robbins "because of obvious signs of nervous disorder:" Of this the Subcommittee declared: "Ambassador Parsons' opinion of Miller's 'nervous disorder' was rendered without benefit of medical advice. This is contrary to Department of State regulations. Competent medical advice was available to the Ambassador and could have been solicited. This lay medical opinion is particularly noteworthy, in that one month later, on October 30, 1957, Miller was subjected to a full medical examination in Washington and certified as *qualified for general duty.*'"

"In light of all the evidence available," concluded the Hardy Subcommittee, "the conclusion is inescapable that Haynes Miller was 'railroaded' out of Laos because he was close to discovering the truth about Universal, its bribes, its virtual monopoly of U.S. Aid construction projects in Laos, and its woefully inadequate performance."

The Subcommittee report cleared his name, but Haynes Miller knew that his hopes for any future diplomatic career were ended. He had returned to this country in possession of his own reports which contained copies of classified documents. He was "controversial." Said his brother Mayne: "They wrote enough in his TOE [fitness] folder to destroy him from any kind of government service or government credibility and sent him home." Haynes, deeply embittered, left the country; he returned to Paris and married a Frenchwoman. The increasing involvement of his country in Southeast Asia was deeply troubling. It appeared to him that Vietnam was becoming a repetition of what he had seen in Laos, and the reports of corruption, inflation, bribery, black market profiteering bore for him an all too familiar sound. He continued to have contacts in Laos, and Southeast Asian nationals visited him in Paris. On one occasion he called up his brother, Mayne, in Wyoming "to tell me how wrong we were out there and that friends of his had been killed in an American bombing raid or something like that. And he was just out of his mind; he was just wild with anguish over it, as though he were saying members of his own family had been killed."

What happened at USOM/Laos to Haynes Miller had happened to others; and one of them, Daniel J. Harkins, later visited him in Paris and afterward wrote to a mutual friend from the Laos mission, a man who had shared a similar fate: "He drove us out to his residence in Combe-la-Ville where he had purchased a very nice home, in fact a substantially built farmhouse which he and his wife were fixing up. He had severed his earlier connection with a French law firm in Paris, and had set up his own law office in his home. . . . He was very much disturbed that apparently he remained on some State Department 'blacklist.' He told me that he had been encouraged to apply for some civilian staff position with the American NATO contingent but that when the NATO principal made the necessary routine reference to State that 'the black flag went up,' and that when explanations were requested, State was evasive."

Harkins was writing, in fact, to inform their friend that Haynes Miller was dead. At 9:45 on the morning of September 5, 1967, Miller drove his Peugeot into a railroad embankment and was killed, like his father a traffic victim. "I'm not surprised," said Harkins, later. "He drove that little car like a bat out of hell."

But even in death, enigma continues to enshroud the younger of the Miller brothers; officialdom had its final word. The last line written in his ambivalent dossier was fittingly written in doubt. His death on the public highway of Combe-la-Ville, Seine et Marne, is "to be attributed to a suicide," the certificate says, but the words are enclosed in quotation marks, as above, as if this indicates no more than the required opinion of the *procureur* (coroner-district attorney).

It is a rare means by which one might deliberately

end his life and there are those who consider the suggestion a final slander on a man who endured his share in the forty-one years that he lived. There are others who, loving him fully as well, feel that the intensity with which he had come to view his nation's role in Southeast Asia might well have driven him to so desperate an act. He is buried in the cemetery at Combe-la-Ville.

Tommy Osborn

His success with the idea established for him a national reputation, and led indirectly to his destruction. In that final tragedy, laced with irony, Tom Osborn was entangled again with many of the leading characters from his reapportionment drama. And this one, too, ended in confrontation with the United States Supreme Court.

On the brisk morning of March 27, 1962, Z. T. Osborn, Jr., was, in the words of his young friend, Harris Gilbert, "sitting on top of the world." In Nashville, at least, he was recognized as *the* attorney who had made the largest contribution to the success of *Baker* v. *Carr*. The story of that success was streamered across page one of his morning newspaper March 27, the Supreme Court decision having just been announced, and there beneath it was Tom Osborn's likeness, standing before a bank of his law books alongside Molly Todd, his recruited plaintiff since the days of *Kidd* v. *McCanless*. Osborn scanned all this with satisfaction at breakfast.

Then he drove to his office, just off Union Street, where he knew the plaudits would flow from this streetful of lawyers and brokers and bankers and realtors, strung out between the Tennessee Capitol and the County Courthouse–City Hall.

Honors were headed his way. The gangling lad with the humble night-school law degree was soon to be tapped for next year's presidency of the Nashville Bar Association. In August 1963, this would be capped in Chicago with his induction as a Fellow of the American College of Trial Lawyers, one of the highest honors in American jurisprudence, limited to one per cent of the attorneys in any given state. Six months later the whole thing crashed; Tom Osborn was disbarred and stood accused of an attempt to fix the jury preparing to hear the trial of a famous client that his new-won reputation helped attract — James R. Hoffa.

Hoffa's Test Fleet trial took place in Nashville during a nine-week period, from October 22 to December 23, 1962, and produced what authorities have called the most serious assault on the jury system in American history. At the least, the trial, which ended in a hung jury, was one of the most bizarre misdemeanor court experiences on record. During its course, a former mental patient strode into the courtroom and unloaded a pellet pistol at Hoffa's head. Hoffa was unhurt, and his immediate mistrial motions were denied. The jury had been absent when the assault occurred. Toward the trial's end, District Judge William E. Miller held two secret sessions and later disclosed that two members of the jury had been dismissed because plots to influence them had been uncovered. Both were replaced with alternatives, four having been chosen during the jury selection. At the trial's conclusion, Judge Miller ordered a full investigation of these efforts to reach the jury and to fix it. The judge, "frankly astonished at the history of attempted jury fixing in this case," declared he had never seen anything like it; at the beginning of the trial, a third prospective juror had reported directly to Miller an oblique effort to bribe him, too.

Out of the investigation Miller ordered came indictments against Hoffa and five codefendants accused of approaching the two dismissed jurors, directly or indirectly, during this amazing trial. Hoffa and three of the five ultimately were convicted in a second trial, held at Chattanooga to remove it from the highly publicized Nashville hearing. In the meanwhile, Tommy Osborn became one of two attorneys disbarred for jury-tampering activities totally independent of these approaches. On November 19, 1963, Osborn was called before Miller and permitted to hear a tape recording of his own voice authorizing an illegal contact with a prospective juror. The suggestion was made to an investigator Osborn had hired for the completely legitimate purpose of providing background information on the jurors. When Tom Osborn acknowledged that the voice on the tape was his, Judge Miller barred him from federal practice on the spot. That was, as it turned out, Osborn's last day ever to practice law. But he conducted a legal struggle that lasted for years in an effort to reverse the conviction he was soon to receive. In the course of that struggle, circumstances emerged that surrounded the Osborn case with bitter controversy which persists in Nashville to this day. The controversy centers on methods used by the government to "get" Jimmy Hoffa, and in the process Tom Osborn.

Osborn's claim was that he was illegally entrapped and the issues in his case were sufficiently close that on one occasion, a three-judge Circuit Court of Appeals panel voted 2 to 1 in his favor; then the full Sixth Circuit Court — with one of its jurists absent — split 4 to 4 on the same issues; and when the United States Supreme Court finally heard Osborn's case, he lost by a split decision that produced an eloquent dissent by Mr. Justice Douglas against government bugging, wiretaps and paid informers.

Osborn's case, like Justice Douglas's dissent, centered on the circumstances surrounding how the tape of Osborn's voice was acquired. At the instigation of Walter Sheridan, head of Bob Kennedy's so-called "Hoffa unit," an FBI agent, with the judges' approval, taped a recorder to the back of Osborn's jury investigator, Robert Vick, who had reported to Sheridan that he thought Osborn was about ready to make an illegal approach to a prospective juror. The juror, Ralph A. Elliott, was a cousin of Vick's and his name had been brought up by the investigator in an earlier conversation with Osborn. On the damning tape, Vick told of a purported visit to his cousin and said that he felt the man might be receptive to a bribe. Osborn authorized a payment of ten thousand dollars to hang the jury in the event Elliott was selected — five thousand dollars upon his selection and five thousand when the trial ended with the bargain kept.

All this was a fiction, insofar as Vick was concerned. He never contacted Elliott at all, he testified, and his cousin was an innocent in the whole affair. No approach to a juror was proved, but "intent" was enough for the law. The tape was also more than enough to suggest strong action to Judge Miller and his colleague, U.S. District Judge Frank Gray, in whose court Hoffa was to have been tried on the jury-tampering charges. The judges called Osborn before them on November 15, 1963, and told him they had information "of a substantial nature indicating that efforts were being made to improperly influence members of the jury . . . and that [Osborn] himself was personally implicated."

Tom Osborn denied the implication during this audience with the judges and once again he denied complicity before a playing of the tape in his presence during a formal hearing prompted his admission. He had lied the first two times, Osborn later testified, in an effort to protect Vick, not knowing of the tape. He confessed deep shame and expressed hope that he would never have gone through with the scheme: "I was susceptible to this thing. I was conditioned for it. . . . I had gotten to the point where I was completely out of a lawyer's position. I honestly had no plan as to what I would do if he [Elliott] was seated. I hope and pray that if I had come to my senses I would have myself challenged that man."

Osborn said he had come to look upon Hoffa as an underdog, persecuted by a government that "was abusing people." After going through the first Hoffa trial, he said, "I had sort of an opportunity to see Hoffa on a different basis. I really graduated over gradually from lawyer for him to a point where I had a respect for him and then friendship and an identification with him. That is about the best way that I can describe it."

"I walked right into the trap." That was to be Tom Osborn's defense from the day of his disbarment, announcement of which shocked Nashville almost as deeply as headlines the following day: President Kennedy had been assassinated in Dallas.

A federal grand jury in Nashville returned a three-count indictment against Tom Osborn December 6, 1963, and his trial was conducted before District Judge Marion S. Boyd from May 25 to May 29, 1964. Convicted on the one count involving the Vick recording, he was sentenced June 19, 1964, to three and one-half years in prison and was fined five thousand dollars. The high court denied his appeal on December 12, 1966 — at the same time it considered Hoffa's appeal — and Osborn was ordered to prison March 13 and began his sentence March 20 at Texarkana, where he remained for several months before his permanent transfer to the federal prison camp at Maxwell Air Force Base, Alabama.

But the Osborn story was far from finished. Even before the Supreme Court received his case, Tom Osborn learned from Harry A. Childress, an Indianapolis Teamster friend of Robert Vick's, that Vick had boasted of certain rewards promised him by Walter Sheridan and of government payments made to the informer. For assistance in the fight he intended to continue from prison, Osborn called on an old friend and neighbor who had begun the Tennessee reapportionment battle with him, Maclin P. Davis, Jr. Davis, declining a fee, entered into his friend's cause with the same crusading zeal he had shown against Jim Cummings in the 1955 legislature. In the next few years he filed a maze of motions and petitions in an effort to reverse Osborn's conviction.

The turning point in this legal battle came when the government demanded a full Court of Appeals hearing after its three-judge panel had split 2 to 1 for Osborn. After this full hearing in April 1968, the court entered an order "in which they said they were evenly divided, 4 to 4, and that as a result of this, they were evenly divided also as to the effect of being evenly divided," said Davis. "They didn't know whether [the deadlock] reinstated Judge Boyd's decision against us or the three-judge court's for us. So they ruled they were just going to hold the whole thing in abeyance — this whole second motion for a new trial — until we had a hearing on a motion to vacate sentence which I had filed while the second appeal was pending."

It took Davis eighteen months to unravel the legal tangle, but in September 1969, the Sixth Circuit ruled against both his motions — the one for a new trial and the other to vacate Osborn's sentence. By this time, that sentence was finished: Osborn had been paroled the preceding April 16.

It was his obsession, now, to reverse his conviction and, possibly, to escape total and final disbarment from the practice of a profession with which he was also obsessed. Four days before the Sixth Circuit upheld his conviction, however, he was permanently disbarred, and in mid-January 1970, the Supreme Court of the United States wrote the final line of his case by refusing Mac Davis's last petition for a review of the Sixth Circuit finding.

Two weeks later, Tom Osborn died. During the afternoon, Dottie Osborn left their home at 4001 Wayland Drive to go shopping. Upon her return, unable to find her husband immediately, she became distraught and called Mac Davis at his office. Davis hurried to the Osborn home. When he arrived a young policeman, ashen-faced, stepped out of the attached garage of the Osborns' ranch-style brick house. Tom Osborn had entered the garage and placed the muzzle of a police revolver beneath his chin. He was fifty when he died.

Hobart Atkins

The idea of reapportionment obsessed him, and he remained involved in it to the hour of his death.

For many years, death was never very far away from Hobe Atkins; he lived with what physicians have called "the living death" — emphysema — and his case was so extreme that oxygen was his constant companion. His frail body was so consumed by the disease that for the last seventeen or eighteen years of his life to attend his law office was a major ordeal and to appear in court was an act of courage. Yet from the day this much older man joined three Young Turk attorneys in the Tennessee case of *Kidd* v. *McCanless*, he seldom missed a planning session or one of those many days in court. He fought the battle through four terms of the Tennessee Senate during those same years. And from *Kidd*'s beginnings in early 1955 through the *Baker* decision in 1962, and to its final implementation in 1965, the year that he died, Hobe Atkins "never received one penny of remuneration from one person" for his legal labors with reapportionment.

Miss Mildred McRae, who served as Hobart Atkins's Boswell for a quarter of a century, knew that this was true. For she kept his books, managed his investments, bought his clothes, drove him back and forth to work and operated his office for all those years. When *Kidd* and later *Baker* v. *Carr* took him to Nashville or to

Washington, she was always along. She often carried his heavy law books and she attended to the oxygen supply for the inhalator he kept beside him at all times.

"Most of the world's work is done by men who do not feel very well," U.S. Senator Everett McKinley Dirksen once said when a plague of ailments prompted talk of his early retirement. Hobart Atkins was one of those men. From the age of twelve, when he left home to take a construction job, his life was spent in work; during most of that time, he did not feel very well.

Hobe Atkins was the shadow figure in the reapportionment revolution, the constant character who appears in every scene of the play but always a bit off center stage, the actor who is never assigned the leading role, but inevitably carries a speaking part. That was his niche in life, too — the silent partner, the reliable pillar who was always there in the peripheral vision of the beholder in need.

He was a mountaineer bachelor whose struggle for education never erased the droll brogue of the Union County hills of his birth. His expensive tailored suits took on a rumpled look the moment he donned them, and his tousled, skinned-up-the-sides haircut was that of an unkempt countryman. His thin lips opened to a toothy eye-to-eye smile with gaps on the sides. Hobart Atkins looked like the hillbilly he was and made no apologies for being. When he took to the law, they flocked around him, and his criminal law clients were rumrunners, bootleggers, moonshiners — often quite violent men.

Life had hammered down Hobe Atkins's physique. From the age of five or six his lungs were afflicted, he was accident-prone, and crutches and braces and medical paraphernalia became, off and on, a part of his everyday life. Yet he managed through work, a keen mind, and a shrewd business sense to amass a fortune before he was forty. When the Great Depression wiped it all out, he picked himself up and built a new fortune. Money just seemed to flow his way. "He didn't need money and didn't want it," said Miss McRae, but all the while Atkins was building things — dams and tunnels and sewer systems — acquiring, investing in stocks and real estate, the silent partner of this one and that.

"He who would control cities must first learn to control himself," he told Miss McRae one day when she "flew off the handle" at a trying client. Hobe Atkins could not spare the breath to raise his voice, so he never did. As his reputation grew, he didn't have to. In the *Knoxville News Sentinel* Dana-Ford Thomas wrote:

NASHVILLE, May 22, 1965 — An absolute hush came over the Senate Chamber.

Not a paper was rustled. All whispering stopped.

It seemed for a moment that everyone knew that the words that were to come would open a clear path to solution of the many problems. . . . The heated debate on Senate Bill 10 had been going on for more than an hour.

Sen. Hobart Atkins, of Knoxville, rose slowly and with some difficulty to his feet. As he stood, he leaned against his desk for support. . . .

As the frail Republican Senator paused to gain new strength for his voice, Senators and guests in the chamber seemed to want to reach out and help him.

Hobart Atkins was serving the last of four terms in the Tennessee Senate when that was written. During his final session and the one two years before, he had had to interrupt his service, ride home in an ambulance and regain his strength, again, in the hospital.

The speech Atkins made was his last effort to get the Tennessee legislature to reapportion itself and redistrict the Congress as required by the lawsuit he had three years before helped to win, *Baker* v. *Carr*. When they didn't, he went back to court again. This second lawsuit, *Baker* v. *Clement,* brought by Atkins and Walter Chandler, sought to equalize the population in Tennessee congressional districts which the legislature had left with disparities running as high as 111,830 persons. A second thrust of the suit sought to block the Assembly from breaking up metropolitan legislative delegations, elected at large, into small districts. On November 19, 1965, Atkins and Chandler won the congressional-district part but lost the legislative portion. His adversary on the Senate floor had been Jim Cummings. Among the three judges handing down that decision was William E. Miller. Two days later, Hobe Atkins died.

His obituaries in the Knoxville newspapers said Hobart Atkins died without knowing he had won the major premise of his lawsuit. The papers were wrong, said Miss McRae: "He knew. He knew because I told him. I went into his room and he was barely conscious and I said, 'Mr. Atkins, can you hear me?' And he nodded. I said, 'You won your lawsuit, Mr. Atkins,' and he smiled. He knew."

"Hobart might not have been the man he was," said his brother John, "if he hadn't had to struggle so hard all his life. But he learned to fight things out and never give up. He had to learn that. Hobart was never a quitter."

His final lawsuit confirmed it. "The bill passed by the 1965 Extraordinary Session of the Legislature," his pleading read, "discriminates against the first four named [East Tennessee] districts, without rhyme or reason, and in favor of the Sixth, Seventh, Eighth and Ninth [Middle and West Tennessee] Districts. This is invidious discrimination."

He came from the poor ridgeland of the Cumberland country, an unlettered asthmatic boy of twelve, to set up a law firm that catered to those whom some would call riffraff while he went about behaving like Horatio Alger. It was entirely fitting, for his last lawsuit, that he should take his argument from Madison's No. 57 of the *Federalist Papers:*

"Who are to be the electors of the Federal Representatives? Not the rich more than the poor; not the learned more than the ignorant; not the haughty heirs of distinguished names more than the humble sons of obscure and unpropitious fortune. The electors are to be the great body of the people of the United States."

INDEX

[332]